WHAT A CITY IS FOR

What a CITY Is For

Remaking the Politics of Displacement

MATT HERN

The MIT Press
Cambridge, Massachusetts
London, England

This book was set in Helvetica Neue and Chaparral by the MIT Press. Printed and bound in the United States of America.

Library of Congress Cataloging-in-Publication Data

Names: Hern, Matt, author.
Title: What a city is for : remaking the politics of displacement / Matt Hern.
Description: Cambridge, MA : MIT Press, [2016] | Includes index.
Identifiers: LCCN 2016000394 | ISBN 9780262034883 (hardcover : alk. paper)
Subjects: LCSH: Urbanization—Social aspects. | Real estate
   development—Social aspects. | Gentrification—Social aspects. | Community
   development. | Sociology, Urban. | Equality.
Classification: LCC HT361 .H47 2016 | DDC 307.76—dc23 LC record available
at http://lccn.loc.gov/2016000394

10 9 8 7 6 5 4 3 2 1

This book is dedicated to the memory of Joice Taylor, 1949–2016

CONTENTS

ACKNOWLEDGMENTS AND GRATITUDE

Most of this book was written in Coast Salish Territories. I want to express my gratitude to the Musqueam (xʷməθkʷə ̓y ̓əm), Squamish (Sḵwx̱wú7mesh), Tsleil-Waututh (səlil̓wətaʔɬ), and Sto:lo (Stó:lō) nations for their generosity in hosting my family here on their unceded, occupied, and traditional territories.

The book wasn't written exclusively here though; major parts were also worked out in Sydney, NS (props to Burt and Irene), Montreal, Saskatoon, New Orleans (with gratitude to Liz Lichtman), Edmonton (thanks to the hospitality of the BWCC Cru and the exemplary care of Dawit, Seble, and family), Whitehorse (where Dan and Sarah could hardly provide a warmer place to stay), and of course 9724 Glynnwood (love to Joan, Adele, and Riley—rest well Pops—as always for the loving care).

At its heart this is a book for and about Albina, and it is to that place that I owe deep gratitude. I was so startled when I first encountered the story of Northeast Portland that I just kept returning, over and over again over the course of several years. Joice Taylor, John Washington, Fawn Aberson, and everyone at NNEBA were my first contacts in the neighborhood, and through the years they have been

so fun, generous, profane, brilliant, and kind to me—in short, they
have been great friends. This book would never have been written
without them. Similarly, Lisa Bates, Walidah Imarisha, and Ibrahim
Mubarak have been unbelievably generous with their time and
energy and constantly patient with all my questions and emails. I
hope they hear their voices in here.

There are also a good number of people whom I interviewed and
spoke to at length in Portland, Vancouver, and elsewhere, and they all
show up both explicitly and implicitly in the book: Lily Grewal,
La'Tonya Garrett, Terrence Feathers, John E. Davis, Izzy, Sharese
McDaniels, Mike Lewis, Andy Yan, Avi Friedman, Bob Williams, Fiona
Jackson and Michael Rodgers from the CHFBC, Skeeter Wright, Elvin
Wyly, Nick Blomley, and Paul Knauls. My thanks to all of them for
their kind attention, time, insights, and counsel. As well, the good
folks at the MIT Press, especially Beth Clevenger and Kathleen Caruso,
have been exceedingly gracious with me from beginning to end, and
have contributed significantly to the book's evolution.

Many other people have responded to parts of this book, in whole
or in part, and have influenced it significantly, in so many ways. They
include all kinds of students and audiences from all kinds of places
who have generously considered and critiqued my ideas and pushed
me toward clarity. But of course it's always friends and family whose
opinions I listen to most carefully. Sobhi and Tamam Al-Zobaidi,
Chuck Morse, Khelsilum Rivers, Kanahus Manuel, Cecily Nicholson,
Leanne Simpson, Richard Day, Erik Swyngedouw, Nathan McClintock,
Geoff Mann, Mark Douglas, Mark Jacobs, Isaac Oommen, Josiane
Anthony, Aklilu Mulat, Joe Sacco, and Am Johal have all offered
significant readings, critiques, and challenges. This book would not
have existed without their sagacity and friendship.

While writing a book about urban displacements, I have found it
almost impossible to distance any part of the writing from my own
experiences here in East Vancouver and Coast Salish Territories. Our

lives here on the fifteen hundo block have been inseparable from my thoughts as I was writing: you know who you all are. Keith, Ashley, Shane, Skye, Diana, Sarah Lum, Mica, Dan, Sarah G., Jesse, Layla, Annah, Justin, Magnolia, Alejandro, Dorone, Sarah, Basma, and many, many more who have lived here with us over the years—this was written with you all in my heart and head, and of course none more so than Selena, Sadie, and Daisy.

I

UNDER ALL IS THE LAND[1]

I'm standing in the bright Oregon sunshine, blinking and squinting in the early afternoon glare. It's the northeast of Portland and I've just strolled through an expectedly bucolic Portlandian community, wandering up and around Mississippi and North Williams Streets and then over along Alberta Street, amazed at the sheer number of bars, cafés, restaurants, and food trucks serving craft beer and local food. There seem to be a dozen cool-looking and tastefully hipsterized eating spots on every block, each of them attractive and distinctive, each branded smartly and each full of magazine-quality fare.

For a hungry visitor this is great news, and after I've eaten too much I zigzag back though the neighborhood, walking off the food and admiring the scenery. The scale is classic Portland: low-density, low-rise, overwhelmingly single-family houses with a few four-story

1. This is the first line of the preamble to the Code of Ethics and Standards of Practice of the [U.S.] National Association of Realtors. The next lines read: "Upon its wise utilization and widely allocated ownership depend the survival and growth of free institutions and of our civilization. Realtors should recognize that the interests of the nation and its citizens require the highest and best use of the land and the widest distribution of land ownership" (http://www.realtor.org/sites/default/files/publications/2014/Policy/2014-Code-of-Ethics.pdf).

mixed-use developments here and there. The requisite bike lanes lace the community, the light rail is close by, and overall it is everything Portland urbanism has become famous for over the past few decades: sweet, walkable, neo-pastoral compact (or "complete") neighborhoods that look and feel eminently livable, dully predictable, and very, very white.

But I'm not here to eat or wander; I've come to hang out with John Washington and Joice Taylor of North NorthEast Business Association (NNEBA), which essentially functions as a voice for the embattled and endangered African American businesses in the district. You see, the inner Northeast, in the neighborhoods around Martin Luther King Jr. Boulevard that most people call Albina, has historically been Portland's only clearly Black community, an area into which African Americans were pushed over the past century, then contained via exclusive zoning, predatory lending, racist containments, and disciplinary real estate practices.

In three distinct waves through the 1900s, Black people were aggressively funneled into Albina via official and unofficial consortiums of city officials, realtors, bankers, landlords, insurers, and appraisers. Black movement out of the neighborhood was severely restricted by a range of compulsions from physical violence to economic disincentives to legal restrictions on homeowners, while bankers and realtors enforced segregation fearing a "destruction of value" should Black people to start inhabiting other neighborhoods. In 1919 the Portland Realty Board declared it "unethical" to sell property in white neighborhoods to Black or Chinese people, and "The City Club of Portland's 1957 report, 'The Negro in Portland: A Progress Report, 1945–1957', documented what was generally understood: 90% of realtors would not sell a home to a Negro in a White neighborhood."[2]

2. Lisa K. Bates, Ann Curry-Stevens, and the Coalition of Communities of Color, *The African-American Community in Multnomah County: An Unsettling Profile* (Portland, OR: Portland State University, 2014).

While intracity mobility was severely restricted, simultaneously aggressive redlining meant that Black people were denied bank loans for homeownership or repairs, even within Albina, often having to turn to highly risky and predatory lenders.[3] Thus, Black families had great difficulty leaving Albina and were made wholly unwelcome elsewhere in the city, all the while being denied tools to build where they were.

Concurrently, in a classic contain-and-disinvest strategy, there was an ongoing, systematic withdrawal of public and private capital from Albina that led to a slow overall community decline until the late 1980s when the area was down enough that, in a classic rent-gap scenario, it was primed for new investment: "The gap between the value of properties and what they could potentially earn was large enough for speculators to line up to buy tax-foreclosed properties in Albina."[4]

As inner-city, west-of-the-river Portland continued to become more expensive, speculators, investors, businesses and the young gentry increasingly turned their eyes to the northeast and its eminently attractive possibilities. The neighborhoods in Albina were cheap, but full of promise: the district was blighted, but had all kinds of "historical charm" and plenty of properties were available. Young

3. "NE Portland Activists Blame Blight on Lenders: 1990 Blueprint for a Slum Series," *Oregonian*, September 11, 1990, reprinted August 24, 2014, http:// www.oregonlive.com/portland/index.ssf/2014/08/neighborhood_activists _blame_b.html#incart_story_package; "Buyers Say Home Loans Refused as Too Small, in Wrong Part of NE Portland: 1990 Blueprint for a Slum Series," *Oregonian*, September 10, 1990, reprinted August 24, 2014, http:// www.oregonlive.com/portland/index.ssf/2014/08/buyers_say_home_loans _refused.html#incart_story_package; "Major Lenders Discourage Homeownership, Aid Decline of NE Portland: 1990 Blueprint for a Slum Series," *Oregonian*, September 10, 1990, reprinted August 24, 2014, http://www.oregonlive.com /portland/index.ssf/2014/08/major_lenders_discourage_homeo.html#incart _story_package.
4. Karen Gibson, "Bleeding Albina: A History of Community Disinvestment, 1940–2000," *Transforming Anthropology* 15, no. 1: 6.

whites were ready, willing, and eager (knowingly and/or ignorantly) to take advantage of the combination of historical segregation, community trauma, and ongoing neighborhood disinvestment that set the stage for its gentrification.

Over the past two-plus decades, these dynamics have created a startling turn in neighborhood demographics as the trickle of young, mobile white folks looking north turned into a steady stream, then into a flood. New businesses and community design features arrived to serve them, and property values and rents spiraled up, with housing prices tripling and sometimes quadrupling (!) between 1990 and 2000 alone.[5] And—bam!—in the time it takes to order a locally brewed, kombucha-and-bacon-flavored donut, the African American community has been scattered, mostly out and across the city's edges. Now there is no longer a single minority-majority neighborhood left in Portland,[6] quite possibly the only major city in North American that can claim that, and it is certainly the whitest city in the country.[7] Its Black community is decentered and dispersed, with NNEBA and many others left trying to hold the pieces together, trying to rebuild the vibrancy and cohesion that has been so recently lost.

And it happened so fast. In 1990 just under three-quarters of Albina residents were Black. In 2010, just twenty years later, the number had fallen to less than 25 percent and by every measure, official and vernacular, has continued to drop sharply and relentlessly since

5. Ibid., 20.
6. Portland Plan, "Population and Demographics," http://www.portlandonline .com/portlandplan/index.cfm?c=52257.
7. There's plenty of documentation of this in variously shifting countings, from Al-Jazeera to the *Washington Post*. John has a theory that as other cities, particularly in the East and South, become Blacker and more Latino, whites are fleeing, coming to Portland as the surest bastion of white values and safety. He's not alone; see, for example, http://www.newgeography.com/content/001110 -the-white-city.

then.[8] In a short generation a whole racialized community has been, and is being, cleared out. It's a phenomenon that has to be understood not as an unfortunate set of circumstances, an unforeseen confluence, or some bad luck, but a deliberate, methodical effort. "In other words, it is not just a cultural or social phenomenon reflecting a lifestyle trend—it reflects systematic reinvestment by financial institutions and the public sector. In Portland, the Black community was destabilized by a systematic process of private sector disinvestment and public sector neglect."[9]

But make no mistake, it wasn't just Black people moving out, it was whites moving in to take their place—very often literally. Within the census tract that roughly corresponds to what most people recognize as Albina, the population of residents who identify as "white-only" has shot up from 23 percent to a hair under 60 percent with commensurately dramatic "gains in average gross rents, median home prices, household income, and educational attainment figures."[10] Over those critical two decades, at least ten thousand African Americans left Albina.

And those who left didn't move to nicer areas. Pushed out by gentrification, most settled on the city's eastern edges, according to the census data, where the sidewalks, grocery stores and parks grow sparse, and access to public transit is limited.

8. L. Bates, A. Curry-Stevens, and Coalition of Communities of Color, The African-American Community in Multnomah County: An Unsettling Profile (Portland, OR: Portland State University, 2014).
9. Gibson, "Bleeding Albina," 6.
10. J. Jordan, "An Examination of Gentrification and Related Displacement of Black Residents in Portland's Boise Neighborhood, 1990–2010" (undergraduate honors thesis, paper 16, Portland State University, Urban Studies and Planning 2013).

As a result, the part of Portland famous for its livability—for charming shops and easy transit, walkable streets, and abundant bike paths—increasingly belongs to affluent whites.[11]

A 2015 study by the Portland Housing Bureau found that "only whites and married couples with children have median incomes high enough to withstand rising housing costs in most parts of town."[12] The report clearly outlines that since racialized communities haven't experienced the same wage growth as whites, their housing choices are limited both economically and spatially: "Housing options are severely constrained for lower income households, people of color, and single mothers and seniors. When earning median income for their Census tract, single mothers have almost no chance of renting a home with more than one bedroom in Portland. A median-income Black household can't afford to rent anything bigger than a studio apartment outside the 122nd and Division neighborhood. Median-income Native American households are limited to studio apartments in Parkrose or Cully. And very low-income people are out-priced of the private housing market across the city."[13]

It is important to note that this current round of displacements was very explicitly catalyzed and designed by The Albina Community

---

11. Nikole Hannah-Jones, "In Portland's Heart, 2010 Census Shows Diversity Dwindling," *Oregonian*, April 30, 2011, http://www.oregonlive.com/pacific-northwest-news/index.ssf/2011/04/in_portlands_heart_diversity_dwindles.html. See also Erin Goodling, Jamaal Green, and Nathan McClintock, "Uneven Development of the Sustainable City: Shifting Capital in Portland, Oregon," in *Urban Geography* 36, no. 4 (2015): 504–527, for a terrific explication of Albina's gentrification and East Portland's ongoing devaluation.
12. Lee van der Voo, "Report: Average Black and Native American Households Priced Out of Portland," *Investigate West*, May 7, 2015, http://invw.org/2015/05/07/report-average-black-and-native-american-households-priced-out-of-portland/.
13. Ibid.

Plan, which was commissioned in 1990[14] by The City of Portland Planning Commission and published in 1993[15] with a long lead-up of public admonishments about the state of Albina and the requisite flag-waving for "urban renewal." The result was a startlingly effective rendition of the kinds of "slum clearance" that have been so common across North America since World War II, maybe with more starkly effective results than most. It is worth noting that the two signatories on the final version of that report were the then mayor Vera Katz and the then commissioner of public safety Charlie Hales. Interestingly, Hales was the sitting mayor as I wrote this book, so over the course of many visits over several years to Portland I repeatedly attempted to interview him on this issue. I was ignored, deflected, and otherwise rebuffed until early 2015 when his communications director engaged me in a sort of substantive email conversation. After a series of PR-style, cut-and-pasted responses to my sort of polite questions, I sent a rather direct and focused question to the mayor's office.[16] After that,

14. Approved Community Plan Process, City of Portland Bureau of Planning, May 1990, https://www.portlandoregon.gov/bps/article/91270.

15. Adopted Albina Community Plan, City of Portland Bureau of Planning, October 1993, https://www.portlandoregon.gov/bps/article/58586.

16. This is the text of that email:
So I guess after having a good read of your response, discussing with several Black leaders I was spending time with yesterday (and having them explain the intricacies and histories of the investment you detail) and thinking it over in light of my research, I'd just like to note your claim that "No council ever intended to encourage displacement." I guess we could parse the word "intended," but the facts are clear: In 1990 Albina was 70%+ Black. In 2010 the number had fallen below 25% and by all accounts continues to fall, with that population almost exactly replaced by whites, with a matching, catastrophic decline of Black-owned businesses and enterprises. The neighbourhood has subsequently experienced a massive revival economically by every possible measure. It is a story of Black displacement and white replacement, of racialized disinvestment and reinvestment. And while there is a whole matrix of conditions that precipitated that, the clear pivot is the Albina Community Plan (launched in 1990 and issued in 1993) that planned and executed this systematic displacement. This displacement is and was not accidental. That plan had two signatures on it: Mayor Vera Katz and Commissioner for Public Safety Charlie Hales. I am sure both are lovely people, but if the current Black community and leadership fundamentally distrusts the City and this Mayor one can hardly be surprised. I appreciate any comment you might have. Thanks!

the line went thoroughly dead, despite several follow-up attempts on my part.

Exuberant reinvestment has occurred since the area was "renewed," and it shows. Money and commercial activity and construction are apparent all over the district, crime is down, new housing developments are flying up, every bar seems packed at night, and streams of people are riding their bikes and walking. But many wonder where all that investment was when these were Black neighborhoods. I ask John Washington this question. He scowls at me: "I knew Black people were fucked as soon as I saw the bike lanes. That's when we knew Black people weren't welcome here anymore." Joice adds: "And the community gardens. That's another bad sign for the African American community. We always gardened. We always shared our gardens and our food. We didn't need 'community gardens.' That's a white invention."

As a longtime advocate for both bikes and community gardens, that's a little rough to hear, but land use has to be understood in historical and political contexts. Gardens and bikes are not just value-neutral, benign goods; they can be and often are the instruments of racialized dispersal. As Joice explains to me, "In the early 1990s, Albina was blighted for sure. The housing here was in such bad decay that the city offered to help people move out, they helped Blacks find new places in other communities. They offered money, paid off their debts, helped them to move out and find affordable housing out in the suburbs, but now they will not help them move back!"

In the grand tradition of slum clearance and urban renewal that has festered in essentially every city in North America, Albina residents were moved out in the name of a master-planned urban regime of rationality and modernism that is inextricable from racialization, with little regard for what was being lost. The sin that those Portland planners from a generation ago fell prey to, like so many planners everywhere have for so long, was hubris: the belief that they knew what was best for Albina and its residents, a racist hubris that gave them permission to exercise their prejudices. Their arrogance displaced the city's only Black community, maybe forever, and broke something that cannot be put back together again.

In retrospect, the same hubris that has fractured neighborhoods in so many cities in such similar ways seems so awfully regrettable, but it is matched by the arrogance of today's planners and civic activists who are so convinced their ideas are the right ones. Listen to how Joice puts it:

> Now there is no minority neighborhood in the city: and that was intended! They created this! Now you don't see anything to distinguish one neighborhood from the next—it's all the same—it's a very bland society. It has to do with bicycles, environmental people, younger city people who are energetic and have new ideas. They want to make changes too quickly and they don't want to hear what was here and working before.
>
> There really is no Black community anymore. Albina is just too expensive here for most Black-owned businesses and Black families. Before this, we could understand our own problems— now the kids are lost, the children have no connection. We used to feel like we had ownership of the community. There are different ways to own, yes, but it's hard. It's scary, it's happening so fast—we used to know the families, the histories, and people took care of each other. Now I have neighbors who moved here from Minnesota. They voted for Obama but don't want to talk to me—they wave at me, but that's it.

And of course, this story is so tiresomely familiar. Gentrification is endemic to every city, particularly global cities and/or cities that are perceived to be success stories, which Portland most certainly is. It is the unfettered logic of the market: to the winners go the spoils, and

to the plans go the powerful. If a neighborhood is in trouble, predatory capital sees an opportunity for profit.[17] If a neighborhood is an
attractive, energetic place that gathers attention, those with money
will buy in. Either way those without the requisite cash and/or social
capital will just have to move along. This is a global phenomenon: in
every city I have ever visited, the incipient threat of displacement
winds its tentacles in. Everywhere is vulnerable, nowhere is immune.

And of course there is a very significant body of theorizing around
gentrification, from graffiti and blogs, to street conversations and
community organizing, to scholarly research and journalistic investi-
gations. Cities across the globe are convulsed by urban displacements
as residents and observers try to figure out what the hell is happening. At some levels it's pretty obvious and predictable, but in every
place the causes, contours, and structures are significantly nuanced.

Neil Smith is often cited as the foundational theorist of contemporary gentrification: his work on rent-gaps and new urban frontiers
have formed a baseline for most contemporary analyses of urban patterns of displacement.[18] Smith's work has been augmented and challenged from the cultural and consumptive perspectives of people like
David Ley, Monique Taylor, and Loretta Lees,[19] and nested in larger
arguments about globalization and world cities by Sharon Zukin,
Manuel Castells, and Saskia Sassen, among many, many others.[20] But

17. Sometimes it's an area or district, or even a whole city. See, for example,
Detroit.
18. See, for example, Neil Smith, *The New Urban Frontier* (New York: Routledge,
1996) and/or *Uneven Development: Nature, Capital and the Production of Space*,
3rd ed. (Athens: University of Georgia Press, 2008).
19. See David Ley, *The New Middle Class and the Remaking of the Central City* (Oxford: Oxford University Press 1996); Monique Taylor, *Harlem between Heaven
and Hell* (Minneapolis: University of Minnesota Press 2002); Loretta Lees, Tom
Slater, and Elvin Wyly, *Gentrification* (New York: Routledge, 2008).
20. See Manuel Castells, *The Urban Question* (London: Edward Arnold, 1977)
or his *Information Age* trilogy: *The Rise of the Network Society*, vol. 1 of *The Infor-*

honestly, pretty much everybody's got an opinion on gentrification, and usually you have to go to the streets to get the most sophisticated analyses.

There is some evidence that the same basic processes of displacement have been occurring since Roman times, but a new set of postmodern, postindustrial circumstances are in front of us now, and the current spasms of gentrification are really late capitalism writ material, or as Rachel Brahinsky puts it: "Gentrification is capitalism playing out in the landscape. It is essentially our economy's urban form."[21]

As I look around Albina, my mind turns to home, to East Vancouver in Coast Salish Territories. The parallels could hardly be clearer, and I feel a foreboding dismay. I have lived in East Van my whole adult life; my family has rented in one ten-block area for twenty-five years, and I have worked almost exclusively in a single two-mile stretch of the city. I have spent those two-plus decades pretty focused on community organizing: running neighborhood schools; founding youth centers, youth exchanges, and neighborhood festivals; building a training institution for alternative economic enterprises; growing community gardens; and a few other things. And, immodestly, I think many of our efforts have been successful. My colleagues and I have labored long and hard on projects that have really improved the

mation Age: Economy, Society and Culture (Oxford: Blackwell, 1996); *The Power of Identity*, vol. 2 *of The Information Age: Economy, Society and Culture* (Oxford: Blackwell, 1997); and *End of Millennium*, vol. 3 of *The Information Age: Economy, Society and Culture* (Oxford: Blackwell, 1998); Sharon Zukin, *Loft Living* (Baltimore: Johns Hopkins University Press, 1982) or *Naked City: The Death and Life of Authentic Urban Places* (Oxford: Oxford University Press, 2010); Saskia Sassen, *The Global City* (Princeton, NJ: Princeton University Press, 1991), or *Losing Control: Sovereignty in an Age of Globalization* (New York: Columbia University Press, 1996).
21. Rachel Brahinsky, "The Death of the City?," *Boom: A Journal of California*, Summer 2014, 52.

neighborhood. We've added funk and flavor, created lasting places for low-income kids, resisted car culture, and nurtured networks of ethical enterprises. I'm proud of most, maybe all, of that work.

And it hasn't gone unnoticed. I'm one of thousands of organizers and activists working away here, in ecological and social initiatives, as artists, musicians, and artisans, in small businesses, organizing for justice, equity, and inclusivity. Take my neighborhood of Grandview-Woodland, one small piece of East Van, which has historically been a working-class and immigrant landing spot. Tough and resilient, its low rents have always attracted political and artistic types, people looking for alternative renditions of the good life, and it long been a center of radical politics. It remains my home, and it still reflects so much of what I think a good city should look and act like.

But it's under siege, like almost all of East Van. Over the last ten years my neighborhood has become steadily gentrified. Culturally for sure: there are bougie restaurants, slick clothing stores, bars that few people I know go to, even a Starbucks. But it's a lot more brick-and-mortar than that: it's our houses. Real estate ads trumpet the "edgy" and "vibrant" neighborhood for new condos— a repercussion of the "new urbanism," a revival of city living that has seen a stunning reversal of the postwar rush to the suburbs that has been bought hook, line, and sinker by huge swaths of the (now) urban elite. It's not the overt militarization of Los Angeles, it's not a legally enforced segregation, it's not ghettoization—it's just the market doing its thing. It's simple supply and demand, and if that means displacement, well so be it.

But wait. You know this old saw. You've heard the same damn story time and again, from the Mission to Marais, Beyoglu to Bo-Kaap, Palermo to ... well, anywhere plausibly cool, really. Every urban neighborhood on every continent is vulnerable if it has any single or combination of preserved architectural features and housing stock, "creative city" institutions, walkable high streets, public transit access, concentrations of consumer services, easy access to downtown, convivial urban design, cultural vitality or cachet, depressed housing values, and/or other capitalizable assets. The tropes of gentrification and displacement have been a (perhaps *the*) central focus of urban geography and urban studies for a generation, but I want to insert something both ontological and strategic here, and use it as a pivot for an investigation into land, property, and sovereignties.[22]

I'm frankly not all that interested in Portland.[23] It's a fine place: not really my style, but I always have a lot of fun, and so many wonderful people, and now friends, live there. I suppose that could be said about pretty much anywhere, but I keep returning to Portland in part because Albina is one of the clearest and starkest examples of displacement that I have ever encountered. That the cold dispersal of the city's Black community has taken place in such an ostensibly liberal milieu makes it a particularly useful tableau for understanding capitalist urbanism—here, there, and everywhere. I submit to you that rethinking what we are talking about when we talk about displacement is the right route to more fundamental questions about cities.

I want to keep asking that question: *What is a city for?* and the clearest avenue for me is to ask historico-ontological questions about gentrification. Considering displacement is to ask who deserves access to land and why, and those answers, or at least those questions, strike me as right at the heart of what a city should be for. Cities should be setting us free, and in many ways and for many of us, they do. But all cities are built on colonial plunder, and most, certainly those in my part of the world, have been built on the backs of racist dominations and unearned privilege.

---

22. Lots more to come on this, but the working definition for sovereignty is "supreme authority within a territory."

23. Nor do I expect you to be all that interested in East Vancouver per se, but stay with me; something particularly illustrative is going on here.

It is impossible to understand the great wealth of cities without understanding dispossession. I am convinced that the city is the right starting place to account for these histories, to take repatriations and reparations seriously, but that project necessarily demands a rethinking of the uncertainties of sovereignty, development, property, and ownership. The buying and selling of land is closely related to the buying and selling of bodies, each giving permission to the other. Imagining otherwise requires some theory, some poking around, some looking hard at what is presumed inevitable, and a lot of listening to stories.

One of the central themes of gentrification thinking, both scholarly and popular, is asserting the capacity of people to stay in place, to resist displacement. You hear it all the time—the other morning in my kitchen, for example, one of my young adult kids bemoaned that she doesn't know if she'll be able to stay in "her" neighborhood, the place where she was born and raised. Of course I empathized for her sake and for mine, but I also wondered *Who made this yours?* I heard my voice in hers and that's something I have certainly said myself, and I wonder how that sounds to, say, an Indigenous person whose people have lived here for millennia. Just because my family has resided and rented in this neighborhood for a generation, that makes it *ours*?

It strikes me that security of tenure is essentially what most all of us are after, personally and socially. We're all hoping for the ability to self-determine when we stay and when we go: to not have something as intimate as our homes left to the mercy of something as capricious as the market. But there is also something in there that makes me uncomfortable. A big part of what makes great cities so great is the flow of new people—flows of immigration, of mobility, of strangers, of alterity and hybridity. As soon as neighborhoods become stilled, fixed in historical space with notions like "ours," then things start getting a little dicey for me. I'm there and I understand, but that's tricky. Talking about community in language that rests on an "us" always means there has to be a "them": people who are not us, who reside outside our borders, and whose entrance we may or may not assent to. And this starts to edge up against ugly xenophobia, and all the racialized prejudices that uncovers.

Far too much anti-gentrification thinking slides easily into uncluttered renditions of private property and ownership, slipping into righteous justifications of voice and authority, about who can speak for a place. I can grasp and maybe even sympathize a little bit with the feeling, or at least the NIMBYesque impulse. People who have lived in a neighborhood or on a comprehensible area of land for a long time do tend to have a subtler, more entrenched, deeper-held kind of care for it, and probably do have a greater stake in its future than those who are passing through. But there has to be a permeability, an openness to flows of newcomers that mirrors the generosity with which so many Indigenous people welcomed settlers to this continent.[24] This suggests more nuanced renditions of sovereignty, or better: alternative or post-sovereignties, far beyond blithely letting the market make those choices, and then positioning them as "natural."

In critical ways almost all of us are implicated in narratives of displacement. Take me, for example. For twenty-plus years I have been doing what I can to contribute to this neighborhood, to be of service. And where my efforts have been successful, where they have made this a better place to live and work, they have plainly contributed to the gentrification of this community. There is little doubt that I have directly and indirectly accelerated the pricing out of my neighbors, my friends, my family, my children, myself. I intended the exact opposite of course, and my efforts have always been attached to a radical politics, but I don't want to sugarcoat it: in undeniable ways I have betrayed my family and neighbors, and

24. For one good starting point on this subject, see Richard White, *The Middle Ground: Indians, Empires, and Republics in the Great Lakes Region, 1650–1815* (Cambridge: Cambridge University Press, 2011).

myself, particularly those of us who are not homeowners. In lots of ways I am precisely one of those settler-activists Joice describes as moving too fast and not listening to what was here.

The joke I often tell is that maybe all this time I should have been chucking garbage around, kicking in some windows, advocating for street widenings, opening a Burger King. Those projects would have made the neighborhood a lot less attractive (to certain kinds of capital at least) and thus maybe suppressed rents sufficiently to allow more of my family and friends to stay here, to feel more secure in our tenure. It's a joke that simultaneously mocks and covers for my dismay, but it's a very real strategic question. How could and should we act? How can we "improve" a city without destroying it? Almost anything can become a selling point: bikes, transit, tattoos, diversity, racialized difference, radical political movements, run-down housing stocks, angry artists, poor people, violent histories. Almost anything can be recycled as edgy marketing.

That's maybe the core of capitalism's durability—its agility and malleability—and so it is with its expression as gentrification. It's not always clear exactly who is responsible. Sometimes the culpability is explicit and stark; at other times, it is highly incremental and pervasive. Displacement often comes sneakily, subtly, as Taiaiake Alfred puts, as a "fluid confluence of politics, economics, psychology and culture."[25] People tend to point at whoever is a little wealthier than they are, at someone, anyone else, and those fingers tend to pin the blame on specific subsets of individuals. Precarity of tenure can induce us to take the personal and extrapolate it to the general. This tendency toward the countercultural blaming of yuppies, hipsters, gentry, whoever, is appealing because it allows somewhere to aim our frustrations and someone to identify by the food they eat,

---

25. Taiaiake Alfred, *Wasase: Indigenous Pathways of Action and Freedom* (Peterborough, ON: Broadview, 2005), 30.

the clothes they wear, the cars they drive, the facial hair they have. But it also obscures the structural conditions that make gentrification, and typically racialized gentrification, not just an unfortunate issue policy makers have to scramble to ameliorate but an inevitability, nay, a *requirement*, of late capitalist urbanism.

Gentrification is the landed expression of displacements and dispossessions from our neighbors, our labor, and our bodies, but I remain unconvinced that "gentrification" is sufficient language with which to build a politics of urban land. I think we need something more, something deeper, something that calls to account the colonial accumulation our cities are constructed on and the kinds of labor that built them.

The domination of land enables and ennobles the domination of people, but the reverse is equally true. Undoing our commitments to one means undoing the other, and all too often gentrification scholarship of all kinds stumbles along, untroubled by the historical narratives all around us. Displacement is the water we're all swimming in, the logic that ensnares us all. As urbanity staggers under the weight of the global rush to urbanize, it is easy to claim that cities are just another site for the social and economic reproduction of inequalities. I suspect the peril is actually much worse: that the liberatory potentiality of cities is a weapon being turned on itself, and ourselves.

EQUITY AND ITS DISCONTENTS

It needs to be said that gentrification and displacement are not universally maligned malaises. Many people welcome rising property values and better-off arrivals for some very good, very definable reasons. Local businesses, for example, love having more people with disposable income around. Crime tends to decline in gentrified neighborhoods. Local politicians are thrilled with increased tax bases. Neighborhood watch groups trumpet "cleaning up" the neighborhood. But more than anyone, gentrification directly benefits homeowners.

Rising property values are the holy grail for almost everyone who owns a house. Obviously people who are engaged in speculation and property flipping rely on it, but more importantly for so many everyday people who have purchased homes, their hopes, their retirements, and most (sometimes all) of their equity is bound up in their houses. In every urban market there are huge numbers of people who have pushed all their savings, all their financial futures, into a single property. The ramifications of any serious value declines, especially for recent immigrant and working-class homeowners, can be brutal. It doesn't take all that much to trigger a foreclosure frenzy, and it's always the poorest of homeowners who get hit first and worst.

The precarity of so many mortgage holders puts them in particular (and peculiar) kinds of binds. Homeowners are forced to defend their property values, sometimes against their best instincts and interests. This often translates into tacit or even explicit support for gentrification and displacement, for regressive policy, or revanchist social milieus. And you can see why. To protect themselves, homeowners, often lower-income owners, believe that they *have to be* antagonistic to any "affordability" policies at scale, because widespread efforts to affect housing affordability will necessarily undermine and push down property values, a prospect many folks just can't stomach.[26] And

---

26. Or at least people *perceive* that increased affordability provisions will drag their home values down by adding cheap, subsidized supply. That's potentially the case, and may be specifically true in certain markets in certain places at certain times, but it's more complex than that. As John Emmeus Davis once said to me:

I'm not at all convinced that building out the affordable housing and social housing sector will reduce the property values of existing owners all that much. It's not a zero-sum game. If a given market was able to differentiate or segment and create more diversity in supply, say a one-third rental, one-third private ownership, and one-third social economy housing split, instead of 50/50 renters/owners, I doubt there would be much effect on market values. There is never just one market—there are always many micro-markets, not just geographically, but in types of tenure. The simplistic belief in supply and demand obscures market complexities. Classical economics, which assumed impermeable market boundaries, cannot account for this properly.

homeowners certainly have to be highly attentive to all the sociocultural contours that affect local property values. Driven by economic exigencies and precarities, this specific regime of land allocation necessarily pits neighbors against neighbors, demanding homeowners think first, second, and third about preserving their own equity.

The key vector that both complicates and exacerbates these simple algorithms has been the explosion of cheap credit over the last generation or two, and the belief that credit is a "fundamental human right."[27] The combination of explosive deregulation in the banking industry and globalized access to agile financing in essentially every sector has birthed a volatile formula for housing markets (and markets in general) everywhere. Thrown into the mix are enforcing narratives of homeownership (perhaps most aggressively articulated in the United States) and the neoliberal stoking of consumptive credit as the engine of economic resiliency: the result is a set of economic and cultural expectations around credit and the ownership of housing that are, at very best, highly distorted.[28]

Let me give you an example from my life, a pretty common contemporary middle-class kind of story. Two of my close buddies moved into the neighborhood at the same time my family did, in the early 1990s. Soon after, Buddy #1 got married, he and his wife both with solidly middle-class social service professional incomes. They got some money from their parents and bought a sweet little place just off a slightly sketchy street for just over $200,000.[29] Twenty years later that house was assessed at just over $920,000, despite

27. As per Muhammad Yunus, among many others.
28. For great explications of debt and credit in the contemporary world, see David Graeber, *Debt: The First 5000 Years* (Brooklyn, NY: Melville House, 2011) and/or Marizio Lazzarato, *The Making of the Indebted Man* (Los Angeles: Semiotext[e], 2012).
29. Please bear in mind that these numbers all come from Vancouver, the most out-of-control real estate market in North America. I know the prices seem too outrageous, but they're true.

them making no significant improvements to the place. They just wanted a place to live, and took care of it, but had no intention of turning into millionaires. They've paid it all off now and think it's something of a dirty joke that somehow that little house is now a goldmine.

Buddy #2 also has a partner, and both of them also have solidly middle-class careers and incomes. They held off buying a place, for whatever reasons, until fifteen years after couple #1. They purchased an equally nice, equally modest house just a few blocks away, but by then (mid-2000s) the price was $780,000 and this couple had to stretch wildly, borrowing every last cent they could from every corner of their extended families (which ended up being a huge amount), and still carry a pretty intimidating mortgage.

Then there is me and my family. We have always rented; neither my partner nor I could ask our families for anything like down payment money. That's not to say we or our families are poor—that's not case. It just hasn't worked out that we have ever been close to being able to buy, nor have we ever really wanted to or made the kinds of life/career decisions that would make it possible. We have been very fortunate to have rented the same house for eighteen years now and it has been perfect for us, but in early October we always have a couple of weeks of incipient tension and then everybody cheers when the landlord asks for another year of checks and decides not to sell the house.

Let me be crystal clear here: no one should shed a tear for any of these three families. All of us are doing great, we're all profligately privileged, and we are all solvent and probably will remain that way.[30] But we are on very different paths to accruing wealth. Buddy #1 has seen his financial cards fall into place, and things look great long-term for that family. Buddy #2 is doing fine as long as everything stays the course for the next decade or two. He and his partner are

30. Touch/knock on wood.

steadily paying down their mortgage and are currently stable. We are great too: we have no mortgage and not much debt, we have no assets, we own nothing, and we pay a fair amount in rent—rent that has paid off our landlord's mortgage and contributed significantly to *his* wealth.

Which gets to two core points. First, this particular kind of market has put the interests of the three of us in direct conflict. Buddy #1 is in good shape pretty much no matter what but has a long-term hope that property values stay high. Every day his wealth is accruing, but it is largely contained in his property. Buddy #2 desperately needs the financial and social architecture around him to continue to support his property value. They are pouring equity into the house, hoping it sticks; any significant turbulence and things will start to look very problematic very quickly. My family, on the other hand, would love to see property values collapse (or at least decline rapidly) so that we can either figure out some way to buy something, maybe with friends, or more likely, see our rent stabilized/reduced.[31] Three pretty similar families in many ways, with similar sorts of incomes, but our interests are in direct conflict based on our relationship to capital and homeownership. And our wealths have diverged very sharply.

Second: this is what happens in rich cities with (currently) fast-rising property values. In poorer places that are out of favor with urban elites, the logic is the same; it's just that the ramifications are starker and the consequences more dire. People are forced to make searing choices, to instrumentalize their homes, reimagine them as

---

31. I know I said it already, but let me repeat. In no way do I mean this to sound as if I am whining about my or my family's situation. We could scarcely be more grateful for how our lives have worked out, but a lot of it, especially our housing situation, has just been dumb luck, mediated by privilege, white and otherwise. Our complete lack of financial assets is the product of specific and explicit decisions, none of which I regret. Mainly, I want this example to illustrate the binds we are all in and the conundrums of certain interpretations of what constitutes wealth and value.

property, and then navigate that commodification based on incomplete market information and limited options. Take the example I just offered of three middle-class, middle-aged couples in a prosperous city in Canada and the clearly divergent wealth trajectories we are on, then extrapolate that to poorer places and poorer people with less capital of all kinds to access. And then imagine those divergences extrapolated one step further *between* places. Think about how that swift divergence in wealth—so evident in just a couple of decades of my life with repercussions for successive generations of our families—is accelerated and deepened in all kinds of ways in all kinds of places. And *then* consider how that divergence gets wielded in the service of racialization, white supremacy, and displacement. And then historicize those exact processes on colonized land as the prime wedge of inequalities in both the micro and macro senses.

Small differences become huge differences become generational inequalities become globally intransigent inequity. Or as it has been so clearly demonstrated, the oft-extravagant rate of return on capital creates classes of entrenched rentiers that beget further generations of even-wealthier rentiers. But I don't want to get fixated on individualized examples. I want to point to the structural conditions that leave all of us maneuvering to protect our own interests, constantly edging us into contention with our neighbors and undermining the best possibilities of urban life.

In Vancouver this makes for a social policy milieu where currently 52 percent of all dwellings are rented, approximately 66 percent in my neighborhood.[32] This bifurcation is underlined by income: the median income of renters is $34,000, owners $66,000, which is both

32. Statistics Canada, 2011 census data. In 2013, 69 percent of Canadians owned their houses. According to a report by the Joint Centers for Housing at Harvard University, in 2012 rentership sat at 35 percent across the United States, with Los Angeles (52 percent) and New York (48 percent) the highest among major markets and St. Louis (30 percent) the lowest.

cause and effect. Vancouver is often perceived as a rich city—and justifiably so. Its housing market remains one of the most expensive in the world, comparable to cities like San Francisco. But it is critical to differentiate between housing *stocks* and *flows*. While the housing market has created whole classes of millionaires and multimillionaires here, a quick glance reveals that Vancouverites' average income is far down the North American scale, in line with cities like Nashville and Reno, places that are rarely considered wealthy.[33] It's a weird contradiction: an absurdly expensive housing market blowing up in a city of decidedly modest incomes. Clearly the local housing market has decoupled from the local economy.

Some classes of people, who may or may not live or even ever visit here, are making fine profits from owning property in Vancouver. As I write, 17 percent of condo owners in Vancouver and Toronto have purchased a second investment unit, numbers that don't include Canadian and out-of-country investors who own units in these cities but do not live in either place, while 12 percent have a stated intent to flip their current residence for a profit.[34] But the median income levels of residents point to a majority of the population who are entirely left out of this property = wealth equation. The housing market remains fundamentally out of reach for everyday people here; or worse for some maybe, the scratching, clawing pursuit of "getting and staying in the game" is distorting their lives and finances grotesquely.

This is just one example from one Canadian city with one seriously problematic housing market, but you get the point. In every market the interests of renters and homeowners are necessarily at odds, which simultaneously creates and is exacerbated by tremendous differences

---

33. This is Andy Yan's fine research, cited often in pieces such as James Surowieki, "Real Estate Goes Global," *New Yorker*, May 26, 2014.
34. "17% of Condo Owners in Toronto, Vancouver Bought for Investment," *CBC News, Business*, August 8, 2014, http://www.cbc.ca/news/business/17-of -condo-owners-in-toronto-vancouver-bought-for-investment-1.2731289.

in both income and wealth. This fundamental contradiction grips cities everywhere, and is essential to understanding the nature of inequality and all its ramifications, historically, currently, and into the future, but also for bellying up to the exigency of capitalist crises.

As Harvard health scholar David R. Williams among many others has detailed,[35] white social and economic dominance in the United States has been in part maintained and concretized by the postwar boom in white homeownership that was subsidized with a 100 percent tax deduction on mortgage interest. Due to segregation and the racialized lending processes of banks, African Americans were very often shut out of the housing market and thus as taxpayers were relegated to subsidizing white homeownership and wealth accumulation. Little has changed: in 1900 the gap between the percentages of white and Black people who owned homes in America was 28 percent. In 2014 the number was also 28 percent. The overall percentages have risen in both cases, but the chasm remains. The real estate research firm that published these statistics commented: "The racial divide in the United States is a tale as old as time. And remarkably, in terms of homeownership, that tale has been largely unchanged for more than a century."[36] Agreed, but I want to think more critically about homeownership here: as not just an unalloyed good, but a core driver of inequality and a deeply damaging construct in toto.

These same kinds of property stories play out constantly, in every city to a greater or lesser extent. But it is not just that people who have money (and whose families have money) can buy and are financially resilient; it's that owning tends to fix, accelerate and venerate financial accumulation. Not all kinds of property ownership are

35. See David R. Williams and Chiquita Collins, "US Socioeconomic and Racial Differences in Health: Patterns and Explanations," *Annual Review of Sociology* 21 (1995): 349–386.

36. Skylar Olsen, "A Black and White Story, Unchanged for 115 Years," *Zillow, Real Estate Analytics*, February 3, 2015, http://www.zillow.com/research/home ownership-by-race-8851/.

equal though; some do little for building wealth, while other types are straight gold. This is everyday knowledge, but the ramifications tend not to be fully understood or appreciated. In a world now increasingly maimed by explosive inequality, questions of equity are fundamentally questions of land, and there is no way to think of a twenty-first-century urbanism without starting with a politics of land, and thus an interrogation of sovereignty.

The *rent vs. own* pivot is very far from the real issue. That conversation is an individualist's blunt instrument and obscures far more than it reveals. We are all renters in the eyes of the state. All you homeowners—try not paying your taxes, for example, and see how that goes. Or try skipping a mortgage payment. It is time to move beyond the rent/own bifurcation (theoretically and economically) and get to fundamental questions of property and ownership and to consider how normative expectations, especially around land, have been so reduced and so limited. The city is a collective achievement,[37] but so many of us are entirely acclimated to believing that differential and preferential access to the benefits is justified. How unimaginative is that?

UNDERWATER

The racialization of land could scarcely have been clearer to me than in New Orleans some eight years after Hurricane Katrina. I was sitting at the edge of Louis Armstrong Park near where I was staying with a pal in Treme. An older woman strolled by and asked if I need some water. I did (pretty obviously: flushed in the heat and pouring sweat), and she handed me a half-full, half-cold plastic bottle. She scoffed when I asked if she wanted me to pay for it: "I just thought you looked thirsty." She sat down on the bench beside me. "It's Isabella, but everyone calls me Izzy." She said she was Puerto Rican, Afro-Cuban, and Native

---

37. To use a phrase from gentrification theorist Elvin Wyly.

American and had lived there her whole life. She knew I wanted to hear it, so without any prodding she generously told me her Katrina story, and it was as bad as I could have anticipated.

Post-Katrina NOLA is a crisis theory/disaster capitalism case-study in action. Izzy's childhood home was just over in St. Bernard Parish, where her family had lived for at least three generations. Izzy, her aged mother, brother, son and daughter all made it pretty early to the Superdome: "We weren't taking no chances," she recalled. They stuck together to endure five days of hellish conditions, then were evacuated by bus to the Astrodome in Houston where they spent four more days, then (amazingly) all five of them were put up together in a motel off a freeway in suburban Houston and given food stamps and emergency rations. They returned to New Orleans three months later, but their house was gone. "Just gone! A pile of garbage!" So they stayed in a tiny FEMA trailer as long as they could stand it, and then separated into the homes of friends and family in various parts of the city. They had no insurance or savings to speak of, and currently Izzy said they rely on a dense network of church, family, neighborhood, and parish supports to get by. Her mother had since passed, her brother and son lived elsewhere in the city, and she and her daughter now lived with her sister in Treme. The family still had title to the original property, but had no plans to build, and no real expectations of returning to St. Bernard. "That's getting to be a different neighborhood now, honey," she concluded.

That's a pretty standard kind of story across almost every part of NOLA, but far more so in Black communities. In the years after Katrina, "54 percent of African American evacuees returned [to their homes], compared with 82 percent of white evacuees."[38] In 2010

---

38. "Eight Years after Hurricane Katrina, Many Evacuees Yet to Return," *Al-Jazeera*, August 29, 2013, http://america.aljazeera.com/articles/2013/8/29/eight-years-afterkatrinalowincomeevacueeshaveyettoreturn.html.

Amnesty International found that far more money was being paid out to residents of white communities while Black neighborhoods saw a massive (and Amnesty International suggests very likely permanent) decline in public housing and affordable rental stock.[39] Just four years after the storm, rents were more than 40 percent higher,[40] and in 2014 CNN Money called New Orleans one of the hottest property markets in the country.[41] New Orleans and Portland are two very different kinds of scenarios with very similar results: Black communities getting displaced. While both, along with every other similar situation, are often subsumed under sweeping gentrification theories, we need more specific and nuanced explanations and lines of analyses.

As Isabella said goodbye, gesturing for me to rise and give her a hug, I asked her where else I should go hang out in the city. She suggested a couple of places, one in the Bywater, a few in Bernard, one in the Lower Ninth. "You be careful though, son! If you're just walking around places doing nothing, people are going to think you're looking to buy up the neighborhood. We got too many white folks trying to take advantage of people when they're down. Not many of us here appreciate that, if you know what I'm meaning." She stared at me good and hard.

39. "Un-natural Disaster: Human Rights on the Gulf Coast," *Amnesty International*, April 2010, http://www.amnestyusa.org/sites/default/files/pdfs/unnaturaldisaster.pdf.

40. "Eight Years after Hurricane Katrina, Many Evacuees Yet to Return," *Al-Jazeera*, August 29, 2013, http://america.aljazeera.com/articles/2013/8/29/eight-years-afterkatrinalowincomeevacueeshaveyettoreturn.html.

41. "There is still plenty of room for this housing market to grow. The median home price in the metro area was only $163,000 during the three months ended September, more than 20% below the national median. CoreLogic is predicting home prices will increase by 8.6% over the next 12 months, followed by a better-than-average 5.4% increase in the year after that" (Les Christie, "10 Hottest Housing Markets for 2014," CNN Money, January 23, 2014, http://money.cnn.com/gallery/real_estate/2014/01/23/hottest-housing-markets/3.html).

Disaster makes for tremendous opportunity, as they say, often just as much as a booming property market. Shit, if you have money, everything looks like a hot market and a potential windfall. If you don't have much wealth, everything looks precarious and out of reach. There is a very clear and well-understood (empirically and theoretically) connection between land tenure and inequality, but we need to move that analysis several steps further to understand that specific *kinds* of tenure inhere certain *kinds* of social relationships and certain *kinds* of social (and economic, cultural) milieus. Thinking about displacement cannot be an isolated exercise; we have to understand specific processes within more broadly historicized and politicized contexts. Maybe more bluntly: any attempts to ameliorate displacement are doomed if they are not rooted in an aggressively equitable and decolonized politics of land, ownership, and sovereignty. Moreover, the city is the right place to start that project, not as a metaphor[42] but as a material rethinking, reimagining, and reallocation of land.

But what does that mean? What *could* that mean? Good people have been saying "Property is theft" since Plato,[43] but it strikes me that we have to dispense with fuzzy notions like "public space" or "the commons" and get more specific, more possible, and more focused on what we're talking about, and what we *could be* talking about. Maybe the most conveniently available theoretical step is to subsume narratives of gentrification and displacement into postcolonial analyses and view contemporary displacements of urban land as the logical extension of colonialisms. The rationalizations for occupying and dominating

42. As per Eve Tuck and K. Wayne Yang, "Decolonization Is Not a Metaphor," *Decolonization: Indigeneity, Education & Society* 1, no. 1 (2012): 1–40.
43. Okay, fine. So Plato didn't say exactly that. Proudhon did in his 1840 book *What Is Property? Or, an Inquiry into the Principle of Right and of Government*, and he actually called it *robbery*, not theft. But Plato was substantially skeptical about the divisive effects of private property. For a good and accessible introductory historical discussion, start with *The Stanford Dictionary of Philosophy*'s entry on property: http://plato.stanford.edu/entries/property/.

someone else's land for your own benefit flow from the same philosophical presumptions of superiority and supremacy, but that too
needs to be substantially nuanced. All gentrifications are not made
equal, and pretty much all the core concepts that are deployed in those
conversations are worthy of close examination.

Take *displacement* and *dispossession* for example, processes that
are often conflated synonymously. But these functions are nuanced
and have different sets of references and implications. The gentrification that a middle-class white family (justifiably) decries when
considering selling their house in an urban neighborhood where
property values and taxes have risen alarmingly is not the same as the
gentrification experienced by a low-income person who is forcibly
evicted from her single room occupancy hotel. And none of it is the
same as people across the globe who have been dispossessed of their
land by colonialism. It's just not. A settler urbanite having to leave a
neighborhood where his family has lived, maybe for generations,
might be sad and awful and distressing, but ultimately probably
alright. Land-based Indigenous cultures being displaced from their
traditional territory is tantamount to cultural genocide. Those processes may have similar geneses and affects but are not commensurate, and each of those are of course experienced intersectionally and
differently by different people, contingent on gender, sexuality, class
privilege, etc.

I am particularly interested in how those two words—*dispossession* and *displacement*—are deployed, and what they point to: whether
there is daylight between them, and if so what that distance is. My
first instinct here was to think of dispossession as a deeper, more
endemically corrosive technique of power, as per Judith Butler and
Athena Athanasiou's description of dispossession:

> In general, dispossession speaks to how human bodies become
> materialized and de-materialized through histories of slavery,
> colonization, apartheid, capitalist alienation, immigration and

asylum politics, post-colonial liberal multiculturalism, gender and sexual normativity, securitarian governmentality, and humanitarian reason. It might be helpful to consider that in the proper sense of the word, if such a thing exists, "dispossession" originally referred to practices of land encroachment ... "dispossession" offers language to express experiences of uprootedness, occupation, destruction of homes and social bonds, incitation to "authentic" self-identities, humanitarian victimization, unlivability, and struggles for self-determination.[44]

I felt less convinced after reading this. The distinctions and boundaries between all concepts are always permeable and shifting, and there is never a "proper sense" of *any* word. It's not fruitful to attempt to draw and then police firm lines of demarcation. It *is* useful however to pay careful attention to how processes are ascribed and inscribed, and who and what we are naming. Displacement looks very different for different people, and while dispossession is inherent in late capitalism it is very far from a universalizable experience. The core problem with attempting to define and fix clear definitional demarcations, to claim a proper sense of words, is that it denies difference, the possibility of divergent experiences of similar processes, the contingent characters of all relationships, and popular participation in defining and redefining languages and concepts.

But I still wanted some clarity, I wanted to think it through some more, so I went for a beer with my pal Sobhi Al-Zobaidi. Sobhi is a Palestinian scholar, filmmaker, restaurateur, and novelist[45] as well as a terrific friend and sophisticated thinker. He and his family moved to Vancouver after the Israeli occupation made their life untenable in Palestine. Sobhi is from Ramallah and his wife Tamam grew up in the

44. Judith Butler and Athena Athanasiou, *Dispossession: The Performative in the Political* (Cambridge: Polity Press, 2013), 10–11.
45. And lots more, too. Look him up, for real.

Old City of Jerusalem, so the Wall separated their family's homes, constantly burdening work and travel and family with baroque bureaucracies and violence. After so much harassment and trauma they fled Palestine, leaving behind huge lives and extended families. So I figured he was the right person to help me think this through.

Sobhi started by drawing my attention to the debate around people fleeing New Orleans after Katrina: whether they should be called "evacuees" or "refugees." Al Sharpton, among others, furiously refuted the notion that they were refugees: "They are not refugees. They are citizens of the United States. They are not refugees wandering somewhere looking for charity." And many liberal media outlets complied, adopting policies that referred to them as American evacuees.[46]

Sobhi, on the other hand, insists that he, his family, and Palestinians in general are absolutely refugees, and that the term is important in no small part because it is bound up with the *right to return*. To him "evacuees" suggests an emptying out of a place, leaving it vacant, or an involuntary sucking out of its people. "Refugees," on the other hand, leave with the intent to return someday. Refugees have left to find refuge from catastrophe, to seek help, but they carry memory and agency. To be a refugee is to be in a temporary state. Refugees move, they flee. Evacuees are taken. "In Palestinian literature we are refugees, but present in both places."[47]

We tried to apply the same kind of distinctions to *displacement* and *dispossession* but the fit was awkward. It seemed clear to us that there *is* daylight between the two processes, but the two terms are not so easily parsed. Sobhi thought of Palestinians who are now

46. Mike Pesca, "Are Katrina's Victims 'Refugees' or 'Evacuees'?," NPR Reporter's Notebook, September 5, 2005, http://www.npr.org/templates/story/story .php?storyId=4833613.
47. See also here the conversation between Gilles Deleuze and Palestinian author Elias Sanbar from 1982: http://www.versobooks.com/blogs/1684-the -indians-of-palestine-an-interview-between-gilles-deleuze-and-elias-sanbar.

contained within Israeli borders—they are dispossessed of almost everything, but not displaced. They still reside on their land but are forbidden from it. This is a function of settler colonialism and echoes the experience of Indigenous people, many of whom remain on at least on part their land but are profoundly dominated on it by settler states. Then we thought of Roma, Bedouin, and other nomadic peoples and how they would approach those words.

Sobhi also spoke of his own father who between 1948 and 1967 lost the houses, orchards, almost everything he had inherited: "I was born into a web of narratives of loss. All through my youth my father relentlessly talked about how 'we used to do this, we used to have this, we used to ...' My father lived in a refugee camp, separated from his family. The times people in the camps were allowed to briefly return home were called Joyous Family trips—they reconnected with their relatives, their neighbors, the trees, the geography, the animals. They reconnected with their identity and their memory of land. Everything revolves around memory. His was an existential loss: not just a number of objects but everything that constituted who he was."

There's a particular set of relationships in Sobhi's story between materiality and immateriality, between memory and existence, between place and identity. He spoke of "the grammar of settler colonialism," the "tools of cultural dispossession," and the way that so much of Palestine was renamed and invested with new stories. "It is the network of relations that makes us visible—it is who we are—we are a mixture of what we have and what we had. We are networks of relationships between objects and people. But there is not one perfect subjectivity that gets corrupted by loss or gain. Our subjectivities are always in process, but become fixed by various ideologies and/or social forces that aim to dominate and posit themselves above all others."

There is a question in here about what we can be rightfully said to "possess." What about the will to possess? What honestly do we "own"? Can we be said to "own our memories"? Sobhi suggests there is a problem with phrasing it that way.

Because then we assume that there is "me" or "us" outside of memory (i.e., the subject is formed outside of memory then takes hold of it). But in fact there is no subjectivity outside of memory. We do not exist outside of memory; it is the network of relations that constitute our sense of who we are. That question turns memory into an object that can be "owned." I also think that "dispossession" at some level has to do with memory in terms of disruption or loss. This is why when we lose a house or a car we're not dispossessed because they can be replaced, but dispossession is the taking away of the space that contains all the objects that articulate one's memory, and these are not replaceable. Dispossession results in some kind of loss and disorientation.

Something necessarily happens to these words and ideas when the context shifts. Depending on when and how we're speaking—and who is speaking—about New Orleans or Palestine or Albina, something happens to the concepts. When displacement and dispossession are transposed to the urban, they translate easily but not directly. As soon they are fetishized and fixed, the ideas become dogmatic. The experiences of dispossession and displacement are always contingent and contextual, overlapping and entwined. The two concepts should be useful tools for thinking and acting, not weights that bear us down.

The displacement of low-income, working-class, and racialized residents from gentrifying neighborhoods in Canadian cities, for example, needs to be confronted for sure, but in the context of settler colonialism and the understanding that literally all those neighborhoods are on traditional Indigenous land. Thinking about American cities—like, say, Portland—is always entangled with histories of slavery and the domination of Black bodies. Ahistoricity is a prime capitalist strategy: constantly wiping the slates clean so that each successive person, family, and neighborhood can claim ignorance and/or nonresponsibility for what happened previously, even if it was very recent and right under our feet. As William Blackstone famously said about property in

1766: "Pleased as we may be with the possession, we seem afraid to look back to the means by which it was acquired, as if fearful of some defect in our title; or at best we rest satisfied with the decision of the laws in our favour, without examining the reason or authority upon which those laws have been built."[48]

In Portland I have met so many white people eager to complain ritualistically and passionately about gentrification and housing prices in the city, but who are shocked to hear of Albina's ongoing displacement of Black people. I have heard white kids blithely and bitterly complain that they can't find a cheap enough place to live on Alberta Street, apparently oblivious to the stories all around them, even very recent and still unraveling ones. But those stories too also have their historical contexts. If Albina is being remade as a very white place, it is treading a well-worn Oregon trail.

PARTISANALLY CRAFTED

This current round of Black displacements was formally launched in 1990, but it was built on a considerable and consistent historical foundation. Northeast Portland became fully consolidated as the area's dominant African American district after 1948, in the wake of the Vanport flood. Vanport (situated on the southern side of the Columbia between Portland and Vancouver, Washington) was a purpose-built wartime community that was erected in 1942 and swiftly grew into the country's single largest public housing project with 42,000 residents at its max (including 40 percent Black people), making it Oregon's second biggest city at the time. Originally intended as a temporary site, it soon included recreation and shopping centers,

---

48. William Blackstone, *Commentaries on the Laws of England, Volume II, Of the Rights of Things* (Oxford: Clarendon Press, 1766), 2. Blackstone, and this (larger) passage is cited so often as to verge on reflexive requirement in a critical/radical text about property, rights, and ownership, but it is cited so often because it so good.

schools and a college, day cares, hospitals, movie theaters, and other services. As the war ended, the population slowly dropped in half and there was considerable conflict between politicians interested in repurposing the site and a significant number of people who intended to stay put and make it home, including at least six thousand (largely segregated) African Americans. In 1948 the Columbia River settled the issue by catastrophically flooding the community, giving residents only thirty-five minutes to escape, wiping out the community and killing fifteen residents.[49] The Vanport refugees crowded into the city, with more than a thousand Black families impelled into Northeast Portland, bulging its population dramatically.[50]

The real estate board, local politicians, residents, and banks made certain that these new Black arrivals were welcome in Albina only, but almost immediately upon their arrival the neighborhood was further constricted. The construction of a new sports stadium at the south end of the community "revitalized" a whole section of the neighborhood, pushing Black people and Black-owned businesses further north. Then another round of "slum clearance" made way for the I-5 highway through the southern and western edges of Albina, and the construction of a new hospital further squeezed residents so that by 1960 four of five Black Portlanders lived in one 2.5-square-mile area of Albina and its four elementary schools were more than 90 percent Black.[51]

49. The connections between Vanport and NOLA's Katrina experience are unmistakable. See, for example, Portland community radio KBOO's special on Vanport: http://kboo.fm/vanport.
50. Manly Maben, *Vanport* (Portland: Oregon Historical Society Press, 1987); Carl Abbott, "Vanport," *The Oregon Encyclopedia*, http://www.oregonencyclopedia .org/articles/vanport/#.VrZn6HqLf1A.
51. Leanne Claire Serbula and Karen J. Gibson, "Black and Blue: Police-Community Relations in Portland's Albina District, 1961–1985," *Oregon Historical Quarterly* 114, no. 1 (2013): 10.

And of course *this* history itself has to be situated in the larger context of Oregon's explicitly racist history, a state that has had all the pillars of white supremacy formally articulated and enshrined throughout its development. In 1844, for example, Oregon constitutionally outlawed slavery but included an "exclusion clause" that made it illegal for Black people to remain in the state, under threat of lashing—a clause not removed until 1926. In 1849 the clause was amended to allow Black laborers currently residing in the state to stay, but forbid any others from entering. A reentrenchment of the law in 1857 further disallowed Black people from owning land, entering courts, or having legal privileges, and in 1862 all people of color had to pay an annual tax just to live in Oregon. In this kind of atmosphere it makes sense that the state emerged as a longtime Ku Klux Klan stronghold, and that Oregon was one of only seven states that refused to ratify the Fifteenth Amendment, giving Black people the right to vote, and held out until 1959.[52]

As historian and author Walidah Imarisha[53] explained to me, the history of Oregon mirrors the national narrative of white utopianism:

Outside of the state very little is known about Oregon history, but I think it is an incredibly useful case study for the rest of the nation because Oregon was bold enough to write their ideologies down explicitly: it was the only state in the union admitted with

52. For some other good sources on Oregon, Portland, and Albina's racialized history, see *The History of Portland's African American Community (1805–Present)*, City of Portland Bureau of Planning, 1993, https://www.portlandoregon. gov/bps/article/91454; Gibson, "Bleeding Albina"; Cheryl A. Brooks, "Race, Politics and Denial: Why Oregon Forgot to Ratify the Fourteenth Amendment," *Oregon Law Review* 83, no. 2 (2004): 731; Carl Abbott, "Portland: Planning, Politics, and Growth in a Twentieth Century City," *Pacific Historical Review* 54, no. 1 (1985): 102–103, http://gizmodo.com/oregon-was-founded-as-a-racist -utopia-1539567040.
53. And educator, journalist, poet, activist, spoken word performer. She's pretty amazing. Check her out at www.walidah.com.

an exclusive racial exclusionary clause in its Constitution. Oregon has always been an attempt to create a white homeland—it
is a racist white utopian experiment. These ideas are not just
dead and gone in the past: the racial exclusionary language in the
Oregon constitution wasn't removed until 2001—and even then
the removal passed by the slimmest of margins. The Fourteenth
Amendment, which guarantees universal citizenship rights regardless of race, wasn't fully ratified until 1973, over one hundred years after the federal government passed it—again by very
slim margins. These same sentiments of Oregon as a white homeland reverberate today: the idea of Portlandia is as a white liberal
playground—predicated on racial exclusion and oppression.[54]

And of course all *this* history is predicated on the colonization and
domination of Indigenous nations. The state of Oregon was notori-
ous for settler brutality toward Indigenous residents (even in an era
of widespread officially-sanctioned white barbarism) and in 1850
the Oregon Donation Land Act forcibly removed all Indigenous people and offered indigenously held land free to any white settlers, who
within seven years had claimed 2.5 million acres of it including all of
the current city of Portland (the city was incorporated—notably—in
1851). American denial of Indigenous citizenship was maintained
until 1924 but many states, Oregon included, refused to recognize
Indigenous voting rights until the federal government stepped in
with the Voting Rights Act of 1965. More than sixty tribes in Oregon
were terminated by the federal government in 1953, consolidated
into larger affiliations or simply eradicated, and yet through it all
Portland retains the ninth largest urban Indigenous population in
the United States.[55]

54. Personal interview with Walidah Imarisha, March 19, 2015.
55. Anne Curry-Stevens, Amanda Cross-Hemmer, and Coalition of Communities of Color, *The Native American Community in Multnomah County: An Unsettling Profile* (Portland, OR: Portland State University, 2011).

Northeast Portland and Albina sit on the historical site of the village of Neerchokikoo, which Lewis and Clark encountered and which had existed there for uncounted generations. Like so many other places, the current iteration of the community rests on layers and layers of displacement and dispossessions that only become visible the longer you look and the more you ask. Now that's a briskly inadequate history of Portland, but you get my point. The clearance of Albina is no accident, no historical anomaly: the stories we listen to and the stories we tell ourselves, which ones we privilege, which ones we call "official," and which ones we decide are legitimate are no accident.

But ahistoricized ignorance is hardly the exclusive province of self-absorbed hipster kids in Portland, and it's always a good idea to keep interrogating how our own words land and what exactly we're talking about. It's useful to resist taxonomically precise social definitions[56] and instead try to remain alert to how ideas/languages are deployed in particular circumstances, and note closely how they are constructed and in what name and for what purpose they are wielded. All too often tightly controlled but apoliticized ideas get subsumed under soft, ungrounded, and floating meanings that muddy the analytical waters, typically in the service of privilege.

Take the idea of "the commons," for example, which shines brightly throughout all kinds of literature and organizing, sparkling with promise and is almost always unburdened by much contour or depth.[57] It used to be that leftist or progressive urbanists reflexively called for more "public space," and now the similarly ubiquitous

56. Unless in the rare cases in which that precision is in the explicit interest of opening rather than closing down conversation. I am very fond, for example, of Raymond Williams's iconic dictionary of ideas, *Keywords* (Oxford: Oxford University Press, 1984), which I rely on often and which feels like a starting point for investigation, not an end point.
57. Like, say, in lots of my writing. See *Common Ground in a Liquid City: Essays in Defense of an Urban Future* (Oakland: AK Press, 2010), for example.

FIGURE 1.1
John Washington and Joice Taylor of NNEBA. (Photo by Lani Brunn)

refrain is for common space and commonality. But it's rarely clear what exactly it is that is being called for, or how it should be realized, or more often how it is to be "reclaimed."

The way the commons or public space is employed in most urban literature presumes that if the space is open, or public, or not overtly privately secured, then everyone will therefore have equal access. But of course that's patently untrue: many factors constrain or enable a person's ability to access "the commons." Consider, for example, a person's gender identification, which almost always affects their willingness and capacity to hang out, say, in a public square, depending on all kinds of other factors including the time of day, who else is there, what kinds of activities seem to hold sway, etc. The larger idea of the commons holds a similar danger—flattening out subjectivities into one beige-colored "commonality," absent difference or history.

Like seemingly every other tool, theoretical or otherwise, the language of the commons can (and does) easily become weaponized[58] to justify displacement. So many national, provincial, and state parks across North America, for example, have been created under "commons" kinds of discourses while explicitly enclosing, excluding, regulating, and containing traditional Indigenous hunting, fishing, trapping, and spiritual practices. As Leanne Simpson puts it: "Historically, Indigenous peoples have never been involved in negotiations for the establishment of parks and protected areas—our lands are always just expropriated without consent. Indigenous peoples and Canadians would both have 'rights' to the land but in the commons these are always determined by the state not Indigenous nations."[59]

Any talk of the commons has to work through notions of *incommensurability*, of difference, to avoid concretizing patterns dominance. Bike lanes and hospitals for example —both "common goods" in urban planning parlance—are often deployed as instruments of gentrification. But we can demand a lot more from commonality: we can interrogate how it is being mobilized, by whom, and for what purposes, and we can ask why that language so frequently seems to disregard, paper over, or actively deny historicity. Invoking the commons doesn't wipe the slate clean.

58. "As Klee Benally notes, decolonization is often weaponized by settlers in order to justify anti-Blackness." Andrea Smith, "The Colonialism That Is Settled and the Colonialism That Never Happened," *Decolonization: Indigeneity, Education & Society*, June 20, 2014, https://decolonization.wordpress.com/2014/06/20/the-colonialism-that-is-settled-and-the-colonialism-that-never-happened/.

59. Personal communication, July 17, 2015. See also the story she relates in which Elder Gidigaa Migizi (Doug Williams) tells her about the imposition of the 1923 Williams Treaty in Leanne Betasamosake Simpson, "Land as Pedagogy: Nishnaabeg Intelligence and Rebellious Transformation," *Decolonization: Indigeneity, Education & Society* 3, no. 3 (2014): 1–25.

Abandoning the idea of the commons is too fraught though; its possibilities are too powerful, and so I want to find ways to complicate and substantiate it. If we recognize that the lands we want "commoned" are saturated with stories, some of them beautiful, and many of them awful tales of displacement and dispossession, then we're more likely to entwine land and justice. If we think about the commons as full of potentiality, as an unstable, politicized idea, as a "flexible template for talking about the rich productivity of social communities and the market enclosures that threaten them"[60] then maybe we have something to fight for. I want to keep speaking about the commons and commonality, but that's pretty easy coming from a white settler's mouth, one accustomed to wearing his privilege like skin, so I'll do it cautiously and hopefully with humility.

There's more here. To speak of the commons is always to speak of property, and that too is a deceptively but decidedly complicated and slippery word. The literature offers (literally) hundreds of possible definitions, and even more resonances are available, to be able to claim much clarity: "There are too many contradictions and contested meanings, too many loose ends, too much contingency and arbitrariness, to many insecure and constructed subject-positions, mixed in with the order, the certainty, the predictability, and the solidity of (certain aspects of) property."[61] This is all good though; throughout the rest of this book, I'll talk about property from a variety of angles and approaches, but mostly when I talk about property I am talking about land, and most often about land and freedom, and even more so land *as* freedom.

60. David Bollier, "Growth of the Commons Paradigm," in *Understanding Knowledge as Commons: From Theory to Practise*, ed. Charlotte Hess and Elinor Ostrom (Cambridge, MA: MIT Press, 2007), 38.
61. Margaret Davies, *Property: Meanings, Histories, Theories* (New York: Routledge, 2007), 10.

Because "city air is supposed to make people free."[62] I believe that an ecological future has to primarily be an urban future: that eight billion humans have to learn to live densely to carefully share and steward our remaining resources. Our best routes to preserving small-town, agricultural, rural, and wilderness integrities is a robust, imaginative urbanism. Cities can, do, and should free us (in multiple senses), but in late capitalism's global land frenzy the historical ideal of a *civitas*—a res publica agreement that binds urban residents together—is consistently violated and perverted into one more site for capital's predation, ever-deepening inequality, and constant, inevitable rounds of displacement. As Manuel Castells prophesized a generation ago in *The Urban Question*, the advanced capitalist city becomes not just *another site* for capital accumulation, but *another kind of site*, a site that now produces staggering and accelerating possibilities for dispossession and enclosure.

Academic researchers have been relentless, voluminous, and often brilliant at documenting successive waves of gentrified displacements statistically, empirically, and ethnographically. Try reading critical urban studies, planning, geography, or sociology journals and you'll be overwhelmed with data, surveys, and narratives. Any number of more accessible publications do similarly good journalistic work sketching the outlines and repercussions of urban transformations, and it's a formulaic conversational trope at dinner tables and on street corners everywhere. Gentrification is accepted, assumed, and consistently included in discussions about any city.

I appreciate that. The first step is to admit you have a problem, etc., but I'll suggest that collectively we've got to be more imaginative to think over, through, and beyond gentrified aporias. Over and over

---

62. This motto was carved over the city gates of the Hanseatic League, a decentralized and federated network of market towns that stretched across coastal Northern Europe from the thirteenth to seventeenth century.

again I see these narratives of gentrification start by withdrawing into two, typically simultaneous and mutually reinforcing stances of fatalism and nostalgia. First: nothing can resist market-driven displacements (it's just natural), and second, the only real response is a retreat into "good old days" misty-eyed remembrances. Neither of these options sits well.

It is often claimed that no neighborhood has ever successfully reversed gentrification, and depending on how you define "success," I guess that's essentially true. Ideologies of the market are now so pervasively ingrained in our ways of being that it is often hard to think outside that logic: "It's like trying to fix a hammer with the hammer you're trying to fix."[63] But surely we can think and act our way out of this, surely this historical moment is not the sum of our future, and surely we can do differently and better.

Nostalgia is a siren song: appealing and attractive, entirely irritating (especially when I fall prey to it), and dangerous. Invoking halcyon days closes off possibility and collects power as a memory unavailable to those who weren't lucky enough to be there. I appreciate the attraction of sun-dappled days past, but only as a means to conjure something new and as a path to new possibilities, to conceiving an altermodernity. The right response to displacement and dispossession is a confidently imaginative struggle. For me, that tends to point to very basic questions around how we impute value, and what we speak of when we claim value.[64]

---

63. As Michael Kinsley, writing in the *New Yorker* about dementia, put it in "Have You Lost Your Mind?," April 28, 2014, http://www.newyorker.com/magazine/2014/04/28/have-you-lost-your-mind.

64. For an excellent recent discussion of "value," see George Henderson's *Value in Marx: The Persistence of Value in a More-Than-Capitalist World* (Minneapolis: University of Minnesota Press, 2013).

SOME GRIEVE WHILE OTHERS REJOICE EXCEEDINGLY

Now is a great time to be talking about what and how to value cities. In an era when Thomas Piketty and Occupy Wall Street, financialization, credit-default swaps, and Gini coefficients are in common parlance, our intuitive senses tell us almost all we need to know: that mind-bending income inequality and dominant thinking about land, and especially urban land, are tightly bound up together. In so many cities across the globe, modestly incomed residents cannot reasonably afford reasonable dwellings while as of mid-2014 Bill Gates had enough wealth to purchase every home in the city of Boston (114,212 single-family homes, condos, and townhouses, at a total purchase price of $76.6 billion). The Walton family could purchase Seattle,[65] the Koch brothers Atlanta,[66] and so it goes.[67] In 2014 the wealthiest eighty-five families in the world owned as much wealth as the bottom *3.5 billion*.[68] That was bad enough, but by 2015 Oxfam confirmed that the news was getting steadily worse (to approximately no one's surprise): "The share of the world's wealth owned by the best-off 1% has increased from 44% in 2009 to 48% in 2014, while the least well-off 80% currently own just 5.5%."[69]And in 2016, once again with dully metronomic predictability, Oxfam released new figures confirming that indeed the world's sixty-two richest billionaires own as much wealth as the poorer half of the world's population, and that 1

65. That's 241,450 homes, $111.5 billion.
66. That's 286,629 homes, $78.1 billion.
67. Tommy Unger, "Which Billionaire Could Buy Your City?," *Redfin*, June 5, 2014, http://www.redfin.com/research/reports/special-reports/2014/us-cities -that-billionaires-could-buy.html#.U5EHP_mwJcQ.
68. "Working for the Few," Oxfam Briefing Paper, January 20, 2014, http:// www.oxfam.org/sites/www.oxfam.org/files/bp-working-for-few-political -capture-economic-inequality-200114-summ-en.pdf.
69. Larry Elliot and Ed Pilkington, "New Oxfam Report Says Half of Global Wealth Held by the 1%," *The Guardian*, January 19, 2015, http://www.theguardian .com/business/2015/jan/19/global-wealth-oxfam-inequality-davos-economic -summit-switzerland.

percent of the globe's population really does own more wealth than the world combined.[70]

One of the core lies of classical economics, and one that is often invoked to justify numbers like these, is that economies are like the weather, governed by natural laws—predictable, trackable, calculable—but immutable: that vast inequality is bad, and we can try to respond to it, but it is just natural, always has been, always will be. Working from that perspective, we see that the longing for economic "development" is easily positioned as an unwavering, unapologetic, and universalized desire. Thus we are burdened by a (at least) 250-year-old[71] set of interlocking discourses of land and private property that leaves us with a presumptive burden of fixity: that this supposed economic reality is all there is. But if nothing else, the recurrence and deepening of capitalist and ecological crises should illustrate how urgently very different ways of thinking, acting, and owning are required.

A solid place to start is by aggressively reconsidering the languages we invoke. If "economics," "development," and "wealth" are clearly historically situated discourses like property or the commons, then "value" has to be an equally worthy candidate for interrogation. Homeowners tend to be adroitly suspicious of the idea of value, in part because of the capriciousness of the value of their homes. When a property market rises, or collapses, or does whatever, an owner's equity mirrors that rise or fall, despite their doing nothing substantive to affect the home price. Homeowners tend to do very little to

70. Larry Elliot, "Richest 62 People as Wealthy as Half of World's Population, Says Oxfam," *The Guardian*, January 18, 2016, http://www.theguardian.com /business/2016/jan/18/richest-62-billionaires-wealthy-half-world-population -combined. The original report is at http://www.oxfam.org.uk/media-centre /press-releases/2016/01/62-people-own-same-as-half-world-says-oxfam -inequality-report-davos-world-economic-forum.
71. Please start that narrative clock where you like. I'm not super interested in trying to locate some font of original land sin, but here I chose 1776 and the publication of the *Wealth of Nations*, which is just one possible point of origin.

cause their houses to rise in value and are rarely responsible when they fall. Homeownership simply captures socially created value and fixes it at particular junctures, allowing for differentiated access to and distribution of that equity.

I'm all in favor of people creating a home that reflects their personalities and expresses their subjectivities. The ability to stay in place over duration, over generations, is perhaps a foundational human experience. But that is totally unrelated to ownership. Conversations about tenure can be approached in multiple ways, and the most promising possibilities for better, more ecological urban relationships lie in removing land (in all senses) from the speculative marketplace and seeing the collective achievements of land value commensurately commoned.

That shift is much more than just a question of property ownership or stewardship. Asking questions about land is the right starting point for asking what a city is for, because it demands imagining a different city beyond a simple site for wealth accumulation. Thinking through land *demands* that we ask how possession, and the dispossession that permitted it, was conceived. Thinking about land *as* freedom demands answers for displacements, and it forces rematriations and reparations into the middle of the conversation. It demands we account for sovereignty and consider the city as a pivot point for resisting displacement and dispossession in multiple senses. What if the city *produced* freedom? That question demands a hopeful imagination—a productive creativity—as the necessary foundation for struggle, and thus for the city.

A COMBINATION PIZZA HUT AND TACO BELL[1]

2

It's a cliché to say that "developers run the city." People drop it in most every place I've ever been, and they're mostly right. Politicians have their spheres of influences, local organizers and activists can get noisy, city bureaucracies try hard to keep up, business organizations and chambers of commerce throw their weight around—but in the end it's the guys who own the land (and it's almost always guys) who ride herd on most of the real decisions. Development firms are often corporate conglomerates, sometimes they are families who got into the property business early in a city's history, others are individual cowboy-capitalist types making a big play, and now, with increasing frequency, it's aggressive capital from other sectors bulling their way into promising property markets. But no matter whose name is on the title, banks and financial lenders are always entwined and typically hold the hammer on final decisions.

There are variations on this theme. Some (especially U.S.) cities have community economic development corporations with significant land holdings, plenty of municipalities have major public housing and/or commercial stocks, and in many places the nation-state

1. With apologies to Himanshu Suri, Victor Vazquez, and Ashok Kondabolu.

owns huge chunks of the nonresidential city. In essentially every municipality, various layers of the state own at least some property within their jurisdictions, and many have very significant portfolios. Broadly speaking, in the Global South the delineations between various typologies of urban ownerships tend to be more complex, involving a wider range of state and nonstate actors, from international speculative financiers to squatters, but it is fair to say that developers of various configurations hold sway in every city everywhere.

And of course ownership imparts relative control over decision making, not just over specific properties but suffused through the sociocultural, political, and economic choices that affect and are affected by property (ergo, everything). Much of the residential market in every city is controlled by individual property owners in collaboration with their mortgage-holding institutions of choice, but huge and hugely variable proportions of that housing market are owned by larger agglomerations of capital, as are the vast majority of urban commercial, industrial, and manufacturing lands.

The raison d'être of these pools of capital, in endlessly hybridizing and fluid variations, is to relentlessly prowl for profit opportunities. Land speculators deploy dismayingly sophisticated algorithmic and actuarial financial tools—increasingly fueled by big data—to assess and predict land value trends and risks. Looking simultaneously to both the long and the short games, capital is constantly adjusting and responding to any possible differential land value gains and/or losses. Like any aggressive player, capital doesn't just observe and respond: all levels of speculator/investors do what they can to influence and manipulate market opportunities and any larger political/policy milieus that might impact property values.

This creates a happy confluence with the needs and desires of postindustrialized cities that are themselves thrust into a global neoliberal marketplace. In the urban rush, cities across the globe are left with responsibilities and costs vastly in excess of their tax bases and thus are constantly trying to create conditions favorable for internal, but especially external, investment. Hypercompetitive cycles of competition to attract and retain capital require cities to feverishly marshal and deploy arrangements of tax relaxations, incentives, urban branding and marketing, mega-events, and capital-friendly social regimes in order to lure investors, tourists, speculators, head offices, banks—anyone with significant capital is heartily welcomed pretty much anywhere at any time. Cities across the globe understand that they are in a dogfight—if capital doesn't feel wanted or supported enough in one city, there are always alluring possibilities elsewhere.

Thus the interests of cities and those of capital become one and the same, and *development* becomes synonymous with the activities of *developers*. But the presumptive logic rests in the claim that any city *does not have enough*. The starting point is the assertion of scarcity.[2] We are induced to believe that no one and no place has enough, in fact can never have enough, and so all cities are thrust into a churning desire to insert themselves into the flows and cycles of international capital, to brand and be branded as a global city worthy of capital's attention.

The all-consuming yearning for global city status has emerged as such a singular mark of contemporary urban policy and politics that it is now prefigured as the essence of city-ness itself. Thus *development* becomes something patently "natural" and normal, as the unfolding or growth of the sociability of the city, realized through

---

2. Which might actually be the singularly biggest lie of capitalism. Scarcity claims that there will never be enough (no matter how sophisticated a society's production) to satisfy unlimited human desires, and thus ongoing competition for scarce resources is endemic to the human condition. The most influential philosopher of scarcity in the Western world has been Thomas Malthus, primarily via his canonical work. See T. R. (Thomas Robert) Malthus, *An Essay on the Principle of Population: Or a View of Its Past and Present Effects on Human Happiness: With an Inquiry into Our Prospects Respecting the Future Removal or Mitigation of the Evils Which It Occasions*, 8th ed. (London: Reeves and Turner, 1878).

the activities of *developers*, who unapologetically view the entirety of the urban landscape as a play, a gamble of capital.

But who and what actually are "developers"? It's a fluid designation: a big-tent aphorism that can just as easily be deployed derogatorily or wielded as high praise and reconfigured for a variety of political ends, but it is clearly ideologically bound up with what is often referred to as the "development era." Development often tends to refer to the international—the set of acts that poorer (so-called developing) countries are presumed to need to perform to alleviate their poverty—but this process is extrapolated to every geographic and economic scale At the urban it presumes that the city needs to constantly *develop*—and the people that can do it are developers. That's a neat formula, but it presents us with a whole bundle of messes. It's worth taking a moment to trace the idea of *development* a little.

Most genealogies place development thinking as a post-World War II phenomenon that formally commences with Harry Truman's 1949 inaugural speech laying claim that:

> We must embark on a bold new program for making the benefits of our scientific advances and industrial progress available for the improvement and growth of underdeveloped areas.
>
> More than half the people of the world are living in conditions approaching misery. Their food is inadequate. They are victims of disease. Their economic life is primitive and stagnant. Their poverty is a handicap and a threat both to them and to more prosperous areas.
>
> For the first time in history, humanity possesses the knowledge and skill to relieve suffering of these people. ...
>
> I believe that we should make available to peace-loving peoples the benefits of our store of technical knowledge in order to help them realize their aspirations for a better life. And, in co-

operation with other nations, we should foster capital investment in areas needing development. ...

With the cooperation of business, private capital, agriculture,
and labor in this country, this program can greatly increase the
industrial activity in other nations and can raise substantially
their standards of living.[3]

Thus was charted a new path for American relationships with the
world's newly-minted "undeveloped" peoples, putatively based on
sympathy, unapologetic paternalism, charity, and not a small dose of
aspirational securitizing in the hope that a different tack might stave
off another global military conflagration.

Emerging from the wreckage of two World Wars and the abject
interregnum failure to ameliorate Germany's resentments, the Mar-
shall Plan was the debut and touchstone of this new orientation: a
proposition that economic reconstruction, aid, and support would
serve as an alternative to previous rationalities of unalloyed colonial
domination. The claim was that *development*, extrapolated throughout a Global South (once called the Third World, now named *under* or
*un*developed, or develop*ing*) would encourage/manipulate newly
independent colonies to adopt Westernized representative liberal
democracies, conceptions of progress, industrial rationality, and
modernization as operating principles. If that resulted in the opening up of a whole new world of consumer markets, extractivist vistas,
cheap/desperate labor pools, and dependent trading partners, well,
all the better.

Right out of the gate, the "development era" was bound at the hip
with the imperatives of the Cold War as the Soviet and American
blocs played Risk with the global map, seeking to expand spheres of

3. Harry S. Truman, *Inaugural Address*, January 20, 1949, http://www.presidency
.ucsb.edu/ws/?pid=13282.

influence, maneuver tactically, and prevent each other from military and commercial hegemony, focusing on key strategic regions with particularly heavy attention. Nationally orchestrated development aid and support was deployed as (and often in collaboration with) armed forces utilizing their assets, constantly asserting presence via key regional allies, regime installations/collapses, and crude market weapons—and always viewing *development* as an instrument of larger geopolitical economic and military goals.

With the ratcheting down of the Cold War, the development era retained its instrumental value but entered a new phase, less fixated on overtly militaristic goals and more committed to drawing the entirety of the Global South into formalized international trade mechanisms and relationships. With the planetary-scale expansion of neoliberal logics came the subsumption of *development* into discourses of capitalist globalization via the Washington Consensus and aid-for-trade schemes tying development assistance to the willingness of recipients to restructure their national economies around export-led, trade-liberalized, deregulated, privatized market priorities. Thus the ideological constructions of *development*—at every scale—are now thoroughly entwined with the "modernization" assumptions that for poor places to become prosperous they have to adhere to the logics and sociocultural structures that are presumed to have made the wealthiest pockets of the Global North so prosperous.

That's something of an essentialist's narrative though, and it is unfair to declare the entirety of *all* development theory and activity as merely a wolf-in-sheep's clothing rendition of imperial domination of the Global South. The overtly neocolonialist, neoliberal logics and languages of development have always been complicated by legions of sincere field workers, administrators, politicians, and theorists acting with legitimate and deeply articulated interest in poverty alleviation, and genuinely attempting to redress massive global inequities. Development theory continues to go through successive waves and counterwaves, eddies and new channels of thought and practice, so that *development* is now broadly understood as some combinations of good intentions, paths to hell, paternalistic depredations, hubris, nationalistic posturing, colonial residues, trust, poverty reduction, and economic and uneconomic transformation of all kinds. But it is fair to call *development*—from the international to the local—the act of the dominant acknowledging the collective subaltern with the presumption that the "natural" progression of social and economic life is a striving toward the dominant. Of course everyone wants to live like us. Who wouldn't?

Thus development thinking has been always been conceived of as dominant wealth noticing and/or disciplining subaltern poverty—at its best about misery alleviation, solidarity, and friendship, and at its worst, paternalism, dispossession, unbridled arrogance, and colonialist domination in a subtler, more slippery set of guises, All development ideologies enact some complex mixture of all these relationships, plus many more. But it is critical to understand that development aid has been and is *always* tied to capital's goals, visions, and perspectives. Once dominated by geopolitical maneuvering, those positions now tend to adhere (implicitly or explicitly) to renditions of development that posit modernist market fundamentalisms as self-evidently panaceaic.

Just as that program of "progress" is played out internationally, those same kinds of relationships get superimposed intra-nationally at the urban and regional levels, with development identified as those processes that adhere to neoliberal economic formulae and dominant notions of success. The language becomes naturalized: just as a baby develops into an adult, poor places will surely develop into advanced capitalist societies. Just as a seed develops into a fruitful plant, with the right conditions, low-income neighborhoods can be developed into upscale consumer enclaves.

We can identify *development* as an all-consuming disciplinary discourse by how confoundingly difficult it is to think outside of it: if places were not "developing," what else would—what else *could*—they be doing? Development has articulated itself as the only option: there is no alternative. You are either with the program or not, succeeding or failing, developing or dying, but there is nothing outside of it.

Development has become at once its own cause and answer, a tidy self-replicating body of theory: as intensified capitalist development exacerbates inequality, more of the same treatment—more development—is prescribed. As Joel Wainwright puts it, "Capitalism reproduces inequality in the name of *development* ... capitalist social relations come to be taken *as* development."[4] Thus development becomes indistinguishable from ongoing capitalist relationships and at whatever scale we are talking about, from international development to local land development. Disembedding any of our ideas or even approaches to development have to first grasp how ensnared we are within dominatory discourses, and then search for ways out.

THE HIGHEST AND BEST USE[5]

Which gets us back to the city. It is fruitful to view gentrification in urban settings through an interrogation of development: dominant presumptions of how people could, should, and ought to live. So much urban property development in cities across the globe mimics the language of colonial displacements in the Global South, with

4. Joel Wainwright, *Decolonizing Development: Colonial Power and the Maya*, (Malden, MA: Blackwell Publishers, 2008), 2.
5. This is a ubiquitously invoked real estate and urban development mantra, meaning: "In the real estate arena, the highest and best use of a specific parcel of land is not determined through subjective analysis by a property owner, developer, real estate agent, or appraiser; but rather, it is a use shaped by the competitive forces within the market where the property is located. It is ... *the most probable use of land or improved property that is legally possible, physically possible, financially feasible (and appropriately supportable) from the market, and which results in maximum profitability*" (http://www.propex.com/C_g_hbu0.htm; emphasis in the original).

eerily similar justifications. The mass dispersal of low-income and/or racialized residents via urban renewal schemes or the more subtle dynamics of gentrification means less productive residents are moved along to make way for more desirable folks, or at least those who will adhere to better ways of living. As Cecil Rhodes once said of the British: "We happen to be the best people in the world, and the more of the world we inhabit, the better it is for humanity." The same might be said for speculators, high-end consumers, and wealthier property owners—the more of the city they inhabit, the better it is for all of us.

If gentrification can be read as certain kind of colonial logic writ urban, then both postdevelopment and postcolonial theory can be usefully applied[6] to the city to help understand displacement.[7] I want to press the limits here of traditional narratives of gentrification that focus almost exclusively on capitalist processes of accumulation, rent gaps, circuits of capital, and neoliberal restructuring.[8] Those renditions take us some distance but can be augmented and nuanced by attending a little more closely to the racialized colonial/

6. Many others have done so in a variety of ways and places; see, for example, David Simon, "Separated by Common Ground? Bringing (Post)development and (Post)colonialism Together," *Geographical Journal* 172, no. 1 (2006): 10–21.
7. This is a little tricky though, as per my comments in the last chapter about conflating gentrification, displacement, and dispossession. Settler-colonial domination is not the same as urban displacement, and the invasion of an urban neighborhood by yuppies (no matter how loathsome) and the resulting property value and rent rises are not the same at all as the stripping of Indigenous or traditional communities of their land, culture, and languages. They just aren't. I do think we can usefully speak of the ethical values and underlying logics, though, with the clear caveat that the full range of acts and sensibilities are not commensurate.
8. See, for example, Kevin Ward and Jamie Peck, *City of Revolution: Restructuring Manchester* (New York: Manchester University Press; 2002); Jason Hackworth, *The Neoliberal City* (Ithaca: Cornell University Press, 2007); David Harvey, *Social Justice and the City* (Athens: University of Georgia Press, 2009), among many others.

developmental narratives that precede justificatory arguments for economic and spatial restructuring. At the global scale it is international development organizations and financiers who do the storm troop-level restructuring of postcolonial economies, while at the urban scale it is land developers and their financial and governmental/municipal collaborators. But it is hardly any secret that development—whether bound up with (post)colonial internationalities in the Global South or land use ideologies of new urban disneyscapes—has to be understood in close relationship with deepening inequalities.

Theory becomes clearer for me though when I can root it in actual places and see it in front of my face. So I went back to Portland, back to Albina, to witness an unadorned urban property battle. Right in the heart of Northeast Portland, at the corner of Martin Luther King Jr. Boulevard and Alberta Street, is a two-acre lot that has been vacant for as long as people can remember. It is city-owned and was on the market for a long time at an asking price of $2.9 million,[9] but in 2013 the Portland Development Commission (PDC) sold the property to a corporate development consortium for $500,000 to build a complex that would include a large Trader Joe's[10] but also up to ten other retailers and a hundred-car parking lot.

The neighborhood immediately splintered into a pastiche of positions for and against the project, the most public opposition largely fronted by the Portland African American Leadership Forum (PAALF) who mobilized quickly to demand that affordable housing be built on the site. In a letter to the mayor, PAALF decried the

9. Andrew Theen, "Portland African American Leadership Forum Sends Blistering Letter with Demands on MLK Trader Joe's Project." Portland City Hall Round-up," *Oregonian*, December 18, 2013, http://www.oregonlive.com/portland /index.ssf/2013/12/portland_african_american_lead.html.
10. The California-based specialty grocery chain (currently 418 stores) known for its groovy affectations, cheap wine, wood-planked walls, Hawaiian-shirt-wearing staff, and general weird conflation of Jimmy Buffet, surfing and tiki kinds of vibes. See http://www.traderjoes.com/.

ongoing displacement of longtime low-income residents by "non-oppressed residents" and demanded that the city stop tax increment–funded developments in the neighborhood in the service of "urban renewal." They called the Trader Joe's project "fraught with injustice" and vowed that "given the long-standing list of promises made, and yet unfulfilled by the PDC to prevent community displacement, PAALF is and will remain opposed to any development in N/NE Portland that does not primarily benefit the Black community."

While Portland likes to perform exhibitions of sensitivity to issues around gentrification and the displacement of its Black population, in large part to protect its branding as a liberal political milieu, PAALF pointed out that "this decision is the opposite and reflects the city's overall track record of implementing policies that serve to uproot, displace and disempower our most vulnerable community members." The letter continued to suggest that this development would exacerbate "the well-documented and ongoing attempt to profit from development in inner N/NE Portland at the expense of Black and low-income individuals."[11]

The city and mayor reacted with calculatedly theatrical levels of concern and, in a contentious public forum, followed up with a public letter signed by Executive Director Patrick Quinton and Mayor Charlie Hales, the PDC rather remarkably and explicitly acknowledged the agency's role in displacing historically Black neighborhoods (noting "the destructive impact of gentrification and displacement on the African American community").[12] At the same time, the PDC

11. Theen, "Portland African American Leadership Forum Sends Blistering Letter with Demands on MLK Trader Joe's Project."
12. Andrew Theen, "Portland Development Commission Responds to African-American Leaders' Concerns Surrounding Trader Joe's, Acknowledges Past Role in Gentrification," Oregonian, January 13, 2014.

declined to alter its position on the Trader Joe's project and site, claiming that affordable housing was inappropriate for that location and that the proposed development would not represent a continuation of city's regrettable history of gentrification.[13]

Soon a whole host of other public figures and organizations joined the fray in support of PAALF, including NAACP Senior Director of Economic Programs Dedrick Asante Muhammad who wrote the following in a *Huffington Post* op-ed:

> The corrosive effect of gentrification can be found throughout the nation even in the "liberal" whitest city of America Portland, Oregon. Portland is known internationally as a leader in urban design with many boasting of its bike-friendly streets, accessible 20-minute neighborhoods and quaint local business culture. ... Unbeknownst to many, however, Portland is also a case study in gentrification, a glaring reminder that urban economic disparities will persist as long as the structural inequalities of our economy remain.[14]

In the face of a swiftly spreading battle, Trader Joe's backed off, with a smugly passive-aggressive public statement sent to local papers: "We run neighborhood stores and our approach is simple: if a neighborhood does not want a Trader Joe's, we understand, and we won't

13. The more I study Portland, the more I encounter this particular civic strategy of power: liberal affirmations of tolerance, sincere apologies for historical traumas, listening sessions, broad mandates for consultation, and effusive evocations of solidarity, followed up with resolute inaction, re-entrenchment of white privilege, and business as usual. It's a common strategy pretty much everywhere, but Portland has perfected it as a fine art. I suggest that this strategy henceforth be named *the Portland achievement*—the broadly branded maintenance of a liberal reputation amid compelling evidence to the contrary.
14. Dedrick Muhammad, "Must End Gentrification to Advance Economic Equity," *Huffington Post*, January 29, 2014, http://www.huffingtonpost.com/dedrick -muhammad/must-end-gentrification-t_b_4687167.html.

open the store in question." But plenty of local residents did, and do, want the store in the neighborhood, and many complained bitterly that Black people, while clearly historically aggrieved and once the majority in the neighborhood, were no longer living there and thus it should be existing residents who decide the fate of the still-empty lot.

> "Was there a vote? This should be reevaluated," said Kymberly Jeka, an artist who lives a few blocks away. "This is not what the neighborhood people want. This is terrible." Grayson Dempsey, an 11-year King resident who can see the vacant lot from her window, said she tried offering her support at neighborhood association meetings, but her voice was drowned out by the opposition. "I moved here when there were gunshots out the window," Dempsey said. "I appreciate that (PAALF) is trying to talk about the origins of gentrification. That's really essential, but they can't stand up and say, 'As residents of the King neighborhood, this is what we want.' The residents of the King neighborhood want this to happen."[15]

There was a strong thread running through much of the support for Trader Joe's that used the languages of local economic development and participatory planning: that residents should be making decisions about their own neighborhood and driving development choices in their own backyard—but in this case it came with a particular racialized tinge to it. As Nghi Tran, a fifteen-year resident of Albina put it: "All of my neighbors were excited to have Trader Joe's come here and replace a lot that has always been empty ... They

15. Casey Parks, "Trader Joe's Decision to Pull Out of NE Portland Leaves Neighbors, Opposition Dissatisfied," *Oregonian*, February 3, 2014, http://www.oregonlive.com/portland/index.ssf/2014/02/trader_joes_decision_to_pull_o.html.

[PAALF] don't come to the neighborhood clean-ups. They don't [even] live here anymore."[16]

But *they*—the African American community of residents, former residents, and those with a real stake in its future—are hardly of one united opinion either. Trader Joe's offers an affordable and warmly generic-feeling yet California-cool chain-shopping experience that a lot of people both really like and welcome; cheap cheese, friendly shelf-stockers in flower-print shirts, and Two Buck Chuck go a long ways toward building brand loyalty. Many Black people, including remaining residents, argue that having an affordable shopping option is invaluable for locals and that its arrival would stimulate some much-needed economic activity in area. *And on a block that has been empty forever! What's not to like?* Much of that line of argument takes on a class-consciousness patina: poor people love Trader Joe's and only out-of-touch elites clinging to a historical nostalgia would oppose it.

But as John Washington of NNEBA explained to me, PAALF's position was never really about Trader Joe's; it was always about how the Portland Development Commission has historically treated the African American community. His argument is that any discussion around that space has to focus on how it can help Black people develop economic sustainability in the neighborhood: "We are so precarious in this neighboorhood. We have no anchors, no corner-stones. How can we dig in deep enough that they can't remove us? We have to find ways to grow our own economic sustainability because everyone is buying us out. If you don't own your community, you can't really be part of it." Joice Taylor and John concur that the

16. Palash Ghosh, "Trader Joe's Pulls Out of Poor Portland, Oregon Neighbor-hood: Defeat of Gentrification?," *International Business Times*, February 4, 2014, http://www.ibtimes.com/trader-joes-pulls-out-poor-portland-oregon-neighbor hood-defeat-gentrification-1553231.

Trader Joe's argument was a red herring; the real issue is Portland's ongoing unwillingness to really talk about Black displacement.

As I write this, the lot remains empty: gaping and mocking. But maybe not for long. In 2014, Natural Grocers, a Colorado-based chain with four stores already in the Portland area, was retained by the California developer Majestic Realty (who originally contracted with Trader Joe's to occupy the site) to buy the land for $502,000, or the same $2.4 million discount that Trader Joe's was to receive. In addition the developer will receive a $122,750 city development grant toward "design changes" to address community concerns.[17] The city and PDC's insistence that a major food store had to go in there[18] seems to have prevailed, although it remains unclear when the building might actually commence.

Almost exactly a year later, in 2015 with the lot still empty, the city announced that the Natural Grocers plan was still on track and unveiled a plan to build affordable housing on a site about a mile further south on Martin Luther King Jr. Boulevard. The plan, to be executed by a local nonprofit and built by a Black-owned construction company, calls for forty-five to seventy units, supported by ground-floor retail. As the *Oregonian* noted at the time of the announcement, "Nothing is set in stone, and no firm timeline has been set,"[19] and when I called around to ask friends and colleagues

17. Andrew Theen, "Natural Grocers Is New Anchor Tenant at NE Portland Site Trader Joe's abandoned," *Oregonian*, August 28, 2014, http://www.oregonlive.com/portland/index.ssf/2014/08/trader_joes_on_mlk_portland_sa.html.

18. In large part driven by the frequent claim that the area is a *food desert*, which, as Nathan McClintock from Portland State University puts it, "may be true according to the USDA definition and their map—but is a preposterous claim, underscoring the fallacy of such arguments that food deserts can be 'fixed' with a grocery store" (personal conversation).

19. Andrew Theen, "Housing, Grocery Projects Coming to Portland's MLK, Ending Trader Joe's Controversy," *Oregonian*, August 17, 2015, http://www.oregonlive.com/portland/index.ssf/2015/08/housing_grocery_projects_comin.html.

what they thought of the news, there was a certain amount of profanity offered, alongside words like "minimal," "tokenistic," and
"embarrassing." In press conferences the city claimed it is a first step
in a new direction, the start of a reversal of displacement, and that
this time—no really, *this time*—they are taking the African American community seriously. Black activists ask why anyone could possibly believe that, why a couple of dozen residences warrant so much
self-congratulation and so many press releases, and what exactly
have Hales and his crew ever done to engender trust in this supposed "new direction." How'd the last one work out, Mr. Mayor?

The story of Albina—and more specifically that two-acre parcel of
land at the corner of Martin Luther King Jr. Boulevard and Alberta
Street—is both emblematic and compelling for many reasons. Thinking through that story instigates all kinds of queries about value and
how complicated it is to articulate alternatives, which necessarily
surfaces deeper questions about land and authority, about place and
duration, and thus about property. I'm not sure there's any way to
speak of that site without speaking of sovereignty.

PAALF and many Portland activists have always been extremely
clear that they want affordable housing on the Trader Joe's site: they
want low-income folks, and low-income Black people especially, to
have access to Albina, and they want back in on the now economically hopping neighborhood. While I obviously support social housing of all kinds, that rationale seems a little thin in and of itself.

From attending and reading accounts of the public forums, and
talking to scores of people, I can identify a clear bifurcation when it
comes to access—how people, and which people, should have access
to the "new" Albina—but there is a consistent default presumption
that the neighborhood needs development and that those resources
have to come from outside the community. A Trader Joe's or Natural
Grocers or any other recognizably safe corporate behemoth is the
obvious and easiest response to that presumed need. It's exactly the

kind of answer cities and neighborhoods everywhere are dreaming of: a big, bland, stable anchor, or as Lisa K. Bates, associate professor of urban studies at Portland State University puts it, a development that will fit seamlessly with "the turn to genericness."

But the fact that this one lot continues to cause such controversy is both totally predictable and astonishing; it opens up a good space for talking about development, not just instrumentally, but fundamentally. If not that, then what? Are you buying in or selling out? But those conversations are so damn hard in the context of constant racialized exclusion, where every alternative seems puerile or patronizing or just one more mechanism of white privilege. As Lisa told me:

> I live on the upper edge of Albina. There are probably more Blacks in this part of the community—what I notice here is that even though prices remain kind of moderate (by Portland standards), the aesthetics are changing to a degree that is quite intense: coffee shops with mason jars, etc.—changes that are really not appreciated by Black people.
>
> There is really a lot of activity that is coded as "white"—like gardens—that have been lost to Black people. Black people have always gardened, crafted, created cooperative economics. Everywhere I've lived Black people rode bikes because they didn't have money.
>
> We get caught up in counterproductive reactiveness—resistance to "white" activities—even though they have been always important parts of our lives.

That's the real beast of neoliberal muscular malleability. Every coping mechanism, every act of resistance can be smoothly incorporated and defanged. Capitalism has always been as much about land as production, and the relentless search for growth requires territorialization, and the constant search for spatial fixes to crises: new land, new

FIGURE 2.1
Lisa Bates at the corner of Alberta Street and Martin Luther King Jr. Boulevard.
(Photo by Matt Hern)

places to develop, new spots to open up to the logic of markets—and
languages of resistance can always be repurposed for that task. So
then, what the hell? I asked Lisa. She replied:

> I don't think people have enough imagination (myself either)
> about what an alternative to gentrification could look like. We
> see a capitulation to a particular kind of change—markets, mar-
> kets, markets—and resist gentrification on the basis of nostalgia.
> We need something other than seeing this place as a ghetto need-
> ing investment.

We can't just talk about one lot, one neighborhood—we have to talk about a different vision for the city. But even when we start talking about alternatives like land trusts or housing co-ops those immediately get coded as stuff just for old, wealthy white hippies.

And how to argue with that? It's more or less true. It *is* well-off whites who so often are in a position to fill the boards at housing co-ops and smile from the brochures for organic farm CSAs. There is nothing in particular about bikes or community gardens or craft brewing that is inherently problematic, but when they are decontextualized they become one more accoutrement of privilege. Alternatives cannot just be alternatives *within*, they have to be alternatives *to*: acts that in and of themselves are negations—a not that, but this.

DEVELOP THIS

So Lisa and I went back to the corner, just wandering around the empty lot at the corner of Alberta Street and Martin Luther King Jr. Boulevard, talking about the land and possibilities. My mind turned to postdevelopment theory, which has taken me some distance over the years in helping me clarify my own positions. Articulated by people like Arturo Escobar, Gustavo Esteva, Arundhati Roy, Ivan Illich, and Vandana Shiva, and drawing on broadly disparate threads from many others, postdevelopment posits development as a particular kind of discourse, one that traps us in prefigured and choreographed conversations.

The moment the era of development commenced, the battle lines were drawn. The story began with a Western pantheon of rationality, modernism, industrialism, and progress that was so unequivocally superior to the degradation, poverty, and backwardness of the Third World that it was painfully obvious that those poor countries in Asia, Africa, and Latin America would of course want to replicate Western trajectories. It was presupposed as a universalized truth that material advancement was synonymous with Euro-Americanism, and a whole constellation of social relations and institutions was required to transform entire societies in that image. "Poor" countries and regions were described as un- or underdeveloped places that had remained in historical infancy or retardation, waiting and wanting to grow into more advanced developmental stages.

Once the problem had been clearly defined, experts from the Western world were dispatched to make extensive and scientific diagnoses of the specific pathologies afflicting these countries and then to prescribe treatments. These treatments of course included economic prescriptions handed out by the IMF, the World Bank, and a thousand agencies of structural readjustment, but the necessary changes were also social, political, and cultural. Western (and Western-educated) professionals detected and taxonomized abnormalities and aberrations in national characters, social institutions, work ethics, school systems, and cultural patterns and then strategized a whole series of systemic alterations. Development becomes a tautology: these changes are required because they are necessary. As Escobar writes in *Encountering Development: The Making and Unmaking of the Third World*:

> Development fostered a way of conceiving of social life as a technical problem, as a matter of rational decision and management to be entrusted to that group of people—the development professionals—whose specialized knowledge allegedly qualified them for the task. Instead of seeing change as a process rooted in the interpretation of each society's history and cultural tradition ... these professionals sought to devise mechanisms and procedures to make societies fit a pre-existing model that embodied the structures and functions of modernity.[20]

20. Arturo Escobar, *Encountering Development: The Making and Unmaking of the Third World* (Princeton, NJ: Princeton University Press, 1995), 52.

I believe Escobar is essentially correct in his characterization of the development project, but it's not quite as tidy as he describes it here. It would be a misrepresentation to suggest that *every* attempt to alleviate poverty and suffering in the Global South has been driven solely, or even primarily, by paternalism and neocolonial intent. Postdevelopment theory is often (correctly I'd say) accused of overuniversalizing and totalizing the development experience, throwing the baby out with the bathwater, and instigating a kind of theoretical and practical paralysis, a "critique without construction."[21] Those are worthy appraisals, and postdevelopment theory really can (and often does) get absorbed in fancy theorizing to the detriment of material/ structural exigencies.

The struggle is real: brutal poverty exists, and something like one in nine people globally will go to bed hungry tonight while the Global North is awash in overconsumption and overaccumulation. All the discourse theory in the world isn't putting food in people's mouths or roofs over their heads, and critics (both practitioners and scholars) of postdevelopment are correct in pointing to a theoretical quicksand that undermines desperately needed material changes. I am compelled by the calls to focus on everyday materiality but remain wholly unconvinced that an ideology of development can escape the gravitational pull of its colonialist foundations. I do not believe development is a construct worth fighting for and suspect the discourse sets traps that ensnare all ends of the development experience. We need not just new language but new relationships that such language can be invented to describe.

21. See, for example: R. Kiely, "The Last Refuge of the Nobel Savage: A Critical Assessment of Post-Development Theory," *The European Journal of Development Research* 11 (1999): 30–55; Nederveen Pieterse, "After Post-Development," *Third World Quarterly* 21, no. 2 (January 2000): 175–191; Sally Matthews, "Post-Development Theory and the Question of Alternatives: A View from Africa," *Third World Quarterly* 25, no. 2 (2004): 373–384; and Meera Nanda, "Who Needs Post-Development? Discourse of Difference, Green Revolution and Agrarian Populism in India," *Journal of Development Societies* 15, no. 1 (1999): 5–31.

This is especially true for thinking about the city, and the insights of postdevelopment can be useful for thinking about the urban. If lower-income neighborhoods, immigrant enclaves, working-class communities, enigmatically organized areas, or really anything other than hyperarticulated neoliberal consumptive expansionism are perceived as "underdevelopment," then any analysis is immediately blinded by condescension. The presumption that *of course* everyone ascribes to a shared set of dreams and shared notions of prosperity normalizes so-called urban renewal, gentrification, and displacement (both intra- and interurban) as "for their own good."

But postdevelopment thought can be aided significantly by placing it more clearly within the larger constellations of postcolonialisms. There is a larger set of decolonizing conversations that has to be brought to bear more thoroughly here, because perhaps the most important critique of postdevelopment theory is that while it correctly interrogates development it fails to adequately situate itself. Too often thinkers, and very often postdevelopment theorists, fall prey to nostalgic reifications of the past, the precolonial, the premodern, and the local, and then concoct romantic images of lives before the incursions of development. It is often tinged with a strange search for the "authentic" without similarly interrogating the degrees to which traditional societies were themselves marked by hierarchies and dominations. That said, I'd say postdevelopment theory does immensely valuable, even essential, work clearing space for thinking about development in radically different ways. Once distanced from a regrettable pining for a mythical past, rethinking development has to open up new hybridizing postcolonial possibilities.[22]

22. It is also true that I am bringing a number of thinkers together here in the fairly loose category of *postdevelopment*. There is a significant distance between many of these theorists, and since the first salvos of writing that named itself *postdevelopment* emerged in the 1990s, many of those authors have responded thoughtfully to critiques, seen their analyses shift and evolve, and seen their positions differentiate from one another.

It's always problematic for a white dude to be theorizing colonialisms, especially in what is certainly not, especially here on the West Coast of Canada, a *post*colonial lived reality. I live on unceded Indigenous territory where the ongoing, active processes of settler colonization are still very visible and visceral. Speaking of colonial domination in any kind of post facto way here on Coast Salish Territories is distorting: the whole project continues to unfold around us. This can be said pretty much anywhere/everywhere: colonization does not simply disappear, and I find it helpful to think of the postcolonial as a process, a horizon that cannot "end." Understanding a little of the landscapes of colonialism, post- or otherwise, contextualizes urban displacements as something beyond just an isolated rupture here and there, and as an extension of some deeply embedded logics.

I'm in some danger of wading too deeply[23] into postcolonial theory and politics here, so I want to pull on just one specific thread that can be usefully employed in this story. Postcolonialism is a vast and shifting body of theory and practice that resides among the very few profoundly influential and important movements that have transformed virtually every corner of contemporary intellectual and political inquiry. Like gender theory, postcolonial studies is not a discipline itself but crosses traditional boundaries and is part of every serious political conversation, explicitly and/or implicitly. There is just so much writing and thinking in, around, and through postcolonialism that it is useful to parse out a couple of different strands for clarity.

In separating postcolonial thinking into three interrelated pieces—politics, theory, and ethics—Robert Nichols has made one attempt that I find particularly useful.[24] He writes that the direct material unraveling of Euro-colonial *political* relationships and the establishment of replacement structures of self-governance constitutes one

---

23. And simultaneously, far too shallowly.
24. Robert Nichols, "Post-colonial Studies and the Discourse of Foucault," *Foucault Studies*, no. 9 (September 2010): 111–144.

body of work. Another is postcolonial *theory* that has focused on literary and cultural representations of identity, othering, hybridity, non-Western histories, and ways of thinking to decolonize canonical Euro-American approaches and presumptions. Nichols argues neither of these "locations" tends to speak to a possible *ethics*: "the prevailing semantics of 'postcolonial' in the western academy has *not* been in relation to a specific ethical attitude, a manner of living or stance towards oneself and others—an *ethos*. Nor has 'postcolonial' come to refer to a set of *practises* that might cultivate and sustain such a mode of living."[25] This is a really insightful claim, for many reasons, but specifically because I am equally interested in the antonymical ethos: the "manners of living or stances toward oneself and others that see development and displacement as natural." And even more specifically, how confronting that ethos might open imaginative space for trying to figure out a manner of living and a material practice that can sustain different sets of relationships with land.

Glen Coulthard's reading of Hegel and Fanon[26] gets me over a big theoretical hump here in thinking about settler-colonial urban displacements and understanding struggles against colonalisms. He simultaneously privileges both the objective and subjective, material and psychosocial battles, or as Fanon put it, the necessity to be "waging war on both fronts." Coulthard takes on arguments from Charles Taylor and others who argue for liberal notions of intersubjective recognition: that a state can allow multiple national identifications and a diversity of cultures within the context of mutual respect, dialogue, and recognition. That construct is patently inadequate in confronting the structural/economic realities of domination, but a singular focus on the opposite, or purely redistributive, end of that

25. Ibid., 118.
26. See Glen S. Coulthard, "Subjects of Empire: Indigenous Peoples and the 'Politics of Recognition' in Canada," *Contemporary Political Theory* 6, no. 4 (2007): 437–460, and his book *Red Skin, White Masks* (Minneapolis: University of Minnesota Press, 2014).

debate's spectrum doesn't take adequate account of the pernicious-ness of inner inculcations of inferiority and the endlessly convoluted psychological traumas that take on quasi-independent trajectories of their own. He points to Fanon's "stretching" of Marxism to include both personal and collective self-affirmation. The highlighting of *self*-affirmation is critical because simplistic structural approaches misapprehend the centrality of struggle and self-determination. All too often, particularly for Indigenous people, freedom becomes a *thing* that can only be granted to them in the language of "rights." As Coulthard describes it:

> Colonized societies no longer have to struggle for their freedom and independence. It is often negotiated, achieved through constitutional amendment, or simply "declared' by the settler-state and bestowed upon the Indigenous population in the form of political rights. ...
>
> As such they [the colonized] do not have to lay down their life to prove their "certainty of being" in the way that Hegel insisted. The "upheaval" of formal freedom and independence thus reaches the colonized 'from without'. Hence, Fanon's claim that the colonized simply go from "one way of life to another, but not from one life to another"; the structure of domination changes, but the subjectivity of the colonized remains the same when this fight is carried out in a manner that does not pose a foundational challenge to the background structures of colonial power as such—which, for Fanon, will always invoke struggle and conflict—then the best the colonized can hope for is "white liberty and white justice; that is, values secreted by [their] masters."[27]

27. Coulthard, "Subjects of Empire," 448–449.

For Fanon, the colonized have to establish the "terms and values" by which they are willing to be recognized "as free, dignified and distinct contributors to humanity." This is a critical pivot that can be very usefully applied to urban gentrification theory. Resistance to displacement has to articulate and struggle for something much more imaginative than nostalgia, something that poses a "foundational challenge" not just to the act of displacement but to the conditions, ethics, mechanics, and practices that normalize it.

In *The Wretched of the Earth*, Fanon famously turns to land: "For a colonized people the most essential value, because the most concrete, is first and foremost the land: the land which will bring them bread and, above all, dignity."[28] Land is also where most academics and many intellectuals exhibit so much theoretical confusion and timidity, given that their everyday lives are so divorced from dirt and materiality, and they so rarely lay commitments bare anywhere except in ideologies. But if Hegel's slave discovers subjectivity through labor, then social subjectivity has to flourish through relationships with land.

THE EARTH GIVES, WE CREATE, LANDLORDS TAKE[29]

If late industrial capitalism articulates itself best in the defense of private property, then maybe a critical examination of property can lead us toward some originative ideas about land and social organization. Fortunately there's been an abundance of great work done already to destabilize our presumptive beliefs about ownership, but that edges us into some fairly fraught territory, especially in a modern Anglo-American political tradition that positions private ownership as foundational to all liberty and freedom, as the guarantor of all other rights.

---

28. Frantz Fanon, *The Wretched of the Earth* (London: Penguin, 1965), 44.
29. Graffiti, seen in multiple locations, most recently in the gentrifying Beacon Hill area of Seattle.

From Aristotle[30] to Locke[31] to Jefferson[32] to (Milton) Friedman[33] and so many between, private ownership of land has been asserted and reasserted as the font of liberty and the only way to assure free markets, the right to accumulation, and defense of family. Property mythologies have become synonymous not just with capitalism, but with a capitalist ontology: fixed, natural, and objective.

The dominant view (sometimes called the "ownership model") claims that there are really only two kinds of property: collective and private. Collective property decisions are made by the larger community, typically the state that has granted itself these rights. This doesn't mean everyone in that community has equally unfettered access: think of a military base, for example, or a hospital, or a school. State representatives allocate and organize rights to collective property, and include or exclude people as they see fit. Collective property is often thought of as "public" property, and in some instances it does in fact adhere to what is popularly considered *public*, but as Michael Hardt puts it, "It appears that some public property has open and equal access, and then you realize that, no,

30. Aristotle, *The Politics* (c. 330 BCE), ed. Stephen Everson (Cambridge: Cambridge University Press, 1988).

31. See primarily his *Second Treatise on Civil Government, 1689.*

32. Jefferson's views were famously complicated, and on property he slipped around considerably, but in the popular rendition he is closely associated with a "property equals free citizens" relationship. See "The True Foundation of Republican Government Is the Equal Right of Every Citizen in His Person and Property and in Their Management," Thomas Jefferson to Samuel Kercheval, 1816.

33. "The only way in which you can be free to bring your knowledge to bear in your particular way is by controlling your property ... if you want efficiency and effectiveness, if you want knowledge to be properly utilized, you have to do it through the means of private property." PBS interview, 2000, http://www.pbs.org /wgbh/commandingheights/shared/minitext/int_miltonfriedman.html.

in fact the State limits and controls the access and has a monopoly over decision-making."[34]

Private property is owned by individuals, groups of individuals, or artificial individuals (like corporations) who have been granted the right to make decisions about that property, including selling those rights. But those decisions are severely limited by a variety of social constraints. The owner of a residential house, for example, cannot build a high-rise or a power plant, open a shooting range or a bordello, start a mining operation or grow marijuana on the lawn (in most places, anyway). In fact, homeowners typically have to ask for permits for even minor alterations like raising the roof, adding rooms, or extending the deck. Conversely, if someone's private property is violated, the general public pays for someone (police, courts, permit offices, etc.) to defend it for them.

The key here is that property is not a *thing*: it is a *right*, or better, a bundle of rights that are socially granted, whether to itself or to individuals, and protected by the state. And those rights are governed by a vast architecture of legal, regulatory, and social structures and conventions that allocate and distribute land in particular ways that adhere to particular ideological presumptions and formations. Or as Nick Blomley puts it: "The ownership model is not so much constative (descriptive) as performative."[35]

The ownership model is a way of seeing and being that orders the world in certain kinds of ways. And much of that ordering is based around the idea of exclusion—the right to exclude other people from your property is fundamental to the ownership model, but as C. B. Macpherson suggested, isn't the right *not* to be excluded from

34. "Playing Three-Dimensional Chess in the Age of Empire: Michael Hardt on the Poors, the Multitude, and the Commons," a conversation with Andrew Reszitnyk, with questions coauthored by Tyler J. Pollard, published on April 28, 2014, https://www.youtube.com/watch?v=DSXQQa3D4BY.

35. Nicholas Blomley, "Performing Property, Making the World," *Canadian Journal of Law and Jurisprudence* 26, no. 1 (2013): 23.

the use or benefit of something equally persuasive? "A right not to be excluded is as much an individual right as is the right to exclude others. Both kinds may be created by society or the state, and neither can be created otherwise. Both meet the essential requisites of property, in that both are enforceable claims of individuals to some use or benefit of something. An individual right not to be excluded from something held in common is as much an individual property as is the right to exclude."[36]

And hey, I'm fine with a little exclusion here and there. I'm not particularly interested in having random people wandering into my house at any and all hours.[37] I'm quite fond of being able to lock my door periodically. I like it when I get to make decisions about my garden and not feel too worried about anyone from the street coming in to snare my vegetables. There always have to be rules, social agreements, and systems of allocation for land. But there is every reason to ask why *these* particular kinds of rules, and *these* kinds of exclusions. The ownership model is not built on "natural" laws, they are not God-given, and we have every capacity to argue beyond these extremely limited, and frankly pretty narrow ideas about how access to property can and might be understood. The ownership model is confounded by the idea of "common property," which complicates and challenges private property at multiple levels.

As Blomley writes, "Considerable scholarly investment has gone into marginalizing or ignoring"[38] alternative property possibilities, especially notions of common property. Late capitalism, emboldened by the collapse of communist regimes across the globe and the subsequent discrediting of large-scale collective ownership of land,

36. C. B. Macpherson, ed., *Property: Mainstream and Critical Positions* (Toronto: University of Toronto Press, 1978), 202.
37. Although, come to think of it, my house does kind of feel like this a lot of the time. That's another issue, though.
38. Nicholas Blomley, *Unsettling the City: Urban Land and the Politics of Property* (New York: Routledge, 2004), 8.

claims itself as a singularity and insists that there are no other conceivable alternatives beyond the ownership model. Every other intervention beyond private ownership gets derided as naively unrealistic, absurdly utopian, and/or recklessly irresponsible. In part, the aggressive closing off of possibilities is so vigorously pursued because capitalism and private property ownership are essentially indistinguishable and to dispute the ownership model is to dispute capitalism. The foreclosing of common property was—and is—essential to capitalism's emergence and expansionism: "It is only when we enter the modern world of the full capitalist market society, in the seventeenth century, that the idea of common property drops virtually out of sight. From then on, 'common property' has come to seem a contradiction in terms."[39]

Common property refers to resources that are "governed by rules whose point is to make them available for use by all or any members of the society ... The aim of any restrictions on use is simply to secure fair access for all and to prevent anyone from using the common resource in a way that would preclude its use by others."[40] The standard example is that of grazing lands to which everyone has access with their animals, something that seems somehow pastorally quaint, impossible to imagine here and now. But examples of common property can be found everywhere in contemporary urban environments: libraries, plazas, promenades, parks, and bike trails, for example, should be understood as common property. These are commonly held institutional properties whose raison d'être is to increase and maintain access, and they are considered at the heart of the good city.

And really, if you start to count, so many parts of our lives, and so many of the most admirable parts of cities are built on common

39. Macpherson, *Property*, 10.
40. Jeremy Waldron, "Property and Ownership," *The Stanford Encyclopedia of Philosophy*, Spring 2012 ed., ed. Edward N. Zalta, http://plato.stanford.edu /entries/property/.

principles. The magic of a library is that we have access to gigantic literary and digital resources without having to own any of it. It is this simplest of principles that the explosion of (some parts of) the sharing economy[41] is tapping into: from car-sharing to tool libraries to creative commons. Common property relationships tend to be encounters that we move through with familiar ease, in part because they replicate everyday neighborliness and friendship: asking to use a buddy's car for the afternoon, banging on the neighbor's door to borrow a drill. And when we talk about urbanity, we are almost always talking about civic space, and great cities share a common feature: "Evolving within them and crucial to their growth and refinement are distinctive informal public gathering places. These become as much a part of the urban landscape as the citizen's daily life and, invariably, they come to dominate the image of a city."[42]

Two key points can be added here. The first is that common property definitionally cannot be absorbed into profit-seeking rationalities. Privileging the principles of equitable access is the antipode of the advantages that institutions like corporations or pools of capital are created to accrue. The second and related note is that common property is equally foundationally bound by agreements that do an end-run around the classical rationales for the accumulation of property, insisting that it that only the common accumulate.

Some of the apparent designatory differences are highly unclear though. Take my library example. I want to define libraries as common property, but couldn't they equally be viewed as collective property, owned and monitored by the state? It depends. Hardt claims that common property has to offer free and equal access, but he also

41. As awful, predatory, and sad as so much of that is turning into. Although much of what is called the *sharing economy* is nothing at all like sharing and represents the worst kinds of cynical commodification, the essential and best-hearted parts of the sharing economy remain useful and lovely.
42. Ray Oldenburg, *The Great Good Place*, 2nd ed. (New York: Marlowe & Co., 1997), xv.

suggests that its governance has to be open and democratic. Where does that leave libraries? Do they count? Part of the issue here is our really limited scope of taxonomies that tries to force all property into a highly inadequate range of possibilities. In reality, a vast array of property rights and sovereignties are in effect all the time, many (maybe most) of which do not fit easily into the ownership model.

Elinor Ostrom, the 2009 Nobel Laureate in Economics, and her husband Vincent spent a career documenting an incredible range of common property configurations governing irrigation systems, farms, fisheries, forests, and much else. They found hundreds of examples of resource governance and management arrangements (they called them CPRs—common pool resources) that were polycentric, with multiple layers of nested relationships working within and beside one another. But as they echoed repeatedly, "Complexity is not chaos!"[43] While the examples they highlight do not easily adhere to ownership model categories, they are totally familiar to most of us. Fishing in a popular stream, sitting on the front stoop of a building, accessing community gardens, kids running between backyards, and families having a potluck in the park are just a couple of examples of our fluencies with property uses and rights that are unstable and permeable. At another level, the cooperative and (parts of) the sharing movement (among many others) mess with any fixed ideas about how sovereignty has to be understood, destabilizing the certainties of ownership.

Essentially all social collisions about land are rooted in conflicts about what kind of property rights could and should be permitted. Designations of private, collective, and/or common land are not fixed categories: they are always shifting, hybridizing, and typically

---

43. See, for example, Elinor Ostrom, "Beyond Markets and States: Polycentric Governance of Complex Economic Systems," Nobel Prize Lecture, 2009, http://www.nobelprize.org/nobel_prizes/economic-sciences/laureates/2009/ostrom-lecture.html.

misunderstood. Think, for example, of houses built on corner lots—they often have walkers and bikers cutting through the corner of their lawns to shortcut the turn, soon grinding a path that's obvious and beckoning to everyone. That's private property that has been at least temporarily commoned. Think about shopping malls—they may look like public markets and have all the iconography and signifiers of public space, but they are actually privately owned and securitized establishments, a fact that often confuses and shocks people when those private property rights are exercised.

Conversely, city planners view the exteriors of ostensibly private buildings as collective property that falls under the auspices of urban design guidelines: property owners can (sort of) do what they like inside a building, but the outsides are regulated and administered by public restrictions, permits, and licenses. In Vancouver, for example, as in almost all North American cities, there are very stringent rules about what the outside of building can and cannot look like, what kinds of materials can be used, the placement of windows, what view corridors must be protected, and the various exterior aesthetic contributions to the public tableau. In the case of building facades, like so many others, what appears to be very obviously private property just isn't. At even more brute levels, eminent domain laws or its many variants (expropriation in Canada, compulsory purchase in the United Kingdom, etc.) allow states to simply take private property for public uses, often via third parties.

Almost all property contention involves *thresholds*—disputes about where one kind of ownership starts and the other ends. Many owners of stores, for example, like to think that they have jurisdiction not just over their businesses, but over the frontage, and the sidewalks in front of the building as well, leading them to feel justified in shooing away homeless people, teens, non-shoppers, etc. Even though their property technically does not extend into the public realm, they often feel as if it does, or at least should, and when they act accordingly many of us tend to comply.

These kinds of arguments are in full flight about the park beside my house. Victoria Park, more commonly referred to as Bocce Ball Park, is a great place—filled with all kinds of urban residents: families at the playground, teens screwing around, older guys drinking, Italian grandpas playing bocce, street types getting high, hipsters throwing frisbees, dog people doing dog-people things. The whole park is only a single block, so everybody's crowded tightly together and of course not everyone is as thrilled as I am about all the ways people use the place. In particular, a group of adjacent homeowners really object to the presence of the sketchier folks and their sketchier activities. In one rather heated community meeting, an older homeowner stood up and exclaimed very definitively, "This is OUR park. We live here, we have to look at it every day. This is OUR park and WE should get to decide what happens here. It's time for US to take it back." He clearly had an idea that his presumed sovereignty over his property extended to the park. As I write this, I think back to the conversations around Albina about who gets to have a say, and how local residents everywhere feel as if their voices should be privileged.

As Foucault famously once put it: "Territory is no doubt a geographical notion, but it's first of all a juridico-political one: the area controlled by a certain kind of power."[44] It's easy to think of property as a simple, stable *thing* that someone holds, but it is really a bundle of claims to control and sovereignty that are by definition unfixed. Cartographical lines are performance, not statements of fact.

Almost every kind of property has an unstable and contingent set of sovereignties, with various constituencies jockeying, sometime explicitly and sometimes quietly, even unknowingly or abstractly, for control. The crux of these conflicts is always primarily about

44. Michel Foucault, "Questions on Geography," in *Power/Knowledge: Selected Interviews and Other Writings 1972–1977*, ed. Colin Gordon (New York: Pantheon, 1980), 63–77.

exclusion (who gets to exclude whom and on what grounds) and then by extension, about accumulation. Our current neoliberal moment cheerleads enclosure, the pulling of land from the common and privatizing it, and boisterously celebrates the private accumulation of property. Claims of common ownership, or nonsovereignty, are (correctly) perceived as necessarily antagonistic to the ownership model.

Any destabilizing of private accumulation runs in the face of the classical property scholarship that most dominant interests rely on, if usually implicitly. John Locke has long been the most influential Anglo-American thinker in this territory, and while there is very broad disagreement and I'd say endemic confusion over what exactly he meant, his writing is invoked constantly as the baseline for property-rights theory. Locke argued something called "unilateral appropriation," a sort of finders-keepers reasoning that he extended to suggest that any piece of property becomes owned when a person's labor acts upon it. He located property as *presocial* (as existing before and outside human relationships) and said that while the earth was gifted (by God) in common to all people, anyone can annex property and remove it from the commonwealth by working in/on/with it. "Whatsoever then he removes out of the State that Nature hath provided, and left it in, he hath mixed his Labour with, and joyned to it something that is his own, and thereby makes it his Property."[45]

Locke combined what is now known as a "theory of first occupancy" and a privileged interpretation of the significance of labor to present a justification for accumulation, including colonial accumulation. His general view was that nothing should be wasted—that underutilized resources were an affront, and people should only be allowed to appropriate property that they can directly put to use. The emergence of "durable goods" (stuff that doesn't go bad) however, especially

45. John Locke, *Two Treatises of Government*, ed. Peter Laslett (London, 1689; Cambridge: Cambridge University Press, 1988), II, paragraph 27.

money, allowed for unlimited accumulation without waste or decay since property can thus be "hoarded up without injury to anyone."[46] Locke concluded that accumulating property or land was not wasteful and therefore morally justifiable. While he acknowledged that resulting inequality was a problem, he didn't view it as undermining the essential right to accumulation via occupancy and labor, and claimed inequality was an issue for another day, specifically for governments to deal with.

Locke, writing just as the modern capitalist market society was emerging, considered at length the transition from a "state of nature" to societies with monetary exchanges and central governments. The bulk of his theory of appropriation was concerned with property being pulled from that "state of nature" commonwealth, but he hedged on accumulation by claiming that it was justifiable "at least where there is enough, and as good left in common for others." I am certainly no Locke scholar, but the sheer volume of academic debate about what he meant by "at least" dismays, but also emboldens, me.

Any notion of property is always shifting, always contingent, and always contentious. The ferociousness of arguments over Locke confirms that the core meanings of even single iconic and foundational thinkers are never fixed. Even people who have spent intense intellectual energy deciphering and interpreting his work are in fundamental disagreement about what he meant to say, or what they very much hope he meant to say. Locke's huge emphasis on the unacceptability of waste, for example, remains entirely unclear in the literature: it is read by some as a justification for the consolidation of

---

46. The larger passage reads (in part): "It is plain, that men have agreed to a disproportionate and unequal possession of the earth; they having, by a tacit and voluntary consent, found out a way how a man may fairly possess more land than he himself can use the product of, by receiving, in exchange for the overplus, gold and silver, which may be hoarded up without injury to any one." John Locke, *Two Treatises of Government and a Letter Concerning Toleration* (New Haven: Yale University Press, 2003), 121.

property ownership in the hands of the few who can put it to use most effectively, and sometimes he is interpreted in the exact opposite spirit.[47]

To my reading, Locke could never have anticipated/extrapolated the explosion of capitalism's scope into every nook and cranny of social life. His arguments around appropriation in a state of nature are only partially legible in the context of the conversion of essentially all property and labor into commodities. The translation of property, and especially of land, into revenue seems to run directly in the face of Locke's dictums around labor. But I also remain unconvinced by arguments that rest on the "right of first occupancy" logics. That line of reasoning is too thin, too schoolyardish, and too open to legalistic claims, which is part of why "rights-based" arguments don't resonate so much with me either. The notion of "rights" really means "I'll beat you in court," a claim that performs as an evasive maneuver to avoid asking direct questions of justice.

This gets us to what are called justificatory arguments: that any social institution, like property, needs to rest on moral grounds. As Macpherson puts it, while property is a *right* in that "its enforceability is what makes it a *legal* right, the enforceability itself depends on society's belief that it is *moral* right."[48] There may be legitimate, even administratively logical grounds, for particular arguments about property allocation, but decontextualizing them mixes cause and effect and obscures the better questions about property allocation: what is, and what *should* it be doing? The Zapatistas, for example, understood this acutely when among their very first publicly performative acts was the burning of municipal property records in San Cristobal de las Casas. Space is socially produced and socially

---

47. For perhaps the best overview and most cogently considered reading of Locke that I know of, see James Tully, *A Discourse on Property: John Locke and His Adversaries* (Cambridge: Cambridge University Press, 1980).
48. Macpherson, *Property*, 11.

productive, and we get it ass-backward if we organize ourselves socially around theories of property, instead of understanding property as expressing our social desires.

The scope of Western imaginings of the ethical relationships between land, property, and sociability was established, as you might expect, in early Greece. Plato was pretty clear, in the Republic and elsewhere, that shared ownership and management of land was vital to protect both the commonwealth and commonality in general. He claimed that if individuals were allowed to own separate lands it would necessarily create divisiveness where "some grieve exceedingly and others rejoice at the same happenings."[49] Aristotle, on the other hand, thought very differently, and while he condemned moneymaking and hoarding, he was convinced that private property was necessary to inculcate virtuous behavior and social cohesion: "When everyone has a distinct interest, men will not complain of one another, and they will make more progress, because everyone will be attending to his own business."[50]

Aristotle claimed that private property was "natural" and had always existed, and should be protected in part because it forced people to behave responsibly and thus allowed for charity and benevolence. All kinds of private property advocates since have built on this tradition, using "tragedy of the commons"-style arguments to claim that collective ownership foments greed, resentments, and, ironically enough, selfish individualism. Perhaps the most influential contemporary thinker in this strain of property rights analysis is the Peruvian economist Hernando de Soto, who extends this reasoning further by stressing that in owning property people can use their land as collateral for loans, and that bringing all that

49. Plato, *Republic*, 462b–c.
50. Aristotle, *Politics*, 1263a. Cited in Jeremy Waldron, "Property and Ownership," *The Stanford Encyclopedia of Philosophy*, Spring 2012 ed., ed. Edward N. Zalta, http://plato.stanford.edu/entries/property/.

"dead money" into play is fundamentally what makes modern market economies function. He notes that wealthy countries in the Global North have very high mortgage-debt-to-GDP ratio (often as high as 80+ percent), while poor African and Asian countries tend to have ratios of less than 1 percent. Invoking stats like these as evidence, de Soto claims that for poor people to stop being poor they need formal property titles (and ideally, giant mortgages).[51]

Thomas Aquinas is often cited as working in this private-property-equates-with-virtue tradition, and to some extent that is true. But Aquinas is also famous for his dictum "in cases of need all things are common property." He followed that up with a more thorough and more radical critique of inequality: "There would seem to be no sin in taking another's property, for need has made it common ... Whatever goods some have in superabundance are due, by natural law, to the sustenance of the poor."[52] He further claimed that where the common good was threatened, governments had the authority—in fact the obligation—to appropriate private property and use it for the commonwealth. Collective or individual seizing of another's goods is not theft, says Aquinas, as need is transcendent: "If the need be so manifest and urgent that it is evident that the present need must be remedied by whatever means be at hand, then it is lawful for a man to succor his own need by means of another's property, by taking it either openly or secretly, nor is this properly speaking theft or robbery."[53]

That's a deeply conservative iconic Dominican theologian sounding like a revolutionary insurrectionist. I wonder what old Thomas would think today about the current depravity of the 1 percent. Writing in the mid-thirteenth century, he hadn't seen anything like

51. See, for example, Hernando de Soto, *The Other Path* (New York: Basic Books, 2002).
52. Cited in Susanne M. DeCrane, *Aquinas, Feminism and the Common Good* (Washington, DC: Georgetown University Press, 2004), 82.
53. Ibid.

"superabundance," and I suspect he would find Thomas Piketty's gently muted calls for a "global wealth tax" timid at best.[54] What Piketty has demonstrated is essentially that because owning stuff has become so much more profitable than making stuff, a global class of spectacularly hegemonic rentiers will, if unhindered, increasingly entrench their power. Thus we get our near-weekly parade of ever-more-ghastly inequality stats. But it strikes me that much of the world now patently meets Aquinas's condition of a "need ... so manifest" and we would do well to listen to his prescriptive alleviations.

If nothing else here, I'd suggest a surpassing cynicism about any evocation of "natural laws." Locke's "right of first occupancy," for example, which is (still!) often invoked as a "natural" or "just common sense" kind of dictum, conveniently negates essentially all Indigenous sovereignties, using contortions like "terra nullius" arguments, or invoking claims that aboriginal inhabitants have not correctly used, or "improved" their lands, and thus cannot legitimately own them. Any ethical claims about property allocation that are not based on justice, especially for Indigenous people, are just not particularly useful to me.

Given the conditions facing us, and the crises of late capitalism that are "so manifest," I submit that more than anything, *imagination* is required. The ownership model has demonstrated itself to be far too inconsistent with a free society, and its applications and affects so subtly problematic that we need not an expansion of the same, but concrete and material examples that other worlds of property is possible. As Karl Marx wrote in 1844:

> Private property has made us so stupid and one-sided that an object is only ours when we have it—when it exists for us as capital, or when it is directly possessed, eaten, drunk, worn, in-

54. Thomas Piketty, *Capital in the Twenty-First Century* (Cambridge, MA: Belknap Press of Harvard University Press, 2014).

habited, etc.,—in short, when it is used by us. Although private property itself again conceives all these direct realisations of possession only as means of life, and the life which they serve as means is the life of private property—labour and conversion into capital.

In the place of all physical and mental senses there has therefore come the sheer estrangement of all these senses, the sense of having. The human being had to be reduced to this absolute poverty in order that he might yield his inner wealth to the outer world.[55]

Here Marx points to one of the, perhaps *the* most corrosive results of the ownership model: that we are reduced to either *having* property or *being* property. Private property has been reified as conferring full personhood upon its owners: "Classical notions of the person demand that a person who is able to own property is not herself or himself property (except possibly their own), whereas the human being who is owned is not a person," and thus we are impelled to ask "whether it is possible to rethink the dichotomies of having/being; subject/object; masculine/feminine; and ultimately owner/owned."[56]

Why does it seem to require so much effort for so many of us to think outside the ownership model? Why is it so difficult to reimagine property not as a singular force for divisiveness and inequality but as something else entirely? If unfolding ecological crises driven by late capitalist inequality change everything[57] and we are all faced with gun-to-the-temple kinds of decisions about resource allocation,

---

55. Karl Marx, *Economic and Philosophic Manuscripts of 1844*, 1st American ed. (New York: International Publishers, 1964).

56. Margaret Davies, *Property: Meanings, Histories, Theories* (New York; Abingdon, UK: Routledge-Cavendish, 2007), 108.

57. As per Naomi Klein.

land use, and sovereignties, why can't we imagine property, and especially urban property as full of potentiality, not foreclosures? Echoing Proudhon[58] in 2009, a collection of law professors issued a Progressive Property Manifesto: "Property confers power. ... Property enables and shapes community life. Property law can render relationships within communities either exploitative and humiliating or liberating and ennobling. Property law should establish the framework for a kind of social life appropriate to a free and democratic society."[59] I actually think we can do a lot better than that, but that's exactly the kind of conversation we should be having, and pronto. Conversations can't be the endgame though: we're talking about materiality, about land. It is time to start talking, and doing, restitution, redistribution, reallocation, relanding.

PROPERTY VALUES

Maybe the first requisite for imagination is allowing ourselves to ask *why not?*—to ask why we reflexively shut down particularly novel or transformative possibilities as naïve or whatever, which gets us back to decolonization. The basis, for example, of essentially all North American property law is founded on the lie of terra nullius: the assertion that the lands of Turtle Island were technically unoccupied because even if there were people here they weren't doing anything to "improve" the place. But if we consistently apply Lockean first-occupancy imperatives, there are both legitimate moral and legal claims for Indigenous "ownership" of more or less this entire continent.

58. "Property, to be just and possible, must necessarily have equality for its condition." Pierre-Joseph Proudhon, *What Is Property? An Inquiry into the Principle of Right and of Government* (London: W. Reeves, 1890).
59. Gregory Alexander, Eduardo Penlaver, Joseph Singer, and Laura Underkuffler, "A Statement of Progressive Property," *Cornell Law Review* 94 (2009): 743.

That claim sounds unbelievable on the face of it, but why shouldn't Indigenous sovereignty be rigorously applied? If the state insists on the inviolability of property (i.e., I cannot come and take something of yours just because I want it; that's theft), then how valid is all our property law (and thus all our law) if it rests on a collective and continuous violation of its own basic precept? And in fact, the intuitive moral arguments for Indigenous claims to land are being substantiated in Canadian courts, maybe most famously in the 2014 Tsilhqot'in decision in British Columbia that has verified Indigenous titles based on a broader rendition of "occupation." The court recognized that the Tsilhqot'in people have in fact occupied their traditional territory consistently and that it has never been relinquished. The repercussions of this decision are potentially enormous because as Grand Chief Stewart Phillip of the Union of B.C. Indian Chiefs, says: "British Columbia is comprised of unceded, unextinguished aboriginal-title territory from one end to the other."[60]

The truth of that claim puts us in some very interesting, and potentially totally exciting, territory. A prominent postcolonial initiative over the past couple of decades has been the practice of "countermapping"[61]—the redrawing of borders, the renaming of places both on maps and in language, and the remapping of cartographical lines— all of which is particularly compelling if it sets the stage for a redistribution of sovereignties, if it can move us in the words of Fanon from "one life to another." Living in Canada, where so much colonial dispossession is so new and so raw, I see the challenge of Indigenous claims to territory as foundational, not just because I live on unceded land, but because it forces us all into reconsiderations of property and

60. Dene Moore, "Supreme Court Ruling Grants Land Title to BC First Nation," *Canadian Press*, June 26, 2014, http://www.huffingtonpost.ca/2014/06/26/supreme-court-decision-bc-first-nation_n_5533233.html.
61. Sometimes falling under gentler monikers like critical or alternative cartography and/or participatory, local, or community mapping.

ownership. Paying close attention to Indigenous renditions of sovereignty and alternative sovereignty can inform a theoretically sophisticated set of claims for the commonality of land, which may well hold the seeds of larger social escapes from the traps of the ownership model and toward the possibilities of post-sovereignties.

I'm obviously invested in the theoretical, but I'm impelled by practice. There is transformational value in the empirical: in experimenting, testing different kinds of relationships with land and property, and assessing their intents and affects based on our experiences of justice and radical pluralism. As Colin Ward wrote a generation ago: we need a mass of ideas, not a mass idea. He's right: we need a whole bunch of new ideas about property: long-held Indigenous notions of alternative sovereignty that have demonstrated value and resiliency through millennia; unproven ideas like Henry George's Land Value Tax;[62] new ideas, like some inspiring parts of the solidarity economy; and hybridized ideas of all kinds. The city offers particular sets of social conditions, maybe incommensurable conditions, that open up particular kinds of possibilities. But so does every other kind of settlement: different kinds of occupancies inhere different possibilities, each one worthy of consideration.

Take one of my favorite places in the world, for example: Fort Good Hope in the Northwest Territories, a Dene community 750 miles northwest of Yellowknife, right where the Mackenzie River crosses the Arctic Circle. It is about as isolated a settlement as you're going to find in North America: 515 people in town, part of the Sahtu Region of sixteen hundred people scattered in five communities across 280,000 square km. Most everybody I know in Good Hope has a family cabin and/or a fish camp somewhere out on the land, anywhere from a few hours to a couple of days away

---

62. More on this shortly.

from town. Once on our way to a cabin down the river, as my hosts pointed out various places en route, I asked how people knew where they could build. How did they know where everyone else was? Was there some kind of official process for deciding who got to use what areas for their cabins, for their hunting, trapping, and fishing? As usual, the guilelessness of my questions elicited a kind of amused smile, and to this one the response was "You just find a place you like where there isn't anyone nearby and build there." That sounds awesome in theory, but what if there's a dispute? What if someone thinks you're a little too close? I've never quite got that sorted out, but there are clearly well-understood processes of land allocation that fit a small community with almost no in-migration and almost endless space available.

In the city, that kind of fluid decision making sounds very attractive, but tough to countenance in places with a minimum of available extra room, where heavily bureaucratized and administratively dense procedures are expected to maintain spacing. But that's more or less what everybody does when they go to the beach or to a park: find a space that doesn't impinge too much and sit down. That works for temporary urban property allocations, but the pluralism and fluidity of the city tends to require more formal arrangements.

But does it always? Multiple renditions of property are absolutely possible, and we tend to be comfortable with more kinds of ownership than is usually acknowledged: think of the library again. All you need to get a library card is some kind of ID and/or proof of address (and sometimes not even that); then you are free to borrow, often many items at a time. You are entrusted to remove potentially hundreds, even thousands, of dollars' worth of books from the facility, without leaving a credit card or really any other kind of securitizing information or collateral. A library patron as a tax-paying resident technically owns the books I suppose, but really library books are common property and the institutional practice of libraries works beautifully, pretty much everywhere, in defiance of the ownership model.

Here's another example. My family belongs to a car co-op here in Vancouver.[63] There are currently more than four hundred fifty vehicles shared by more than fifteen thousand members, including cars, vans, hybrids, trucks, and electrics. It is a co-op administratively: owned and run democratically by its members with an elected board and regular members' meetings. A variety of membership plans exist for individuals and businesses, but essentially to get in you just have to buy a refundable share purchase, which lets you use any vehicles you like, paying per hour and per kilometer.[64] Vehicles are scattered all across the city, with locations based on concentrations of members, and parked in designated spots. To book one you just go online (or phone in) and block off the time period you need. Then you fob into the car, use it, and return it to the same spot, with at least a quarter-tank of gas.[65] You can book it for a minimum of one hour and keep it for as long as you want, up to weeks at a time.

The co-op was founded with an ethic of shared responsibility: members are encouraged to clean up after themselves, chill out if the previous user made a mess, make sure you get the car back on time, and be a responsible sharer. Various dispute resolution policies are in place, should conflicts arise, because as you might guess with that many cars and that many members there are often (but almost always minor) conflicts. Say someone brings the car you've booked back late, and you're stuck waiting. Or someone parks it in the wrong spot. Or the car is returned almost out of gas. Or the car stinks. There are all kinds of

63. It's called Modo: http://www.modo.coop/.
64. Right now, it's $500 per share ($250 per share for extra drivers in the household), then four dollars per hour plus forty cents per kilometer to drive. It's a little more complicated than that, with casual memberships available, kilometer charges dropping at certain distances, no charges between 11:00 p.m. and 8:00 a.m., and so on, but you get the idea. These amounts cover all gas, insurance, maintenance, and repairs. You can pay (nominally) into an accident fund, and you have certain parking privileges all over the city.
65. There is a dedicated credit card kept in the car at all times for gas purchases.

possibilities and processes from warnings to fines to eventual expulsion if you keep violating the agreements. But really the whole thing works amazingly smoothly,[66] and one of the pillars of middle-class North American life is reimagined as unowned property.

The car co-op has been kind of a revelation for me and my family. I was skeptical initially—I didn't think we could be that organized, we had kids going in every direction, it seemed a little bureaucratic—but Selena[67] convinced me and it's been brilliant. We have access to all kinds of vehicles, they are always well-maintained,[68] and we don't have to worry about repairs or maintenance, which ultimately saves us money. Possibly best of all, we really do drive a lot less: when we don't drive we don't pay, so we only use a car when we clearly need one. We know in advance exactly how much it will cost us, and it cuts down on superfluous (and expensive) driving.

Technically, it is true that we (cooperatively) own more than four hundred fifty vehicles, but really we own none. We share in the fortunes of the co-op equally. Like everyone else in the organization, I care for the cars and treat them well, but don't fetishize them. I want them to be clean, usable, functioning and efficient, but I have no particular attachment to them as objects. The release from identification with whichever vehicle I happen to be driving, however subtle and pernicious that might be, is sweet relief. They are just cars: as useful to me as any car I have owned, but decoupled from all the cultural, financial, and organizational baggage. It is shared property working every day, without a lot of complications. It feels like the best of a couple of worlds. To be clear, it's not a utopian arrangement. These are still cars we're talking about, no matter how they are owned: still polluting, climate-changing, city-clogging bad ideas with all kinds of shitty repercussions,

---

66. That's assessed as a user, but everything I've heard from people who work in the office suggests that it's a highly functional organization.
67. My partner.
68. Which is a welcome change for us.

but in the having-to-live-in-the-here-and-now sense, the car co-op makes a ton of sense for us.

Could we extrapolate this kind of model for land? Why not? That's what a housing co-op does. In the face of exploding urban unaffordability and displacements, why don't cities just start buying up every residence they can, and leasing them out, long or short term? That's a dominant strategy in all kinds of cities from Switzerland to Singapore, but overwhelmingly the Anglo-American nexus has enthusiastically eschewed publicly held property in favor of private ownership, for some very specific, but also some ephemerally articulated ethical and ideological reasons. The core of the argument though tends to revolve on the building of individual wealth. A co-op for cars is different from houses because cars depreciate—meaning that the net loss of value is absorbed collectively, making the shared loss and shared risk attractive for members, while the gamble of homeownership is that land can (and very often does) appreciate in value. It is a gamble that ultimately costs all of us far too much, and one people tend to cling to until it's too late to change, but it is a gamble that is constantly alluring to people, especially in the contextual paucity of alternatives, with too few new ideas to work with.

But how can new kinds of ideas about land and property inform new kinds of antigentrification struggles? Can new ideas help us here, in New Orleans, in Albina, or in any other place facing displacement? Implying the language of innovation[69] requires caution, and part of me thinks there is little need for new ideas: what is really needed is a shared ethical commitment to doing the right things. Part of me thinks that the last thing any of us should be worried about is new ideas, and that resisting endemic racialized dispersals,

69. Or any other language that the "social innovation," "social enterprise" world has jacked to whitewash or greenwash the relentless commodification of every nook and cranny of human activity.

the global land grab, and metastasizing inequality is a matter of backbone, old-school organizing, and resistance. And in part that's true. An individual good idea here or there is all fine and good, but it won't significantly alter social conditions. It is wholly possible, for example, to have a brilliant and innovative housing co-op that keeps a few old white hippies happily sheltered but does nothing much for anyone else. New ideas have to both emerge from and contribute to larger social conditions. There is a constantly roiling dialectical relationship between the material and the cultural, between on-the-ground action and creating the broader conditions for commonality: a war "on both fronts." Embracing both ends of this struggle simultaneously can stretch traditional social theory and, when applied to our understandings of land, open up a whole range of possibility.

Thinking back on a couple of decades of my own hustling community work, I often wonder about the relationships between formal organizing work and vernacular relationships. I wonder about people's willingness to think urban property differently, and how little surprises often jump out serendipitously. Like this one: I've lived in the same neighborhood for the past twenty-five years and I've gone to the same hardware store regularly—it's the only one nearby. It's small but packed, the staff is convivial and because I do a lot of gardening I'm there often. An old-time Italian family owns the place, and they're more-or-less good guys who have been entrenched in the neighborhood for approximately a century. Some of the staff has worked there as long as I've been around, so we have come know each other, if only in a friendly customer-service sort of way—enough that many of them know where I live, and we wave at each other on the street.

The other day the lock on our bike shed jammed. It's a crappy door leading to a crappy little hovel in the back corner of the house, but it's well-used because everybody in the house rides. We had a cheap padlock on the door and one cold, wet morning, the lock just cramped up. I tugged hard on it, invoked considerable profanity, WD-40ed the hell out of it, without any luck. It's the only way to get bikes out of the basement, so I had to find a solution ASAP. I didn't have many options, so I walked over to the hardware store. There was a kid behind the counter who must have been new because I had only seen him once or twice before. He didn't recognize me. I explained the situation and asked if the store had a set of bolt cutters I could borrow for fifteen minutes. I didn't want to buy them since they surely would cost a lot of money and I need to snip a lock approximately once per decade. I didn't know anyone else I could borrow them from.

The kid looked at me like I was a fool. "Um. ... We don't *lend* tools. ... We're a *store*. ... We don't have things you can *borrow*." I stayed with it. "Yeah, I know. But look I'm a really longtime customer, I live like two minutes away, the guys know me, I'll bring it right back, honest! Like *right* back." The kid was less than moved, except toward condescension. "Um, *no*. Like I said, we don't *lend* out tools." I just stood there for a second, not really sure what my next move was. Then an old-time employee poked his head out from behind a pile of stuff, frowned gruffly at the kid, and said, "Yes we *do* lend tools out. I'll be right back." The kid looked blankly at me as the older guy wordlessly went and got this giant pair of cutters. I didn't say anything, just walked home, snipped the lock, walked back, and thanked the man for his generosity. He only grunted at me.

My point here is that the conditions for trust had evidently been established. If the older guy had never seen me before, he surely wouldn't have lent me anything. Other factors contributed to his generosity: I've spent a lot of money at that store over the years, the store has a long-held reputation for being community-minded, he felt comfortable with my middle-aged, middle-classish white-guy familiarity, he knows where I live, and so on. We all have these kinds of solidarities—sometimes small like this example, sometimes a lot deeper—but linked together, concretized, and extrapolated to larger social and economic milieus, they begin to build a city of generosity. Among the core questions embedded here is how to establish solidarity across difference when our shared histories are so dominated by violent violations of trust and when white people in particular have given others so many clear reasons for suspicion—like say, in Albina, or here, or more or less anywhere. The only answer I can think of right now is that we have to find ways to enact trustworthiness repeatedly and deliberately and consistently.

Small examples of neighborliness are sometimes just that. But in an everyday sense, they create a certain sensibility that sets the larger social conditions for something well beyond life stylism. It is this subjective/objective interplay where new ideas can flourish as part of something much bigger; to think and act a material commonality. As Gustavo Esteva puts it: "The time has come to enclose the enclosers ... Commoning, the commons movement, is not an alternative economy but an alternative to the economy. The idea is to radically abandon the "law of scarcity" construed by the economists as the keystone for the theoretical construction in which economics is based."[70] I admire these kinds of formulations tremendously; they resonate with a certain lyricism and sound so right, but only if "the commons" stays politicized, if incommensurability stays at its heart. The claim is not simply good, or liberatory by virtue of itself, only by what it does. Commonality cannot be a metaphor; it has to start with the rematriation of stolen Indigenous lands and an embrace of reparations, and then be willing to be called to account for displacements, especially racialized displacements, here, in Albina, and everywhere else. Claiming commonality all too often acts as a sleight of hand, a deceptive stalling tactic, a "move to innocence" that bathes the speaker in a soft glow of righteousness while demanding little. While commoning is a start, it "neither reconciles present grievances nor forecloses future conflict"[71] and is only as good as its ongoing commitments.

70. Gustavo Esteva, "Commoning in the New Society," *Community Development Journal* 49, no. 1 (2014): 144–159.
71. Eve Tuck and K. Wayne Yang, "Decolonization Is Not a Metaphor," *Decolonization: Indigeneity, Education & Society* 1, no. 1 (2012): 3.

And thus: I want to reimagine what the city is for, what it might be for. It seems very clear to me that imagination has to be yoked to an analysis that both starts and ends with landed imperatives as the release point for rethinking the city. But thinking new thoughts is not always easy, especially if I'm demanding that imagination materialize itself. So I went looking for some inspirations, some new ideas in action, where imagination meets struggle. Specifically, I went looking for ways to rethink urban land beyond property.

3

JUBILEE: AFTER THE TEACHING STOPS, THE LEARNING BEGINS

The proposition that "no place has successfully resisted gentrification" leaves a lot of interpretive wiggle room and carries a load of ideological/orthodoxical baggage.[1] While I suspect that the core of the claim is more or less (depressingly) true, the larger implication is far more daunting: that neoliberalism is an end-of-history inevitability, that no alternative to economic predation exists, and that should capital turn its eye toward your neighborhood the best you can hope for is to escape with whatever you can carry.

But if that is more than we are willing to accept, the obvious next question is what to do. What should people who are under threat here, in New Orleans, in Albina, or anywhere do? How should cities act to prevent their most vulnerable and valuable residents from getting displaced at capital's whim? If hypercapitalist expansionism is not the end of history, what else is left to propose? It is here that I

1. There are all kinds of counterarguments that might be brought to bear here; does, say, the Cuban Revolution count? The proposition that gentrification is currently undefeated is a provocative and tenuous claim, but the basic thrust is sound and worth considering.

find myself most consistently frustrated by the generalized Left,[2] and even more so by specific elements of the academy and intelligentsia: the unwillingness, or inability, to forward meaningful, non-nostalgic new ideas and proposals for action. The contemporary Left (especially in North America) is consistently paralyzed (in part) by mean-spirited factionalism, a fetishization of abstracted theory, and such a widespread lack of courage that even the most modest glimmers of hope are immediately subject to witheringly cynical analysis.

I have long noted this tendency: the startlingly articulate capacities of critical commentators who are so skilled at critique that any new initiative can be systematically sliced and discursively diced into submission. Ungrounded criticality offers distance: it is possible to hammer away without being subjected to substantive return fire. But as soon as you put new proposals on the table or work to build alternative movements, you yourself are immediately vulnerable to that same critical gaze. Thus so many brilliant commentators hang back, content with argument and analysis, but without much materiality to add and scant commitment to action.

Nowhere is this more evident than in conversations about urban displacement. So many books, articles, and lectures end with the inevitable call to a "new urban politics" or a "different kind of city" or "common front against gentrification" with little else beyond sincere nods and drinks later. Take *The Gentrification Debates: A Reader* for example—a solid collection of previously published and well-known articles edited by Japonica Brown-Saracino that is often used as a primer. It has sections on the who, what, where and why of gentrification but not a whiff on possible responses/alternatives. This is not a criticism of the book, which is a fine one and whose shortcomings are endemic to the field. Consider David Harvey—as respected a radical urban commentator as there is—who often ends talks with "I think I

---

2. Sorry, "the Left" is an entirely malleable and fuzzy term, and I confess to deploying it ideologically here, but stay with me.

know the nature of the problem, but I don't have any solutions."[3] Or Michael Hardt and Antonio Negri (whom I also admire plenty) who spend three major volumes describing new forms of empire, biopolitical control, and what a multitudinous altermodernity might look like, but after all that they defer any "okay, what's next?" questions and conclude that "a book like ours should strive to understand the present but also challenge and inspire its readers to invent the future."[4] With all due respect, for two such boldly brilliant writers known for activist pasts, this is total chickenshit. We deserve better than that.

But that's not fate. Intellectual energy and sophistication can surely be put in the *service* of action, materiality, and on-the-ground activism. I am not talking about abandoning our critical faculties, or shying away from contention, hard choices and political decisions; I am arguing for a scholarship that unapologetically contributes to hopeful movements and a theoretical rigor that supports everyday organizing and community work. I have some thoughts about the endemic quietism and remove of so much of contemporary academic life, in part centered on the reconfiguration of modern universities as industrial production units, but for now I'd like to offer just one line of analysis.

The project of remaking the city requires a collective and individual willingness to surpass sirenic cynicism—a willingness to experiment, to try new approaches large and small, to hazard coalitions, to fail and learn—and to support others who are doing the same. Many of these attempts will not look ideal. Many will not adhere easily to dogmatisms. Many will appear doomed, or quietly reformist, or inconsequential. If the Left (of all stripes, however that might be defined) cannot embrace a plurality of antagonisms, not just theoretically but also on the ground, then neoliberal logics will continue

3. See, for example, "RSA Animate: David Harvey, the Crises of Capitalism," https://www.youtube.com/watch?v=qOP2V_np2c0.
4. Michael Hardt, Antonio Negri, and David Harvey, "Commonwealth: An Exchange," *Artforum* 48, no. 3 (November 2009): 210–221, http://korotonomedya .net/kor/index.php?id=27,316,0,0,1,0.

to enjoy unbridled pillaging of the commonwealth, if only due to a
lack of opposition.

One of the core pieces to remaking the city has to be the recasting
creative production. For a generation now the idea of enterprise has
been closely associated with the libertarian Right and reduced to the
enactment of a Thatcher-Reagan, up-by-the-bootstraps, individualist capitalist ethos of "free" enterprise. That vision of enterprise-as-
avaricious-entrepreneurialism has been deservedly derided from all
directions as inimical to commonality. I'd argue however, in the spirit
of Colin Ward, that this is a perversion of the best implications of
the idea, that enterprise should be understood in the DIY and DIT,[5]
small-scale, cooperative, and collectivist threads that are the best of
the socialist tradition.

> I often wonder how we reached the situation when honourable
> words like 'enterprise', 'initiative' and 'self-help' are automati-
> cally associated with the political right and the defense of capital-
> ism, while it is assumed that the political left stands for the big
> brother state with a responsibility to provide a pauper's income
> for all and an inflation-proof income for its own functionaries.
>
> Ninety years ago people's mental image of a socialist was a
> radical self-employed cobbler, sitting in his shop with a copy of
> William Morris' *Useful Work versus Useless Toil* on the work-
> bench, his hammer in his hand and his lips full of brass tacks.
> His mind was full of notions of liberating his fellow workers
> from industrial serfdom in a dark satanic mill. No doubt the
> current mental picture is of a university lecturer with a copy of
> *The Inevitable Crisis of Capitalism* in one hand and a banner la-
> belled "Fight the Cuts" in the other, while his mind is full of

5. Do-it-yourself and do-it-together.

strategies for unseating the sitting Labour candidate in the local pocket borough.[6]

I'd like to think that our everyday visceral experiences of dispossession (from land, neighbors, our work, our bodies, ourselves) encourage and substantiate the value and centrality of theory. But any explanatory frameworks have to extrovertedly position themselves as routes to action and specifically as routes to action for everyday people every day. To do that work, theory has to embrace a radical plurality, not just of identities and antagonisms, not just of positionalities and sensibilities, but of hopes and dreams.

That suggests a kind of experimental, imaginative, enterprising, hopeful proclivity toward mobilization and action—a milieu that encourages us all to attempt all kinds of projects and organizing from a multiplicity of directions. Lasting social change across multiple scales only occasionally coalesces in mass movements, in very particular historicized confluences. Those moments are preceded, predicated, and predicted by innumerable incremental, asystematic, and asymmetrical small-scale moves that come in fits and starts, bits and pieces, unquantifiable and acategorical. And *that* requires an embrace of a roiling, participatory milieu where multiplicities of people can contribute, constantly in the everyday, in performance and reenactment, episodically and at length, with and without leadership, with and without direction.

The reimagining of city residents as producers rather than consumers of the city requires trust, flexibility, and generosity—or neighborliness. It is absolutely true that we are all socially producing space all the time, and I want to extend that to the material, to suggest that everyday people can and do build and rebuild the city around themselves all the time. Emboldening ourselves as producers

6. Colin Ward, "Anarchism and the Informal Economy," in *Reinventing Anarchy, Again*, ed. Howard Ehrlich (San Francisco: AK Press, 1996), 229.

of the material and immaterial city means recognizing the disciplinary state as primarily antiproductive[7] and encouraging creative production from below; it means not making room for unfettered capitalism, but for the subjectivity of the city as a constantly unfolding site of creative assemblages.

Common wealth is constantly being produced. The commons is not just a thing: it is a set of social relations that is constantly expanding and/or contracting, moving, unstable, sometimes in place, sometimes not. To realize a social commons requires an embrace of that multiplicity, of that incommensurability, not just in theory but in the material, in the everyday, which is *always* to speak of struggle. The means has to reflect and mimic the ends—but that end is a horizon, not a heaven.

This in part is why I am so ambivalent about the popular contemporary use of the Right to the City (RTC) trope. Flowing from the ever-allusive and elusive Henri Lefebvre, the notion has emerged as highly fertile territory across multiple disciplines and sites. The phrase gets invoked as an all-purpose banner to organize under, from activist groups to critical geographers to its enshrinement in Brazil's constitution to social movements across the globe. For many the Right to the City has emerged as the most promising of new urban possibilities, and yet still, after reading Lefebvre rather closely and then several books examining his oeuvre, as well as several concerted attempt to understand its deployments, I am unconvinced I know exactly what to think about it. Actually, I remain unconvinced I even know what the slogan actually means, beyond its obvious rallying cry potential.

If people find RTC a useful organizing umbrella, then I'm all for it—especially for people who have had basic human needs systematically

7. As per Gilles Deleuze and Félix Guattari, who describe the state as an "apparatus of capture." *A Thousand Plateaus: Capitalism and Schizophrenia* (Minneapolis: University of Minnesota Press, 1987).

and viciously denied to them—but into that conversation I want to keep asserting the primacy of struggle, an imperative that the call to "rights" subtly undermines. Rights are a highly legalistic and individualist framework, not easily adapted to the social. To claim that you have a *right* is to declare a legalistic faith, and rights discourses inherently appeal to a higher body for affirmation and application—the legal system, the state, the United Nations, God—somebody. This suggests a particular kind of approach to social change that demands inclusion, recognition, and acceptance into existing conditions and now, ultimately, a submission to Westphalian cartographies.

A transformative politics of an alternative modernity has to be intent on remaking the core assumptions of the capitalist project, not just asking for equality of inclusion. Claiming a Right to the City strikes me as a potentially valuable start, what David Harvey calls "a weigh station," but we need much more than that. When our imagination is limited to inclusion in existing social conditions, our struggle is reduced to pleading. As Glen Coulthard put it: "This is what I take Taiaiake Alfred to mean when he suggests, echoing Fanon, that the dominance of the legal approach to self-determination has, over time, helped produce of a class of Aboriginal 'citizens' whose rights and identities have become defined solely in relation to the colonial state and its legal apparatus."[8]

A legal, rights-based strategy has to be just that: a strategic route to a far more imaginative struggle and perhaps the Right to the City is a platform for our collective imaginative capacities. But if I am going to take up my own challenge—if I am able to theorize in the service of action and unsettle the colonialist assumptions I carry with me about property and sovereignty, I want to stay curious about how we can think outside of ourselves. If our current urban regimes of land allocation and property sovereignty have proven disastrously inadequate, how might we learn new ways of being?

8. Glen S. Coulthard, "Subjects of Empire: Indigenous Peoples and the 'Politics of Recognition' in Canada," *Contemporary Political Theory* 6, no. 4: 452.

EVERYWHERE ALL THE TIME

In the spirit of the chapter, I want to float an epistemological trial balloon. In order to think outside ourselves, to think outside predatory colonialist capitalism, space has to be cleared for a radical plurality of possibility—particularly when it comes to learning new modes of thinking and action. After a couple of decades of working with young people, one of the few things I feel sure about is that I have no idea how people learn, and I'm pretty sure that no one else does either. "Learning" is a grossly inadequate word to describe the innumerable ways people acquire new skills, ideas, insights, and capacities. Some people may well be perceptive in observing how certain kinds of people grow in certain kinds of circumstances under certain kinds of conditions, but I am exceedingly suspicious of anyone who claims to taxonomize universal learning styles or skills.

We are all unclassifiable bundles of predispositions, positionalities, and personalities that are unstable and shifting. We are constantly making and remaking ourselves, and how we "learn" is similarly permeable and unfixed. How people learn new ways of acting and being entirely depends on an uncounted array of factors and tensions, and rather than understanding learning as a necessary and contingent by-product of teaching, we should be asking about the conditions under which people can grow, thrive, and learn. Universalizing any part of that equation reduces the vast horizons of human potentialities to a set of technical exercises in the service of biopolitical control: humans producing humans. The modernist educative project to standardize a universally reproducible production of teaching inevitably runs aground in the face of ineffable multiplicities. Learning is not the product of teaching.

One of my favorite experiments in this vein is Sugata Mitra's Hole-in-the-Wall project. Mitra is an exuberantly polymathic Bengali physicist, computer scientist, and inventor who in 1999 installed a computer in the wall outside his Kalkaji, New Delhi, campus, which backed onto an urban slum. A (then) high-powered PC was contained within the wall and a monitor and touch pad were accessible from the street, located at a child's level. No instructions, details, or information were provided; the computer could access the Internet with a web browser; but all the systems were in English.

Within hours an eight-year-old child was observed showing his six- year-old sister how to browse, and within days constant crowds of slum children gathered around the monitor, watching one another use the machine. It was quickly evident that large numbers of kids, many of whom were functionally illiterate, most of whom knew little English, and almost none with previous computer skills, were able to work with one another, without adult intervention, with competency. For the next five years Mitra and his team installed similarly arranged computers in twenty-three locations across rural India from the desert west to the mountainous north to the humid south, and the results demonstrated over and over the same thing: children were able to learn to use computers and the Internet on their own without teacher supervision. The key was that it had to be a social activity. The groups that crowded around the monitors were self-designing, and despite sometimes having only minutes of individual access a day, small packs of kids working together and surrounded by larger groups observing and advising were all able to build complex sets of skills. These results were "irrespective of anything": class, geography, cultural or religious background, any variable Mitra could factor in had no significant impact on the results.

In subsequent years Mitra, now a professor of Educational Technology at Newcastle University in England, has expanded the project to Cambodia, eight African countries, hundreds of locations across India, and innumerable smaller experiments. The results have led Mitra to call learning a "self-organizing system," a thesis that echoes generations of alternative education thinkers across the globe. More provocatively, he frequently quotes the sci-fi author Arthur Clarke to claim that "Every teacher that can be replaced by a machine should be."[9] For a techno-Neanderthal like me, this is a tough pill to swallow, but turn it a little and it becomes compellingly urgent: what can a teacher do that a machine cannot? That's a challenge I'd extend to anyone who spends time with kids: what makes you not a machine?

There is a clear connection to urban life here. Just as learning can best be understood as self-organizing, so can city life. If we can reliably rely on children of all ages to learn complex skills in small self-organizing social systems, is it possible that small groups of city residents can learn the skills necessary to care for their neighborhoods and substantially govern themselves? If learning is not the product of teaching, is it possible that convivial neighborhoods are not the product of planning?

To learn new ways of thinking about, understanding, allocating, and using urban land, consider the Hole-in-the-Wall example as one compelling route to imagining productive, self-organizing, self-governing systems of urban relationships. Countless small and mid-sized groups of people across the world have proven themselves able to coordinate and flexibly manage common resources of all kinds with complex governance and service arrangements. There is every reason to think that imagining an equitable set of accesses to urban property can be an equally successful social project—a route to remaking ownership.

I am not forwarding a libertarian narrative, nor am I advocating for a radically laissez-faire Wild West imaginary, but for moving urban land beyond the logic of the market and beyond the disciplinary state. I am convinced that people are absolutely capable of

9. Here are three Mitra lectures: "Kids Can Teach Themselves," February 2007, http://www.ted.com/talks/sugata_mitra_shows_how_kids_teach themselves; "The Child-Driven Education," July 2010; http://www.ted.com/talks/sugata _mitra_the_child_driven_education?language=en; and "Build a School in the Cloud," February 2013, http://www.ted.com/talks/sugata_mitra_build_a_school _in_the_cloud.

governing commonly held land, and that every cook can govern with subtlety, generosity, and hospitality.[10] Of all the many examples I could invoke here, I can think of none better than the Right 2 Dream Too (R2D2) camp.

THE RIGHT TO REST

On several of my visits to Portland, I've stopped in at Dignity Village,[11] an intentional community founded and run by more than sixty homeless residents. The village started as a squat in downtown Portland but since 2001 has had a permanent space on some semirural land out by the airport. The land is owned by the city, but it is self-governed by elected residents. It is a sweet little spot: brightly painted tiny houses, shared social services, showers, gardens, and an overall tidy, almost quaint feel to it. In a lot of ways it is a tremendous success story of homeless people organizing and resisting, building networks of support, and carving out a solid, functioning community for themselves.

Soon after one of those visits a local buddy took me aside: "Look, DV is fantastic, but you've *got* to go check out Right 2 Dream Too. Dignity Village has done everything right, but they're now way out of town, out of sight, and out of mind. R2D2[12] is staying in the city, right in everyone's face. and it's not going away." So the next day I went downtown to hang out with founder and chairman Ibrahim Mubarak.

I've since spent considerable time with Ibrahim and R2D2, and my pal was right: something important is going on there. In 2011 a small group of homeless people established the camp, on private property,

10. As per C. L. R. James's famous essay: "Every Cook Can Govern," *Correspondence* 2, no. 12 (June 1956).
11. Sometimes by myself; sometimes with a crew of grad students in tow.
12. Among the all-time great acronyms.

right next to the paifang at the entrance to Old Chinatown.[13] It's a corner lot right on West Burnside, which is one of the busiest commuter routes and in and out the downtown core. Initially it was just a bunch of tents lined up in tidy rows on a gravel lot that the owner, due to a complex set of beefs and motivations, allowed to stand,[14] but in short order it was built out into a fully functioning tent shelter and community. Almost the entire site is now covered with an elaborate series of tarps and tents, subdivided into a warren of differentiated spaces. There are porta potties, a kitchen, a library, a laundry,[15] a dumpster and composting, Internet access, two communal sleeping areas (men's and women's) plus couples' tents. In the summer, garden beds and bikes are available, and on two sides of the property stands a brightly colored zig-zagging fence made of old doors, inscribed with inspirational/aspirational messages that are sponsored by local schools and nonprofits. There's twenty-four-hour security, everyone has to check in and out, strict drinking/drugs/ violence/sex prohibitions are in place, and every time I've been there it seems to run like a tight little ship.

It's just a single corner urban lot, but it's a multidimensional, breathing, shifting project that sort of gets bigger the longer you look. The

13. Interestingly and illustratively, the camp was set up in large part because the Occupy Portland project had taken over the space where homeless people had previously gathered and did not particularly welcome their presence. R2D2 was built in direct response to that strange displacement, but Ibrahim and the Right 2 Dream Too folks were generous in rebuilding that relationship and giving the Occupy Portland crew clear communication about how they could support one another.

14. The owner had knocked down an old commercial building with the intention of installing food carts, but after he was denied permits due to the gravel surface, he decided to lease it to Right 2 Survive (R2D2's governing nonprofit) for one dollar per year. He obviously is being generous, but mostly he really wants to piss off the city.

15. Sleeping bags are provided and are laundered twice a week on top of being sprayed with bleach and tea tree oil every night.

core difference between Dignity Village and R2D2 is that the former is a permanent settlement and the latter a shelter, which means that the sleeping spots are available on a first-come, first-served basis. Every evening registration opens at 5:30 p.m. and at 8:00 the names of the lucky winners are announced.[16] There are spots for seventy-five people, and they are full every night.[17] If you don't make the cut, you're given a blanket and told to come back and try again tomorrow. Very early one wet December morning, I walked a widening gyre of concentric circles around the site and counted forty-seven people in doorways and under benches, just within a few blocks.

It took me a little while to recognize the organizational efficiency at work. The key to the whole thing is the back area of the site: a cluster of individual tents where twenty staff people live full-time, semipermanently. The camp is run by these volunteer residents who do all the security, cleaning, monitoring, and maintenance of the place, with the leadership of Ibrahim. The total budget for R2D2 is something like $1,500 monthly, all of it coming from private dona-tions, grants, and ad hoc fundraising,[18] and the biggest line item by far is the laundry. The staff has to be seriously sharp to work with a population that is occasionally a little volatile, totally in need, and overwhelming at times, and do it with very limited resources. Ibra-him described their mandate like this:

> Our main goal is to protect people's right to rest. We make sure people know they are not the problem and they shouldn't blame themselves. The problem is the problem; it is a system that is failing people. We're providing a place where people can get a good night's warm, dry and safe sleep because so many home-

16. There's also a dedicated twenty-four-hour sleeping tent for people who want to sleep during the day. Some people living there work night shifts.
17. Including a number of people with full-time jobs.
18. T-shirt sales, in-kind donations, fundraisers, and so on.

less people are so sleep-deprived that it's hard for them to
think. Once they are rested they can start to rebuild their lives.
We recycle plastic, cans, and paper—we need to recycle people's
minds, and getting sleep is the first step.

Unsurprisingly, an ongoing set of battles surround the project. This
part of the story is tiresomely predictable: the threats and bribes from
the city, the blustery fumbling of municipal officials, the deadlines,
the missed deadlines, the revised deadlines, the bullshit deadlines, the
lawsuits, the angry local businesses, the public meetings, the false
resolutions, the failed attempts to relocate the camp, the arbitrary
applications of bylaws, dire predictions from local landowners, public admonitions—all of it could have been scripted.

But the unexpectedly exciting twist is that R2D2 keeps winning,
keeps digging in its heels and staying highly visible. It sued the city
and in 2015 won an $846,000 judgment,[19] with which it was given
another deadline of two years to move. It is currently reviewing its
options and looking for another spot, but the central axial is to stay
in the city center. As Ibrahim told me: "We want to stay close to
where there are employment services and food options because we're
trying to transition people to new lives. We want people walk past
and people see us. We want homeless people to know where we are,
and for other people to see how we're organizing."

We've all seen tent cities that look like this. Squats, homeless
camps, refugee settlements, protests, Occupy sites. There have
always been houseless people self-organizing in temporary shelters,
and there are always people like me: middle-class do-gooder types
who observe with a sympathetic eye and help where we can. And
most of the time people like me implicitly condescend. Smile and

19. Andrew Theen, "Right 2 Dream Too Homeless Camp: A Year and $846,000
Later, Still in Same Spot," *Oregonian*, February 25, 2015, http://www.oregonlive
.com/portland/index.ssf/2015/02/right_2_dream_too_homeless_cam_3.html.

nod, offer some platitudinous banalities, tell our friends about this inspiring place we have seen, maybe donate a little time or money, and keep moving along. Most of the time our observations come with no small dose of paternalism and amazement that these marginalized folks can pull this thing off.

Every time I leave R2D2 I feel an unsettling mess of emotions. Some guilt, some sympathy, some empathy, some good cheer, some energy, some simultaneous embarrassment and gratitude for how soft my life is. But maybe the only really useful feeling I have is a simmering, ill-directed rage. I live in city with a relentless homelessness crisis. You probably do too. Portland is no different. There are an estimated four thousand homeless people[20] in that city of something like two million.[21] So one out of every five hundred people in Portland doesn't really have anywhere to go at night but it is illegal to sleep outside in Portland, a bylaw that is enforced in both the legal and everyday senses.[22] So what the hell are homeless people supposed to do if the shelter and R2D2 are full?

It's how unnecessary homelessness is that most angers so many of us. It is easy to think of people on the street as a sad but "natural" reality that always has been true and always will be so. But it is these tacit assumptions that consistently trap us. We come to believe that political choices are not our choices at all but foregone conclusions that we can at best accommodate. These beliefs seep into the deepest parts of ourselves. And the worst of these beliefs are often the most intransigent. Like most everyone, for example, I find it near impossible to

20. According to the City of Portland Housing Bureau, 2014, http://www .portlandoregon.gov/phb/60643.
21. Like all sprawling metropolises, where the city starts and ends is rather capricious, so it depends on where and how you measure. The 2010 US census gives these numbers for Portland: 583,776 for the city proper (and an estimated 609,456 for 2013), 1,849,898 for the urban area, and 2,314,554 for the metro region.
22. Cops yelling, shoving, hassling, moving folks along.

think all that much about starving kids and still function usefully. It's infuriating to live in a world where just under a billion people go to bed at night malnourished and almost three million children die of hunger every year.[23] That's brutal enough, but this happens in a world that produces at least 1.5 times as much food as it needs[24] and is performatively awash in profligate wastage.[25] Just as kids across the globe are dying in the name of our political choices, four thousand people in Portland wonder every night where they should sleep, but not because there are not enough beds or buildings to shelter them. It is a wholly unnecessary exercise.

Somehow in this political milieu a small group of highly marginalized people with a total paucity of financial or material resources and just an empty gravel lot are able to do what the City of Portland cannot manage. How is it that all the university degrees, all the sophisticated language, all the money, all the good intentions, all the municipal departments filled with well-meaning, plaid-wearing, thick-eyeglass-sporting, liberal-reading, rich-friend-having, network-accessing, land-having, bylaw-writing, really-very-nicely-compensated urban officials

23. Not to be overly righteous, but three million! That's approximately the total population of Armenia or Toronto or Mongolia or Iowa. Kids dying, every year. If one year everyone in Armenia died, and then the next year every last person in Iowa passed away, and then the next year everyone in Toronto died, what would the response be like?

24. "The food crisis appeared to explode overnight, reinforcing fears that there are just too many people in the world. But according to the FAO, with record grain harvests in 2007, there is more than enough food in the world to feed everyone—at least 1.5 times current demand. In fact, over the last 20 years, food production has risen steadily at over 2.0% a year, while the rate of population growth has dropped to 1.14% a year. Population is not outstripping food supply." Eric Holt-Giménez and Loren Peabody, "From Food Rebellions to Food Sovereignty: Urgent Call to Fix a Broken Food System," *Food First Backgrounder* 14, no. 1 (Spring 2008), http://international.uiowa.edu/files/international.uiowa.edu/files/file_uploads/bgrspring2008-FoodRebellionstoFoodSovereignty.pdf.

25. According to the Institution of Mechanical Engineers, "As much as half of all the food produced in the world—equivalent to 2bn tonnes—ends up as waste every year." http://www.imeche.org/knowledge/themes/environment/global-food.

cannot match the organizational sophistication and effectiveness of a few dozen homeless folks with $1,500 a month to work with?

Look, I'm not about taking gratuitous potshots at Portland's smug self-satisfaction.[26] And it does no one much good to fuss about my own regrettable capacity for smugness, or to point out how complicit I am in the rampant inequality that stains my own city and neighborhood. All of that is essentially futile. But it might be very useful here to ask what the rest of us can learn from R2D2.

Conversations about marginalized or poor or homeless people are all too often coded renditions of "How can we get these people to act like middle-class taxpayers?"—which is of course another development discourse variant. The assumption that they are dysfunctional and in need of professionalized treatment is so banal as to be unsaid, but following postcolonial and postdevelopment analytical strategies, what happens if we park our arrogance briefly and consider what these folks are doing that we are not, or cannot, seem to do? That question sometimes gets reduced to a noble savage effort, but in this case it is pretty easy to be specific, direct, and disciplined with the question. R2D2 is having quantifiable, consistent success at providing incredibly cost-efficient shelter to a very-difficult-to-house population. And they are doing it while creating on-the-job training in a convivial, supportive organizational context, and on commonly held land that they do not own.

What are they doing that traditional social service agencies so often cannot seem to? Is it just that Ibrahim has a particular kind of genius and charisma? That's part of it, but that's not how he sees it. "I'm Black, Muslim, and homeless—the three worst things you can be in this society. If I'm out here creating places where people can live—then lots of other people can too." He's right and wrong on that point, I'd say. Wrong because not many people have the kinds of skills and experience he does, but essentially he is correct. The reason for

26. Okay, maybe a little.

R2D2's success might be intention, because as Ibrahim says, professional service providers need people to be dependent on them: "There's a real gap we see between city officials, academics, bureaucrats and the grassroots organizations. We don't dictate people's lives. We ask them how can they become productive and then surround them with support as they move from consumers to producers. Everyone makes mistakes, but we believe in people. We look at how people can care for one another. The homeless community is a real melting pot, there's a lot of difference here, but that's life."

Whenever I talk with Ibrahim or think about R2D2, it feels as if real insight is just sitting there about what a city of generosity and hospitality could look like. I'm not entirely convinced I know exactly what that insight is, but I do know that the touchstone ideas I keep returning to when I ask what a city is for seem to be entirely alive in that wet, tarped up, scrappy city lot. When I think about the conundrums and contradictions of urban land, displacement, and dispossession, my mind keeps returning to R2D2.

A TIME AND A PLACE

The objections to these kinds of examples tend to be twofold. The first suggests that it is easy to scan the globe, cherry-pick a few sweet scenarios (typically from highly marginalized populations) that demonstrate common land principles in action, and then recklessly extrapolate to the general. Most everyone has encountered an amazing cooperative farm or housing complex, a squat or intentional community, but it is surely faulty logic to assume that just because one experiment has been successful in alternative land arrangements that others (or *any* others) will therefore necessarily be so.

More so, these kinds of examples typically involve relatively homogenous populations, like my Fort Good Hope example from chapter two. Right 2 Dream Too fits this description in that the participants all share an existing shared set of commonalities to

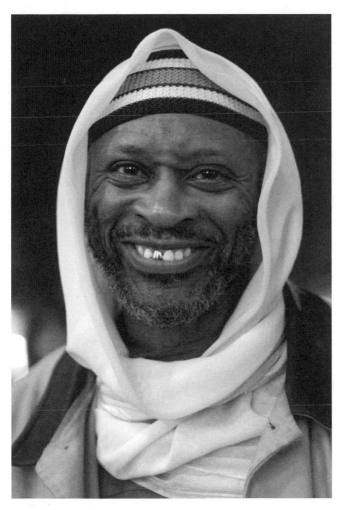

FIGURE 3.1
Ibrahim Mubarak. (Photo by Intisar Abioto, The Black Portlanders)

build around: homelessness in the latter case, shared cultural identity and geographic isolation in the former. In both cases conceptions of alternative sovereignties have emerged among clearly identified and differentiated populations.

It would be naive to point to selected existing working alternative juridico-political land arrangements and then claim that people in general are predilected to cooperative social relations. I could just as easily cite a greater number of awful, crassly predatory renditions of property relations, from people shooting strangers who ring their doorbell to neighbors brawling over minor transgressions, to Robert Frost,[27] to entrenched major land disputes, and conclude that we need to radically strengthen the ownership model, not destabilize it.

The second major drawback to highlighting compelling yet isolated examples like I have done here is the problem of scale. I, like the Ostroms and so many others, have used small-scale, bounded, and comprehensible units in the Schumacherian, small-is-beautiful sense. But as David Harvey puts it:

> The possibilities for sensible management of common property resources that exist at one scale (such as shared water rights between one hundred farmers in a small river basin) do not and cannot carry over to problems such as global warming, or even to the regional diffusion of acid deposition from power stations. As we "jump scales" (as geographers like to put it), so the whole nature of the commons problem and the prospects of finding a solution change dramatically. What looks like a good way to resolve problems at one scale does not hold at another scale.[28]

27. "Good fences make good neighbours." Robert Frost, "Mending Wall," in Robert Frost, *North of Boston* (New York: H. Holt, 1914).
28. David Harvey, *Rebel Cities: From the Right to the City to the Urban Revolution* (Brooklyn, NY; London: Verso, 2013), 69.

This is essentially correct: it is obviously untrue that management configurations at one scale will automatically "cascade down" or "aggregate up" scales, that we could simply transpose the strategies for managing a shared farmland to a metropolitan region or a household. Complexities and specificities are inhered not only in every scale, but at every site. It is equally untrue that inter- or intrascalar solutions are automatically replicable either.

But to throw out the baby with the bathwater here is a very strange response. The examples of R2D2, of any of the thousands that the Ostroms documented, or of countless others we might invoke should not be romanticized or nostalgicized, nor should they be framed simplistically as blueprints. Each of these examples offers plenty to learn from, not just functionally, but as examples of dual power and living breathing places of alternative renditions of ownership. The point is to demonstrate possibility, perhaps extrapolate in part, but more to build the soil of an alternative modernity.

The traditional Left continues to hamstring itself with fantasies of salvific sweeps, a position that derides everything beyond mass action as insufficient or reformist. The claim that "socialism in one city is impossible" may or may not be worth talking about at one level, but at another it is exactly the all-or-nothing acid that dissolves radical thinking and action, and at still another level is just plain untrue. Just as the construction of a new solidarity economy has to be built piecemeal from the ruins of late capitalism, so too might emerge a commonwealth, with some old, some new, some repurposed elements, from workplace to workplace, neighborhood to neighborhood.

Socialism, or any other rendition of radically egalitarian and/or utopian social relations, will wax and wane, swell and subside, be fought over and defended, built and rebuilt. If we perceive the commonwealth as an artifactualized *thing* that we either have or we don't, then we're doomed to an endless loop of disappointment and recrimination. The commons, or a socialism from below, or a radically democratic pluralistic altermodernity, or whatever, has to be understood not as a secular-socialist heaven, but as a horizon that keeps bending at the edges, a build-the-road-as-we-travel *ongoing act* of emergence.

Functioning examples, in the particular as well as the generalized, offer inspiration and models to learn from. But more than that, imaginatively constructed alternatives act as lodestones, attracting and fertilizing new kinds of relationships. Sites where commonality is asserted act as nodes in constantly appearing, reconfiguring, and reconstituting networks of social economic and political exchanges. Torre David[29] may or may not have much to teach recovered urban spaces elsewhere, but squatters, social organizers, and housing activists everywhere learn from it, directly and indirectly. The multiplication, expansion, and deepening of those networks is the emancipatory horizon.

Carving out space for imaginative possibility is exactly what the ownership model suffocates: the relentless march to enclose, privatize, own, and claim property asserts itself as the one and only. Every intervention is a break in those clouds, whether it's a small art installation or a temporary autonomous zone, a protest, a squat, a worker-controlled factory occupation, a housing cooperative, shared gardens, or the creation and armed defense of a regional autonomous zone like those in Chiapas or Rojava—all of those and everything in between opens up space—in both the socially produced Lefebvrean sense, but also the boots-on-the-ground everyday material sense. It is the strength of the relationships within and between these interventions that either isolate or socialize the possibilities.

---

29. An amazing forty-five-story recovered office tower in Caracas, Venezuela. It is the third-tallest building in the country and was planned as a luxury development project but failed after the death of its founder and the Venezuelan banking crisis. It was taken over by the government in 1994, and after lying abandoned until 2008 it was occupied by over 750 families. They have built it into a spectacular and functioning vertical favela with full-time security, shops, a doctor's office, barber, chapel, soccer arena, and much more. See *Torre David: Informal Vertical Communities*, ed. Alfredo Brillembourg and Hubert Klumpner (Zurich: Lars Muller, 2013).

In that spirit I want to consider three specific threads—one existing, one old, and one new(ish) idea. To realize the city as a space of commonality and participatory unfolding, there have to be pushes and pulls, carrots and sticks, limits and ambiguities, attempts and failures, but none can be a totality, and in fact hoping for systemized "solutions" is exactly where we get all bound up.

GROUND RULES

Contemporary urban planning as a rationalist social exercise was born out of the social rubble of the first waves of the Industrial Revolution. Cities, most acutely those in Western Europe and the American Northeast, were besieged by workers pouring out of the countryside and colonized territories to chase the promise of work, with profoundly inadequate housing or civic services to accommodate them. This flood disrupted every aspect of social and cultural life in ways that cities were wildly unprepared for. The resulting Dickensian squalor, overcrowding, infrastructure failure, and rampant exploitation so threatened existing urban fabrics that dominant classes panicked. With anarchist and socialist organizing in the air, communist revolutions fomenting in Russia, and the swift growth of radical unionism in urban Europe and the United States, bourgeois urbanists acted quickly to undercut the potentially insurrectionary foment. Motivated in part by revulsion in the face of widespread proletarian and immigrant moral turpitude, in part by fears of political mobilization or even revolution, in part by racialized prejudice, and in part by the burgeoning poverty of urban social conditions, planners began to reorganize the city in comprehensive and systematic ways.

The explicit goals were to fix certain activities and certain people in their rightful places: to concretize dominance, to maintain order, to carve out space for industrial profiteering to proceed unhindered, to house and service people sufficiently so they could settle down, to allow for the mercantilist flow of goods, to make room for the automobile, and to cleanse the city physically and morally. Like all movements there was a shifting mélange of intentions, motivations, and orientations, but the connecting theme of urban planning has always been asserting the ability of municipal authorities to shape the form and functions of the city along ideological contours. Mobilizing every resource available—commissions, ordinances, blue-ribbon panels, social organizing, media blitzes, political contortions, moralizing, and new systems of zoning and taxes—urban regimes of permitting and planning congealed by the early 1900s to construct and control modern cities.[30]

If the urban crisis precipitated by industrialization birthed the modern era of city planning and theorizing, then perhaps our current interlocking sets of crises should not be wasted. And it's not hyperbole to call existing conditions crises: ecological devastation, climate change, and explosive inequality are bound up with the greatest rush to cities the world has ever known. I stand by my contention that this represents a unique confluence of possibilities and hopeful potentialities, but that requires a reimagining not just of ontological questions about what a city is for, but of social commitments to land.

That's not a particularly difficult claim to make in many ways, but what exactly that means is another matter altogether. It's clear that we have to be talking about limits. The best and bluntest tool available for municipalities to govern with is taxes: the basic mechanism for encouraging some kinds of behavior and discouraging and/or limiting others. The shock of the late 2000s financial crises goosed a

---

30. Some of my favorite and most-relied-upon general histories of urban planning include Peter Hall, *Cities of Tomorrow*, 4th ed. (Chichester, UK: Wiley-Blackwell, 2014); Leonie Sandercock, *Making the Invisible Visible* (Berkeley: University of California Press, 1998); Lewis Mumford, *The City in History* (New York: Harcourt, Brace & World, 1961); Murray Bookchin, *The Limits of the City* (Montreal: Black Rose Books, 1986) and *Urbanization without Cities* (Montreal: Black Rose Books, 1992).

suddenly enthusiastic upsurge in conversations about regulating financial markets, from reinstating mothballed legislative tools to a bouquet of FTT (financial transaction tax) proposals to far more transformative proposals, none of which really ever got much traction but brought a tiny breath of fresh air into the most stagnant of atmospheres. For a moment, it seemed possible to talk in a broad-based, popular way about real political choices and real urban transformations.

That moment has temporarily subsided and the Euro-American Global North remains stuck in a curious paralysis—in the face of some the most confounding crises ever encountered by humanity, the range of thinking has tended to remain resolutely cautious and incurious. Even in the midst of calamitous economic convulsions, the options in 2009 were reduced to a little bit more Keynes here or a little more Smith there, with the progressive Left's "We're all Keynesians now!" approximately the most depressing rallying cry ever.

Which is why the slogan "Another world is possible!" when echoed from Tunis to Occupy to Porto Alegre is so bracing: but when, and how, did any of us ever come to think otherwise? The sliver of light the financial crisis opened appears to have been squandered, but every sprawling exurban wasteland to every grossly overpriced downtown condo development blares: "Another city is possible!" I am no fan of catastrophism—I want to believe that it doesn't take tragedy or collapse to force social change—but the historical record is not much on my side on this point. People are so tremendously resilient and so adaptable that most of us will suffer fairly significantly before shifting our dogmas, but there is some evidence amassing that people in all kinds of places are open to thinking differently, even very differently, about what their cities could and should be.

Maybe the simplest pivot point is to talk about taxes. I remain convinced that the municipal is the right locus of the political, but that is problematic when in essentially every nation the vast bulk of taxation revenues flow to higher levels of governance. Most cities across the globe are faced with exploding sets of burdens but very limited options for raising taxes. They are thus forced to desperately offer themselves on the global marketplace, doing anything and everything to make themselves an attractive landing spot for internationalized capital, whether in the form of foreign direct investment (FDI), tourist classes, property speculators, or multinationals looking for welcoming investment regimes.

This begins to look like a tautology, or at least a really irritating inductive bind: cities need revenues, revenues have to come from investments, investments only come when a city is attractive to capital, and cities that are attractive to capital will inevitably price their most valuable residents out. Sincere municipalities try to continually balance the presumptive pulls between people and profit, hoping to find some ideal middle ground or at least to negotiate a kind of compromise. But that logic is of course always bound to the same capitalist tendencies to cyclical crises, deepening inequality, and private accumulation on the backs of everyday labor.

Henry George made the argument throughout the late 1800s that there are routes to thinking outside these logical dead ends and the best place to start is to reform the logics of property taxation. A revival of interest in Georgist economics has welled up over the past decade, and it's not hard to see why. George's foundational idea, best articulated in *Progress and Poverty* (1879) is a land value tax. He argued that the state is taxing the wrong things by allowing people to accrue unearned rewards via property appreciation and speculation, both of which require no effort and add no real value. Instead, to fund itself, governments are forced to tax labor excessively, which inhibits real value-adding activities.

This sets up a whole economic ecosystem of misplaced priorities and incentives, whereby landowners are desperate to maintain their property values and will cheer rising housing prices, even though they understand it to be deleterious to non-owners. The pull to privatize the socially earned wealth of the land means that any improvements, including tax-funded infrastructure, increases the value of privately held property and the value-adding activity of all of our labor (including community organizers and activists) increases the unearned wealth of landowners.

This sets up a perverse tide of wealth aggregation in propertied older generations to the direct detriment of unpropertied younger people, creating a kind of desperation among non-owners to get into the market—somehow, anyhow, no matter what it takes, sooner rather than later, because buying in is only going to get more painful.[31] Of course this kind of frenzy is only in the interests of certain classes of people, and everyone knows that. Everyone understands that current housing prices (in Vancouver for sure, but in essentially every global city) are far beyond most everyone's reasonable budget, and any kind of downturn—let alone a bust, prolonged recession, or depression—will damage the most recent purchasers (and taxpayers) the most, which in itself adds fuel to the fire to get in quickly before things go sour. Exploding housing prices induce a wild sort of risk-taking impulse among everyone.

In fact, the housing cycle adheres very closely to the definition of a pyramid scheme: the more people who can be seduced to buy into the scheme, the more already existing enrollees in the pyramid benefit. The goal is to get pushed further up the pyramid, which both increases profit and mitigates risk. The scheme works as long there

---

31. I recently had a locally prominent developer come and speak to one of my graduate housing policy classes. He was asked what advice he would give to young people living in midst of Vancouver's current housing mess. He started pacing and waving his hands in the air like a revivalist preacher: "Get into the market! Now! Do whatever it takes! Move to the deep suburbs, buy a 300-sq.-ft. condo, quadruple up, remortgage your parents' house! Do *whatever* it takes, because that house will be more expensive tomorrow, and even more next week!" It was a compelling performance, and he left a class full of students with eyes like saucers, running to their phones at the break to check real estate listings. I tried to talk them down, but I don't think I had much success. It was exactly the kind of pressure people are subjected to constantly, and it's easy to see why it is so effective.

are constantly more members joining. As soon as that supply of new participants falters, then the value of everyone's investment in the scheme is under threat, which is why any affordability initiatives or nonmarket housing provision at scale is resisted so furiously by homeowners, realtors, developers, and bankers. But all pyramid schemes eventually collapse, some sooner rather than later, depending on the scale of their ambition. Essentially no value-adding activities are happening in pyramids—little labor is involved, and the claimed generation of wealth is fictitious—and so they have to crumble. And thus we get the late 2000s mortgage-fueled crisis that metastasized to so many other sectors so swiftly. These crises are inevitable because land speculation and the contemporary credit cycle drive one another.

But don't take my word for it, ask Martin Wolf, chief economics commentator for the *Financial Times* and probably the world's best-known English-language financial journalist, and exceedingly far from a wild-eyed pinko. He calls "the land cycle" and the "private appropriation of the fruits of others' efforts as a prime route to wealth" a "ruinous way of running our affairs," and says the following: "Whatever one thinks of the *justice* of this arrangement, the *practical* consequences have become calamitous. Do we want to start yet another property-fueled credit cycle as soon as the debris of the present one is cleared away?"[32]

The answer, says Wolf, is a land value tax. He's hardly alone though—LVTs are the sweetheart of economists everywhere, and across the ideological spectrum, from Joseph Stiglitz to Polly Toynbee to George Monbiot to Winston Churchill.[33] The basic idea is simple: tax

32. Martin Wolfe, "Why We Must Halt the Land Cycle," June 29, 2013, https://www.youtube.com/watch?v=g5kc9RepC1Q.

33. "Roads are made, streets are made, services are improved, electric light turns night into day ... and all the while the landlord sits still. He renders no service to the community, he contributes nothing to the general welfare, he contributes nothing to the process from which his own enrichment is derived."

the value of unimproved land. The value of land is commonly created and so any gains in value should be as well. Henry George spent a career both refining and proselytizing on behalf of the theory, but the essentials are as simple as they are defensible.

> We have traced the unequal distribution of wealth which is the curse and menace of modern civilization to the institution of private property in land. We have seen that so long as this institution exists no increase in productive power can permanently benefit the masses; but, on the contrary, must tend still further to depress their condition. ...
>
> Deduction and induction have brought us to the same truth—that the unequal ownership of land necessitates the unequal distribution of wealth. And as in the nature of things unequal ownership of land is inseparable from the recognition of individual property in land, it necessarily follows that the only remedy for the unjust distribution of wealth is in making land common property.[34]

George published *Progress and Poverty* in 1879, and it sold over three million copies that at the time might have made it the best-selling book ever written by an American author. He was one of the prime intellectual drivers of the Progressive Movement and ran for several offices, including coming in second in the New York City mayoral election of 1886.[35] The LVT was hardly the only piece of his philosophy but was the core of it, largely for his belief in its ability to ameliorate inequality and correctly reward labor.

Winston Churchill, 1909. Cited in Robin Harding, "Property: Land of Opportunity," *Financial Times*, September 24, 2014.

34. Henry George, *Progress and Poverty* (New York: Robert Schalkenbach Foundation, [1879] 1958), 328–329.

35. A fairly narrow loss that Georgists then and now fervently believe to have been a fraudulent election.

I do not propose either to purchase or to confiscate private property in land. The first would be unjust; the second, needless. Let the individuals who now hold it still retain, if they want to, possession of what they are pleased to call *their* land. Let them continue to call it *their* land. Let them buy and sell, and bequeath and devise it. We may safely leave them the shell, if we take the kernel. *It is not necessary to confiscate the land; it is only necessary to confiscate the rent. ...*

There is but one way to remove an evil-and that is to remove its cause. Poverty deepens as wealth increases, and wages are forced down while productive power grows, because land, which is the source of all wealth and the field of all labor, is monopolized. To extirpate poverty, to make wages what justice commands they should be, the full earnings of the laborer, we must therefore substitute for the individual ownership of land a common ownership. Nothing else will go to the cause of the evil-in nothing else is there the slightest hope.[36]

Socialists, anarchists, ecologists, and the Left in general tend to love George for his emphasis on land, inequality, and commonality, but libertarians are stangely drawn to him as well. Milton Friedman grudgingly admitted the need for taxes and called an LVT "the least bad tax" in large part due to its efficiency. This kind of attraction to Georgist taxation is in large part because of its simplicity: Land value taxes cannot dampen the supply—there will always be essentially the same amount of land—in the way that, say, an income tax purportedly dampens the desire to work. Extra costs should not be passed on to renters since supply and demand relationships would remain unchanged. If property taxes were commensurately reduced,

36. George, *Progress and Poverty*, 405 (emphasis in the original). In the italicized lines, he does not mean "rent" as in money paid to a landlord; he means *economic rent*, or activity that makes money without adding anything productive.

"improvements" to property could be accurately rewarded and thus an LVT would create a real incentive to use land fully via the tax penalties on vacant lots, thus boosting the supply of houses. You cannot move land, so you cannot dodge an LVT. Its simplicity begets a certain kind of elegance.

So what's going on here? When something seems too good to be true, it usually is. How can it be that a simple, fair, efficient tax could have such potentially revolutionary social implications, yet remain essentially ignored? How is it possible that such a powerful instrument for reducing inequality and poverty be beloved by so many across the ideological spectrum, yet remain so obscure? Is it true that an LVT holds so much promise?

The simple answer is that yes, an LVT really *is* that promising, but what is primarily lacking is the political will to confront the property ownership model. The necessary motivational conditions, however, made themselves evident during our most recent financial crises when all kinds of people were sent scurrying looking for legitimate responses, and legions of closet Georgists emerged with new confidence. As the subprime crisis in the United States triggered a series of multisectoral global financial contortions, it became immediately evident that shifting some, or even much, of the tax burden to land— whether via LVT or more traditional techniques—would substantially stabilize the housing market, and thus larger markets as well.

But that was where dominant economic analysis got cold feet and retrenched itself. The conventional claim remains that the late 2000s crisis was essentially a financial crisis: Wall Street capital run amok, a regulatory failure, the shadow banking system out of control, the financialized economy Frankensteined. That approach is partially correct, and a critical interrogation of the financial landscape is obviously desperately needed. But what most economists—including Piketty—continue to either disregard, downplay, or peripheralize is the centrality of land to both the previous crisis and our current entwined crises of inequality and ecology. As Clifford Cobb puts it:

Since economists such as Shiller, Krugman and Stiglitz have already included real estate as an intermediate factor in booms followed by destructive busts, the key question is not whether real estate is involved in economic crises. The question that needs to be addressed is whether real estate speculation is the central cause of those crises. In simplified form, the issue is whether causality flows primarily from real estate bubbles to banking, or vice versa. They almost certainly interact, but, for economists, the question should be where the core of the problem lies. For policymakers, the issue is whether bank regulation or land-value taxation is the more effective means of limiting speculative bubbles.[37]

I actually see this as obfuscation in some ways—the chicken-or-egg search for original economic sin—but the core point is correct. It is the interaction between land and financial speculation that has perverted our economic thinking about value and allocation beyond recognition. If the intent is not just to prevent crashes or relentlessly recurring macro- and microeconomic crises, then the real goal should be to reimagine both land and financial flows, simultaneously and in concert.

So are LVTs a silver bullet? Not really. They cannot be positioned as panacea in and of themselves. There are very few places where a true land value tax has been implemented, and although there are scores of municipalities worldwide that have attempted versions, these have mostly attempted to tweak economic growth by encouraging landowners to "improve" vacant properties, which is a plausible ancillary benefit. In and of themselves, LVTs have real value if deployed strategically, but their full potential is realized only if

---

37. Clifford Cobb, introduction to *After the Crash: Designing a Depression-Free Economy—Selected Works of Mason Gaffney*, ed. Clifford Cobb (Malden, MA: Wiley-Blackwell, 2009), 14.

they are rolled out in combination with other policy instruments designed to undermine inequality.

George claimed that the imposition of an LVT would make it possible to abolish all other taxes[38] and took to calling his idea the single tax, the tax that would raise enough revenues to make all other taxation unnecessary. Most economists who have examined this claim have found that a simple land tax, even a really aggressive one, would not produce enough to entirely replace existing state tax bases, but as Paul Krugman puts it: "Believe it or not, urban economics models actually do suggest that Georgist taxation would be the right approach at least to finance city growth. But I would just say: I don't think you can raise nearly enough money to run a modern welfare state by taxing land [only]."[39]

While I concur with Krugman, he substantially misses the point here. The primary goal should not be to dredge up enough revenue to fund an amelioratory welfare architecture, but rather to imagine a free society where inequality is reduced to irrelevancy. George made substantial progress in this regard by enlarging his taxation proposals to include the proposition that all natural resources should be held in

---

38. As with pretty much all prophetical voices, he often got a little carried away: "What I, therefore, propose as the simple yet sovereign remedy, which will raise wages, increase the earnings of capital, extirpate pauperism, abolish poverty, give remunerative employment to whoever wishes it, afford free scope to human powers, lessen crime, elevate morals, and taste, and intelligence, purify government and carry civilization to yet nobler heights, is—*to appropriate rent by taxation.*" George, *Progress and Poverty*, 405–406 (emphasis in the original). Easy there, big feller. Look, as you now know, I am a firm proponent of LVTs and remain enthused about their truly radical potential. However, this is exactly the kind of thing a discerning reader has to pass over and hopefully forgive the man for, recognizing wild proselytizing for what it is. LVTs are essential but not sufficient, as they say.
39. Quoted in Michael Moore, "This Land Is Your Land," October 20, 2009, http://www.psmag.com/politics/this-land-is-your-land-2a060d28bd4f#.7hxm66y5x.

common,[40] which makes intuitive sense to most people, but currently there are very few jurisdictions ready to really attempt *that* project. As the *Economist* put it in 2014:

> But if LVTs are so great, why are they so rare? One explanation is that it is too difficult to value land separately from what sits on it. There is not much of a market, for example, for undeveloped land in central London. However, some think this can be overcome. The 2010 Mirrlees Review of British taxation argued that bean-counters could compare the price of similar buildings in different locations, for instance. In any case, the efficiency of the tax does not depend on accurate valuations. The bigger barrier is political. LVTs would impose concentrated costs on today's landowners, who face a new tax bill and a reduced sale price. The benefit, by contrast, is spread equally over today's population and future generations. This problem is unlikely to be overcome. Economists will continue to advocate LVTs, and politicians will continue to ignore them.[41]

And that's the point I want to emphasize here: the barrier is political. All kinds of subtle issues of implementation and introduction are at play, and absolutely it's not a straight money shot, but there is considerable evidence demonstrating that LVTs and the socialization of land and resources is an obvious, necessary step. The project is well-understood, well-documented, and well-strategized, but it involves a

---

40. Which raises the question: By whom? Who should hold which lands in "common" and under what premises? The easy formulation that "natural resources are part of the commonwealth" conveniently skips over colonial expropriation of land. More on this point coming, but it's closely tied to earlier critiques of the way *common* is invoked.

41. "Why Land-Value Taxes Are So Popular, Yet So Rare," *Economist*, November 10, 2014, http://www.economistcom/blogs/economist-explains/2014/11/economist-explains-0.

very substantial shift of power, money, and resources. As a result, there is substantial resistance.

A portfolio of conditions needs to be in place for an effective introduction of an LVT, but the dominant requirement is desire. The ownership model of property has such a firmly hegemonic hold on the contemporary imagination, especially in the Euro-American West, that denting it, let alone assaulting it, is tantamount to heresy. But there's nothing like getting priced off your own street; nothing like getting evicted; nothing like seeing your kids, cousins, parents, friends moved along; nothing like housing anxiety; nothing like seeing the local grocer close after thirty-eight years; nothing like yet another low-income house getting torn down; nothing like whole neighborhoods functionally disappearing; nothing like ongoing endemic displacements; nothing like the ongoing colonial domination of Indigenous lands to help shift attitudes.

The current experience of displacement is so profound in so many places that speculative tax proposals are now popping up with surprising frequency. In many ways speculative taxes are straight Georgism: socializing private land may be too unsettling, but socializing any value gains from here on out is perfectly reasonable. The basic idea is to cut the legs out from the housing speculation that is making so many cities feel so precarious, and not surprisingly, San Francisco, the home of so much volatility around tech sector-driven displacements, voted in November 2014 on Proposition G, a gentle and elaborately hedged antispeculation tax.

The proposition was simultaneously both highly courageous and very delicate. It would have imposed "an additional tax on the total sale price of multi-unit residential properties that are sold within five years of purchase or transfer"[42] Essentially it was an anti-flipping

42. "City of San Francisco Transfer Tax on Residential Property Re-sold in Five Years, Proposition G (November 2014)," https://ballotpedia.org/City_of_San _Francisco_Transfer_Tax_on_Residential_Property_Re-Sold_in_Five_Years, _Proposition_G_%28November_2014%29.

measure, with the tax penalties decreasing over time from an additional 24 percent if the seller had owned the property for a year or less
and decreasing to 14 percent for sales between four and five years
after that. And there were a raft of exemptions: neither single-family
homes nor condos nor those with more than thirty units were included;
newly built housing was exempt as was any subsidized or social housing, or if the owner used it as a primary residence for at least one year
immediately prior to the sale. Many other provisions and compromises were made to the proposal, which was sold as both widely palat-
able and highly targeted at specific kinds of speculative behavior.

By the time the measure reached the ballot, the proposition was
eminently reasonable (to the point of too much compromise) but in
the midst of furious antigentrification struggles seemed highly pass-
able. There was real public debate on whether the initiative was sur-
gically specific enough to achieve its stated ends and even more
question about whether those ends were justifiable, and given the
Bay Area's current fixation on displacements and housing prices,
much of the discussion was pretty sophisticated. Very predictably
though, real estate associations, landlords, bankers, and developers
lost their minds and poured vast amount of money and disinforma-
tion into the campaign, including $800,000 from the National Asso-
ciation of Realtors, $170,000 from the San Francisco Association of
Realtors, and $425,000 from the California Association of Realtors
Issues Mobilization PAC. The No side outspent the Yes campaign 20
or 30 to 1.[43]

Despite significant support from local and state politicians, the
proposition was defeated 54.2 percent to 45.8 percent, which was of
course a failure, but optimistically it was more than that. Introducing
the latent idea of municipalities actively intervening in market

43. J. K. Dineen, "Tenants, Homeowners at Odds over Prop. G.," *SFGate*, October 3,
2014, http://www.sfgate.com/realestate/article/Tenants-homeowners-at-odds
-over-Prop-G-5797591.php.

speculation on land is a critical watershed, born of desperation. Had Proposition G passed there would have been a long way to go still to carve out lasting, legitimately nonmarket space in that city, but opening up the conversation in a formal way is a huge step. It may in fact take an escalating series of crises and dispossessions before those conversations reach critical mass in San Francisco or anywhere else on this continent or before initiatives like this start getting passed, but to my reading it's a big deal.

Here in Vancouver there is constant anxiety about housing costs, affordability, and ownership: we live in the second-least affordable housing market in the world,[44] so there had better be. But aside from some low-grade rumblings, little appetite exists for any punitive taxes on flipping or property speculation. Currently the broad-based frustration with property values is typically expressed in concern around "foreign" ownership. Interestingly this kind of language has crept into all kinds of polite, even progressive conversation, here and elsewhere—in newspapers, call-in shows, TV jeremiads, public forums, and everyday discourses—and in some quarters is almost now assumed as starting point for rectifying "affordability."

It hardly needs to be said, but as soon as the word "foreigners" creeps into any analysis you're about to get a dose of (sometimes veiled) racialization. Out here on Canada's west coast that nudges up against anti-Asian, yellow-scare language, with claims that "rich

44. In 2014, Vancouver achieved this distinction for the sixth straight year! Come on up and collect your trophy, Vancouver! (http://www.cbc.ca/news/canada/british-columbia/vancouver-s-housing-2nd-least-affordable-in-world-1.2505524). This rating is conferred by Demographia, an organization with some highly dubious ideological stances but that does in fact occasionally produce some solid quantitative research. This metric simply divides median housing prices by median gross household incomes: not the most sophisticated of measures, for sure (e.g., it fails to account for transport costs), but useful as a starting point. In 2014, Vancouver once again trailed only Hong Kong, closely chased by San Francisco, Sydney, San Jose, Melbourne, Auckland, San Diego, Los Angeles, and London, in that order.

Chinese" are buying up all the houses, that they don't even want to live here, that they are just parking their money, and so on. As comedian and writer Charlie Demers jokes, when Chinese people first started arriving on Canada's west coast in the early 1900s, it was said that the white man couldn't get a break because the Chinese would work so cheaply and were taking all the jobs. Now it's said that the white man can't get a break because the Chinese have all the money and are buying all the houses.

The housing anxieties, precarity, and displacements in so many cities can push people toward a generalized and/or focused fear of others. Sometimes it is expressed in straight racism, sometimes posturing xenophobia, sometimes in more contoured arguments. In 2014, for example, the accomplished urban geographer David Ley published *Millionaire Migrants*, a solidly data-driven and documented explanation of how internationally fluid capital is distorting housing markets by decoupling housing prices from local employment markets. Looking at cities including Vancouver, Hong Kong, Singapore, London, and Sydney, Ley says, "In every one of these cities the market is being driven by something other than owner-occupiers. Not just new immigrants, but investors, including offshore investment." He found "almost a one-to-one correlation over a 25-year period between Metro Vancouver becoming one of the most unaffordable real estate markets in the world and a surge of international immigration and offshore investing."[45]

In Vancouver (as is pretty common on Canada's west coast), this gets translated into anti-Asian rhetoric, sometimes veiled, sometimes not at all. Ley claims that the target should in fact be Asian investors, because that is where the money happens to be these days

45. Douglas Todd, "Why Vancouver Housing Is So Unaffordable and What to Do about It," *Vancouver Sun*, June 27, 2014, http://blogs.vancouversun .com/2014/06/27/why-vancouver-housing-is-unaffordable-and-what-to-do -about-it/.

(or at least the bulk of the money interested in the west coast of North America). "What's causing high prices is simply an empirical question, and I'm very confident in my data. If we were talking about high housing prices in Kelowna, we would be analyzing the effects of buyers from the Alberta oilpatch."[46] The same kind of sentiments are expressed in housing markets across the globe, but directed at rich Middle Easterners, Indians, Russians, Americans, Japanese, Albertans, whoever. Every market has a segment of "foreigners" who are singled out as the real cause of unaffordability for locals.[47]

And the argument is wrong every single time. It matters not at all where these investors are coming from: overseas, overland, within country, out of country, the next suburb over, wherever. The problem is profiteering from and speculation on land. The answer is not taxes on foreign house buyers.[48] We do not need firewalls against immigrant investors. We need firewalls against rich people, wherever they come from, and specifically in this case, rich people turning land into market opportunities.

The strongest part of Ley's argument is his understanding of the effects of speculative investment, but that activity is equally damaging if the investors are from Chengdu or Calgary or Coquitlam. Eschewing any kind of racialized or xenophobic language should

46. Ibid.
47. But I'm super suspicious even of this sort of couching of the "it's the foreign money" argument. In late 2014, at the height (hopefully) of the hysteria around "offshore Asian buyers" (update from late 2015/early 2016: I was wrong; the hysteria just got ramped up even further), the Canada Mortgage and Housing Corporation (CMHC) reported in its fall rental market report that only 5.8 percent of condominium units in Vancouver's downtown peninsula were owned by foreign buyers, 3.4 percent in the city of Vancouver and 2.3 percent of condos in the whole Metro Vancouver region: hardly the tsunami we are so often warned of (http://www.vancouversun.com/Foreign+ownership +highest+downtown+Vancouver+condos+CMHC+report/10658524/story.html).
48. As have been enacted in a whole variety of different jurisdictions with wildly variable intentions and results.

open space for talking about the real problem—which is speculation in the short and long term, and more fundamentally the private accumulation and profiteering from land, and more specifically, settler profiteering from Indigenous land.

Once the real culprit has been identified, there is still a lot to talk about, but the conversation has to take place in the context of political choices about what kinds of values and behaviors we want to valorize or suppress. In the United States, for example, homeowners are currently subsidized more than $100 billion annually: "Their mortgage rates are subsidized through the government-sponsored enterprises Fannie Mae and Freddie Mac; they get a big deduction on federal income taxes for mortgage interest payments and for state and local property taxes; and they even get favored treatment on capital gains from the sales of primary residences."[49] Renters get no such tax breaks.

The American "ownership society" model, imagined to be a paragon of self-reliance and individualism, is in fact built on the backs of the commonwealth: massive public support and a subsidy that "according to the Congressional Joint Committee on Taxation ... add[s] up to $700 billion in lost (U.S.) government revenue over the five-year period through 2014."[50] In the context of collapsing local budgets, overburdened cities, and the detritus of a mortgage-fueled global economic crisis, perhaps those tax priorities can be shifted elsewhere, but more specifically aimed in the right direction.

But let's speak a little more clearly about urban processes of accumulation. Ongoing regimes of taxation and policy are eagerly transferring existing capital to propertied classes, but the great material wealth of cities has always been constructed on their capacity to

49. Viral V. Acharya, Matthew P. Richardson, Stijn van Nieuwerburgh, and Lawrence J. White, "White Picket Fence? Not So Fast," *The New York Times*, August 16, 2011, http://wwwnytimescom/2011/08/17/opinion/why-we-should-end-homeownership-subsidies.html?_r=0.
50. Ibid.

focus and synergize resources. All cities, and especially global cities, are dominantly built on concentrations of wealth pillaged from near and far. Just as London, Paris, Amsterdam, Barcelona, and the grand cities of Europe are concentrating the wealth plundered over centuries from the Global South, cities like Vancouver and Portland are still fueled by resources extracted from Africa, South and Central America, and all over Indigenous territories in North America.[51]

In this tradition it is no surprise that capital seeks to extract whatever it can from residents, exercising "accumulation by dispossession,"[52] a new(ish) term for the ongoing processes of what Marx termed 'primitive' (or original) accumulation: the churning enclosures of the commonwealth that created a landless proletariat funneling money to propertied classes via land reimagined as capital. The dispossession that accumulates in cities can be local or international, but it is always predicated on the clearing of Indigenous land.

Think back to my briefly sketched history of Portland in chapter 1. The city was founded in 1851, a year after the 1850 expropriation of two and half million acres of Indigenous land that was handed to any settlers who asked for it. The ongoing dispossessions of Black people in Albina have always been intimately linked to the theft of Indigenous land, both materially and politically, each given permission by ideologies of accumulation.

Land or speculative taxes in themselves are not going to call to account that history. They are a limited step, but if applied well they might be a critical piece in unwinding that narrative to provide just a little breathing room in an atmosphere suffocated by property. All of the tools I am throwing on the table here have possibilities, and each has to be willing to square to contending futurities, and to answer to

51. "Top 100 Companies in B.C.," *BC Business*, 2015, http://www.bcbusiness.ca/top100/companies.
52. David Harvey, "The 'New' Imperialism: Accumulation by Dispossession," *Socialist Register* 40 (2004): 63–87.

the displacements that their own rationalities rest on. If originary dispossessions have set the trajectory for all subsequent relationships with land, perhaps an unraveling of property can begin to realize the conditions necessary for a just politics of land.

THE TOOLS AT HAND

Reimagining and restructuring urban relationships with land and property are not just matters of taxation. We need the pull of constructive ideas as much as we need the push of taxation—we need the carrot to the stick, the honey to the hammer—and they need to work in combination; one without the other will not be adequate. The architects of contemporary economic restructuring understand this very well. First-wave analyses of neoliberalism[53] tended to focus on the "roll-back" of Keynesian institutions and policy, mirroring obfuscatory "small government" rhetoric. But it quickly became clear that neoliberalism is not just about the dismantling of social-welfare-state apparatuses, it is at least as much about the "rollout": the construction, consolidation, and defense of new forms of governance, regulation, inter- and intrastate networks, and economic formations. Our late capitalist neoliberal moment is characterized equally by the push and pull of a new architecture of social relations, and thus any credible alternatives must be as well: taxation and regulation of the land market alone is not sufficient.

Pull arguments must exist in favor of nonmarket alternative land allocation mechanisms that make sense, are plausible, equitable, and viable, but also attractive. There has been so much ideological energy expended in defense of the now globalized American Dream and the

---

53. Jamie Peck and Adam Tickell, "Neoliberalizing Space: The Free Economy and the Penal State," in *Spaces of Neoliberalism: Urban Restructuring in North America and Western Europe*, ed. Neil Brenner and Nik Theodore (Malden, MA: Blackwell Press, 2002), 33–57.

ownership model that private ownership has become reflexively connected to specific virtues: individualist responsibility, self-reliance,
stability, Rockwellian hearth-and-home ethics. It is presumed, for
example, without any convincing evidence (and in the face of plenty of
evidence to the contrary), that homeowners make better neighbors
and more involved community members because of their ostensibly
greater commitment to the place.

Arguing for commoned land can't just revert to fuzzy lefty clichés
decrying unaffordability or displacement: we have to make real arguments and have real ideas. It is well-understood and documented
how the ownership model is facilitating a massive transfer of wealth
to propertied classes, conditions that have prompted all kinds of
new thinking on the supply side in every city. Supply-side claims
argue that housing is too expensive because the market is too tight;
so the answer has to be to build more and differently, especially for
young people who will be more likely to embrace housing options
beyond single-family detached houses.

In this milieu, all kinds of innovative new thinking about housing
forms and configurations has emerged: micro-lofts, laneways homes,
tiny houses, shared residences, innovative towers, thin houses, con-
tainers, row houses, etc.—and that's fine—some accelerated supply
probably won't hurt, especially if it is interesting, flexible, and cheap.[54]
But in a globalized environment, the demand can be essentially endless; in many places, especially where the need is most acute, a fixation
on supply provision will not suffice. Innovative urban design is merely
a veneer. The real issues are not a paucity of supply or a lack of cool
housing typologies or poorly designed public spaces. Design cannot
think us out of any crises of displacement, but tends to effectively

---

54. Although many of these models are simply ways for property owners to
maximize their property values and further accelerate the market by doubling
down in borrowing against their existing mortgage.

mask, if not exacerbate crises by contributing unapologetically to rising property values.

A ton of sophisticated socioeconomic thinking and organizing across the housing continuum exists—from shelters to social/assisted housing to rental to collective and supported ownership to market housing. Essentially all of it is useful and worth considering, but I want to focus here on specific configurations that confer lasting, secure tenancy, and create the material conditions for new forms of social relationships. Obviously social housing (of all kinds, from emergency shelters to long-term subsidized housing) is critical for those in most need and should always be part of the picture, but what interests me most here is land tenancy that challenges and alters terms of the ownership model. I will highlight three here—community land trusts, cooperative housing, and squatting—and explain why each has germane implications, not just for housing but all kinds of land uses and relationships.

One of the places new (and old) thinking about urban property tends to cluster is around expanding homeownership (often closely allied with creative design thinking). Lots of people make the argument that we can and should be living in a total-ownership society. It's a fairly simple set of claims sometimes made in toto, often in pieces: that people cannot fully participate in a credit-driven society without a mortgage, that owning a house is a basic human right, that homeownership is the primary way to build wealth, and so on. The best parts of this line of thinking argue for the radical democratization of the homeownership model, making it possible for *everyone* to own a house. All kinds of people make this argument in all kinds of ways.

The *New York Times*, for example, in late 2014 wrung its hands at the steady decline of homeownership in the United States, "from a peak of nearly 70 percent in 2004 to a 20-year low of 64.3 percent recently, the number of owner-occupied homes has barely budged, while the number occupied by renters has increased by nearly 25 percent." The *Times* editorial board looked at these numbers and wondered whether homeownership was overrated and whether it would be a good thing if more people rented. The board firmly concluded no on both points, arguing that owning has always been the primary way to accumulate wealth by forcing mortgage holders into fixed payments on a solid and likely appreciating asset. Theoretically some renters could do the same with disciplined savings and investment, but in practice this rarely happens and renters rarely accumulate much wealth.

The *Times* acknowledged the barriers to ownership for so many, and noted the potential risks involved during downturns, especially after the raw experience of the late 2000s housing bust and foreclosure crisis. They insisted, however, that "the lesson of that debacle is not for individuals to avoid homeownership or for policy makers to devalue its importance. Rather, the lesson should be to foster conditions under which middle and lower-income Americans can sustain homeownership and avoid the ruin of foreclosure."[55]

One of the most articulate advocates of this position is Avi Friedman, a high-profile architecture professor at McGill University in Montreal, who has written extensively on innovative affordable housing prototypes and designed houses across the globe, including the Grow Home and the Next Home, which have received huge media attention, as models for new Global South housing. In 2000 *Wallpaper* magazine named him one of the ten people "most likely to change the way we live," and in 2004 Robert Scully called him "the most influential housing innovator in the world." So after I heard Avi speak about increasing access to home ownership,[56] I called him.

55. The Editorial Board "Homeownership and Wealth Creation," *New York Times*, November 30, 2014, SR8, http://www.nytimes.com/2014/11/30/opinion/sunday/homeownership-and-wealth-creation.html.
56. David Ball, "If You Can Afford to Rent, You Could Be a Homeowner," *The Tyee*, November 27, 2014, thetyee.ca/News/2014/11/27/Afford-Rent-Could-Be-Homeowner/.

He articulated his position clearly: that under capitalism (which he describes as "beyond our control") it has been demonstrated again and again that home ownership is by far the best and most efficient route to capital accumulation, which is especially critical now in an era of significant social service erosion. His claim is that while there is every possibility for almost all renters to become owners given the right economic conditions, "This can never be achieved without government mechanisms—including direct and indirect subsidies—to support people, especially young people in finding ways into the market." He pointed to Singapore as among the places he has visited where state interventions into the market have been tested and proven: "The Singaporean government owns 80 percent of their land in lease-hold arrangements ... because without limits on speculation there cannot be affordable housing. Governments have a moral obligation to help people find secure housing."

At face value, there's plenty to like about this kind of argument, mostly because it is attractive in a straightforward meritocratic way. An economic democracy seems predicated on equitable opportunity, and thus if state interventions can support broad-based access to the land market we'll therefore be in an equitable democracy. It is also clear that owning a house is a reliably viable route to wealth accumulation.

But that logic is all backward—clear evidence has been amassed that accelerating inequality is linked closely to the exploitation of land and accumulation by dispossession—so expanding and enlarging the market control of land can only exacerbate those processes over the long run. Homeownership tends to concentrate wealth, true enough, but it is *private* wealth, pulled directly from the commonwealth and extracted directly from displaced populations, and in any capitalist society, let alone the hyper-accelerated globalized rendition we live in today, wealth of any kind will necessarily accumulate in fewer and fewer hands. Frantic measures to increase access to ownership is exactly the kind of Band-Aid solution that looks good in the short term, but actually accelerates the conditions that caused it in the first place. It is a direct replication of the development bind: capitalist development causes extravagant inequality, but more capitalist development is prescribed to ease it. I appreciate Avi's faith in popularizing access to secure tenure, but presuming that social conditions are beyond us and thus that doubling down on private ownership is the only viable route strikes me as unduly unimaginative, especially when other configurations are so plausible.

TRUST IN LAND

It is into this space where shared or limited equity schemes, probably best articulated by community land trusts, step in. The basic theory is pretty simple and lies somewhere between ownership and rental, in a category that is sometime called a "third-tier" set of options and includes deed-restricted housing, mutual ownership properties, limited equity, and a whole bunch of unclassified vernacularly shared arrangements.[57] The idea is to separate the house or actual built structure from the land in a "dual ownership" arrangement: one party owns the house and another owns the land. Consider the house my family has rented for the past eighteen years. Let's just say on the market it's worth a million bucks (that's probably accurate in Vancouver's current real estate market). However, the physical house itself is, generously speaking, kind of a piece of shit.[58] Any new owner will surely tear it down, and the physical house is probably worth fifty grand at very most, probably a lot less.

---

57. For example, let's say that a young person gets married. The couple build a house on their parents' property. The youngsters (probably) own the equity in the house, but the larger family holds the deed to the land.

58. That's a technical real estate term. Honestly, I love the house and it has treated my family beautifully. It's huge and rambling and leaky and drafty, but it has its charms. I remain totally grateful for and to it.

All the monetizable value of the property is embedded in the ground. And this of course is true for most every house everywhere—it's the dirt, not the shelter, that's valuable.

Shared or limited equity schemes put this bifurcation to use by financially separating the two. One party (the steward) buys and holds just the land; the other party (the tenant) purchases just the building. This allows moderate-income folks to buy a place extremely cheaply (say, in my case, for fifty thousand dollars) while the land is held permanently by the stewardship party. It's a shared win that works by reversing the normalized logics of tenure and ownership. The land retains its value, while the buyer gets to build their equity. Long-term affordability gets locked into the terms of purchase by building resale caps or covenants into the agreement, so that there is no chance of property flipping, or of the house leaving the low-mod-erate income market. As Michael Lewis of the Canadian Centre for Community Renewal put it to me, "You can't argue for affordability if you do not have alternative land tenure with social purpose built in. It is *the* key. There are only three costs to land development: construction, financing, and inflation, but right now the community can't capture the latter (the raise in land values) because it gets pocketed by the 'normal' activity of the market."[59]

Community land trusts build on and institutionalize the model: "The owner of the land is a nonprofit, community-based corporation, committed to acquiring multiple parcels of land throughout a targeted geographic area with the intention of retaining ownership of these parcels forever."[60] CLTs retain the deed to the land and get first rights to repurchase, but the units (which can be anything—houses,

59. Personal interviews and beers, from December 2014 to January 2015.
60. Oksana Mironova, "The Value of Land: How Community Land Trusts Maintain Housing Affordability," *Urban Omnibus*, April 29, 2014, http://urbanomnibus.net/2014/04/the-value-of-land-how-community-land-trusts-maintain-housing-affordability/.

condos, commercial properties, office spaces, industrial, whatever) are owner-occupied with resale caps or formulas. The basic CLT model is an innovation from the 1960s, designed to support African American farmers in Georgia who were locked out of ownership.[61]

The direct result of those initial Civil Rights–era efforts, now called the Institute for Community Economics in Albany, Georgia, is one of the biggest and most progressive seeders and funders of CLTs in the country. Thousands exist across the United States and Canada, in all kinds of configurations, scales, histories, and intentions—some that look like more traditional community development corporations, some that emerge from very localized antigentrification struggles, some urban, some rural, some elegant and complex, others relatively simple and bounded. Sometimes nonprofits are formed for this explicit purpose, but the landholding stewardship entity can theoretically be any community-based organization—faith-based groups, cooperatives, unions, or even a municipality.

A highly sophisticated set of land trust tools—legal, financial, and theoretical—have been developed with the requisite amount of contention and debate about applications and relative effectiveness,[62] but the biggest issue by far remains figuring out how to acquire the land in the first place. CLTs are most effective in heated markets where housing prices are unaffordable, but of course that unaffordability applies to the stewarding organization as well. Land trusts require a whole lot of equity up front just to acquire some property, and equity that will not be recouped, or at least cannot need to be recouped, in the foreseeable future. Once under way, CLTs can leverage their size to acquire new properties, but assembling the initial

61. Although there are all kinds of historical precedents and antecedents that the ideas emerge from, including the Garden City movement, Robert Owen, Josiah Warren, the Diggers, and so on.
62. See, for example, the National CLT Network (http://cltnetwork.org/) or *Shelterforce* magazine (www.shelterforce.org) for a couple of good repositories of info and conversation.

capital, often called the *threshold problem* (how to take commodified property and bring it over the threshold into the social portfolio) is by far the biggest structural issue with all shared equity models.[63]

But you know who almost always owns land, and often a ton of it? Cities. Most cities have considerable real estate portfolios, and because they have the capacity (administrative, legal, financial) to acquire and control land, they are ideally situated to get into the CLT game. Chicago, Las Vegas, and Austin, among many other places, have land trusts in operation, but Burlington, Vermont, is probably the best example where a municipality has facilitated the nonprofit sector in establishing community-based shared equity models. There was a time (actually a lot of times) when the state actively built infrastructure, including housing, so it remains sort of puzzling why so many cities, especially those bedeviled by affordability crises, are reluctant to allocate land for the permanent affordability that CLTs can lock in. Cities are always anxious about losing land-use planning flexibility, and municipal bureaucracies are often queasy about getting into property deals, but the dogmatic intransigence so many municipalities evince is infuriating. Cities hold all the land use planning cards: they have every economic advantage and every policy capacity to assemble property specifically to be held in affordable trust. If every two-bit developer can turn a 15–22 percent profit on every generic condo project they throw up, why isn't the city, any

---

63. When I talked to Michael Lewis about the threshold issue, he put it this way: "Gathering the initial equity to get a CLT or shared equity project off the ground is the real issue in a nutshell. In essence, using publicly owned land for Community Land Trusts is just reallocating common resources in public–social partnerships—as opposed to PPPs—but to make it happen you still need civil society support and technical skill, especially in financing." This is true, as the complexities of financing the social economy often baffle financial institutions as much as practitioners. This simple problem—how to get enough money to get a CLT off the ground—is actually more subtle than it looks. More on this later.

city, every city, doing similar work, but in the service of residents and the commonwealth?

When I asked John Emmeus Davis this question, he didn't dance around it. John has been the senior and most sophisticated advocate for CLTs and shared equity in North America for at least a generation now.[64] He's not just a proselytizer though; he understands housing and land issues under capitalism as well as anyone I have encountered, so I figured he was the right person to ask.

> Cities aren't in on this (and not to sound too crass) because for the most part they are in the back pocket of the developers. Take a city like Philadelphia, for example, at the other end of the economic continuum from Portland or Vancouver. There are 40,000 vacant lots in Philadelphia and 25 percent of them are held by various departments and agencies of the city. They finally got around in the last year to creating a public land bank, so why wouldn't they take all their 10,000+ lots and stick them in the land bank and then as soon as they clear title put it all into CLTs and community-based organizations that will protect affordability in perpetuity? That's the rational response, but it's not going to happen! It's just not.
>
> Politicians are not planning long term; they're planning for the next election cycle. Flashy investments and private sector

64. John's a great guy who publishes prodigiously on housing issues, primarily on shared equity and CLTs, but more broadly on community collective action and local organizing. Since 1993, his main gig has been as one of the founders and principles of Burlington Associates, a consulting co-op that has helped more than one hundred Community Land Trusts get rolling across the United States and internationally. John also has been a longtime key player, via various roles, in the development of the Champlain Housing Trust, which now owns and operates more than two thousand apartments, houses, and commercial buildings in the Burlington, Vermont, area.

cheerleading are the kind of short-term news politicians crave. Good policy is bad politics.[65]

But there are some deeper, more essential issues at play here, beyond just figuring out how to pull off these schemes. As much as I see tremendous value in shared equity and especially CLT models, I'm not wholly convinced they really alter the social terms of the ownership model. Shared equity uses financial and organizational sophistication to untangle the affordability knot for some, but it is the resale covenants that are most powerful. These restrictive covenants are not unique to limited equity arrangements, but really just another rendition of speculative taxes. At scale, CLTs could very conceivably reconfigure the housing market for large swaths of the city, but if participants are just leveraging the opportunity as an incremental step to get into the larger market, it becomes just an equity-building lifeboat for a lucky few. CLTs are only socially transformative if they move housing out of the market, rather than facilitate entry into it. John didn't shy away from my challenge:

> I think that shared equity and CLTs challenge the ownership model within a protected enclave of the social sector, but unless your holdings are significant and combine community ownership with community power [they] will remain isolated. CLTs can be very effective internally, but unless they are scaled up they don't affect larger policy. To be impactful externally, you have to combine a focus on property with a focus on power.
>
> Not enough affordable housing organizations can do this—combine property and power—and are just able to focus on being housing developers. Doing affordable housing is yeoman's work and moral work. It's the heavy lifting of serving people in

65. Personal interview, December 18, 2014.

need, but their impact on larger policies will be limited unless they are doing community organizing in tandem.

John is exactly right here, and there's another way to think this through, which is why housing co-ops strike me as pretty critical, in no small part because they are at the heart of my neighborhood. In the 1970s, a sort of mythical time for social funding in Canada, the CMHC (Canada Housing and Mortgage Corporation) began funding new nonprofit housing co-ops (the funding streams were essentially closed in 1992), and now there are more than 250,000 people across the country living in 2,200 cooperatives comprising more than 92,000 total units.[66] Most of these are in Vancouver, Montreal, and Toronto, but there are several thousand rural co-op units as well. These numbers pale in comparison to co-op housing membership in Europe, especially in Germany, Finland, and Switzerland where the sector is giant, but they remain a significant force in Canada, in Vancouver for sure, and in East Van absolutely, despite the federal funding petering out more than two decades ago.

Co-op housing models also tend to be pretty simple, and while there is a relatively wide range of applications and configurations, the basic formula is not complex. Instead of straightforward state provision of large-scale social housing, the Canadian co-op model tends to finance mixed-income, smaller-scale developments to be managed and ultimately wholly owned by nonprofit corporations. These co-ops come in both equity and nonequity versions. The latter is far more common: once the state has built the project, the nonprofit co-op assumes ownership of 100 percent of the units with members occupying units on a contractual arrangement. Monthly rental fees cover taxes, operating costs, and repairs and ultimately pay down the mortgage so that theoretically, in time the nonprofit

66. As per the Cooperative Housing Federation of Canada (www.chfcanada.coop).

society and its members can own and operate everything debt-free. The important caveat is that despite most co-ops having a mix of market and nonmarket units, the math rarely adds up easily, so to ensure that subsidized units are available for low-income residents the federal government has provided significant support annually.[67] Now that many of these 1970s- and 1980s-era developments have paid off (or are about to pay off) their mortgages, the Canadian government is ending the subsidy program, with many housing co-ops very well-prepared financially for this contingency, and others scrambling for alternative strategies.

In my neighborhood of about 35,000 people, co-ops are not just foundational social architecture; they are a critical bulwark against gentrification. On the west side of the neighborhood is a ten-block stretch (affectionately known as Red Square) that includes fourteen separate three- to four-story mixed-income nonprofit co-ops, with an average size of thirty-five (mostly family) units.[68] While virtually every other housing form is vulnerable, these co-ops cannot be gentrified. Owned by nonprofit societies, the buildings cannot be sold, and individual units cannot be auctioned off; they provide all the security of tenure that individual ownership provides, but it is articulated collectively.

67. The number that tends to be reported is that the federal government has provided $1.6 billion in subsidies annually. However, as Fiona Jackson and Michael Rodgers of the Cooperative Housing Federation of British Columbia told me: "It is not correct to use that dollar figure when talking about housing co-ops alone. It has been used with regards to subsidy programs for both housing cooperatives and nonprofit housing societies—of which there are many more than co-ops—under federal operating agreements. And those subsidies wouldn't have reached a peak figure annually until probably the early 1990s." It's hard to tell precisely how much went to co-ops, but suffice to say that it's a significant amount.

68. There are sixty of these in the larger East Vancouver community, and the average size in British Columbia is fifty-six units.

To be sure there are issues and trade-offs to living in a co-op: all the committees, petty bureaucracies, and collective decisions can be a pain in the ass; there tends to be limited choice around renovations; and most co-ops are kind of generic-looking. Maybe more than that though there are legitimate financial implications. Living in a nonequity co-op means that residents do not personally benefit from any land lift the property might realize. The nonprofit society might benefit, but only in a resale (which doesn't make much sense) or if the lift can be financed for building improvements. Co-op residents also experience a loss of flexibility: once they move into a co-op, the market leaves them behind (or they leave it behind). Instead of accruing increasing equity that might be leveraged to move into another place, co-op residents are treading financial water—unless they are very adept at saving the money they don't spend on a mortgage, or plan to live in a co-op until the end of their days. At a larger level, the organizational work required to develop and maintain housing co-ops can be a little arduous and unglamorous—the infrastructure and fiduciary gymnastics can be complex—especially in an economic and policy environment that tends to view co-ops as anomalous irritants.

All that said, there are some very compelling reasons to think about co-ops personally and socially, and the drawbacks are hardly deal-killers or inevitabilities. There are all kinds of ways to think and act our ways out of the limitations they inhere, and none of what I've catalogued is immutable. Co-ops in East Van have been lifesavers for so many of our friends and neighbors (shelter from the market in both senses), and most of the co-ops I have spent time in are friendly, attractive, and totally appealing, with nothing to suggest that there are untenable compromises being made.

But I'm not here to stump for co-ops in particular (OK, maybe just a little). Sure CLTs and cooperatives require sizable up-front investments, but honestly not really in the larger scope of federal, provincial, and municipal budgets. The amount required for nonmarket housing provision is amazingly modest, and that's without trying to calculate the opportunity costs and sheer loss of human potentiality that are incurred by inadequate housing— not to mention the numbingly immense budgetary repercussions for health care, social services, and community safety that bad housing policy creates. My real point is that models for rethinking and remaking our relationships with housing, and ultimately with land, *already* exist. Not a whole lot new has to be invented when the tools are at hand. Particular regimes of market-based land allocation and use have been constructed for us, and we can construct others, and at scale.

And that's where these kinds of housing innovations strike me as most important: in their specificity for sure, but more so in their intent. Community land trusts, shared equity, and co-ops are slightly different expressions of the same impulse—cutting out land from the profit-seeking marketplace. One adheres more closely to an ownership model, while the other gets more collectivist, but all kinds of possible variations on the theme exist. These are just a couple of configurations but with a focus on dual power. As Mike Lewis puts it: "The key is building reciprocity and solidarity into any land tenure relationships, linking up assets and needs, so that solidarity is infused at a number of levels. If we bring purpose to tenure we can capture the value that is being created and reinvest it into the commons—because almost all that value is currently getting sloughed off by the market."[69]

Capitalism requires dispossession as a normative framework. Without it competitive marketplaces cannot function. Once the idea of the market was radically expanded so that the economic subsumed the social, processes of enclosure became normalized.[70] Thinking about gentrification and dispossession or even softer, more

69. Personal interview with Mike Lewis, December 2014.
70. As per Karl Polanyi, *The Great Transformation: The Political and Economic Origins of Our Time*, 2nd ed. (Boston: Beacon Press, 2001).

generalized ideas of "affordability"—in Albina or East Vancouver or New Orleans or wherever—requires talking about nonmarket tenure. I'm not suggesting that there are no viable routes to action within capitalism[71] but that dispossession is assumed in a capitalist worldview, and any long-term thinking about land as a commonwealth has to begin outside the market, and suture itself to rematriations of land thefts.

In addition to community land trusts and cooperative housing, I want to discuss a third category of possibility: squatting. Sometimes all the organizational and financial contortionism involved in legally extricating land from the market feels a little overwrought. Why not just take it? There is more than enough land in the world. People are not houseless, homeless, underhoused, or poorly housed because there aren't enough houses. People are not landless or evicted from agricultural land because there isn't enough ground. Why shouldn't people who need land just occupy what is available? Isn't that an obvious moral imperative?

A long line of religious, ethical, and economic theory supports the occupation of land or buildings by people who do not have legal permission to use it. In North America especially, squatting is highly marginalized as a policing problem and the province of punks, desperate homeless people, righteous anarchists, or survivalists, but throughout much of the world it is a respected and expected form of tenure. Robert Neuwirth claims that there are more than a billion people squatting today or one in seven people globally.[72] In many cities like Mumbai or Sao Paolo or Nairobi, informal settlements represent major proportions of both land base and population. As Colin Ward put it: "Squatting is the oldest mode of tenure in the world,

71. I find "waiting for the revolution" analyses particularly cynical and irritating. The idea that all action is doomed under capitalism is exactly the kind of anomie I'm writing against here.
72. Robert Neuwirth, *Shadow Cities: A Billion Squatters, a New Urban World* (New York: Routledge, 2005).

and we are all descended from squatters. This is as true of the Queen [of the United Kingdom] with her 176,000 acres (710 km2) as it is of the 54 percent of householders in Britain who are owner-occupiers. They are all the ultimate recipients of stolen land, for to regard our planet as a commodity offends every conceivable principle of natural rights."[73]

That's where squatting is at its best, when it is far more than a simple take-what-you-can-get claim. Remember Aquinas? "In cases of need all things are common property ... If the need be so manifest and urgent that it is evident that the present need must be remedied by whatever means be at hand, then it is lawful for a man to succor his own need by means of another's property, by taking it either openly or secretly, nor is this properly speaking theft or robbery."[74] Squatting answers this moral imperative, creating a rupture not just in the ownership model of land, but in dominant ethical frameworks of property, just ownership, and sovereignties. People taking the land they need to survive, whether it is farmland, parkland, abandoned luxury apartments, empty houses or empty lots reverses what Debord called the "obvious degradation of being into having."[75] And it may well be that even our old friend John Locke, who most position as the foundational thinker of private property, might have agreed, at least in part.[76]

---

73. Nick Wates and Christian Wolmar, *Squatting: The Real Story* (Hastings, UK: Bay Leaf Books, 1980).

74. Cited in Susanne M. DeCrane, *Aquinas, Feminism and the Common Good* (Washington, DC: Georgetown University Press, 2004), 82.

75. Guy Debord, *Society of the Spectacle* (Brooklyn, NY: Zone Books, 1995), 17.

76. That's a much longer set of conversations for people more interested and adept in Locke scholarship than I. The best writing and thinking I know of in this line of analysis comes from James Tully. See his *Discourse on Property: John Locke and His Adversaries* (Cambridge: Cambridge University Press, 1982) and/or *An Approach to Political Philosophy: Locke in Contexts* (Cambridge: Cambridge University Press, 1993).

Squatting is not a social aberration, and it's not hard to imagine how legitimated squatting can fit into a plausible social framework. First, the practice is already popularly accepted all over the world, and, second, why exactly should it be reviled? Even asking that question draws us into franker, less convoluted arguments that are driven by moral and ethical imperatives. Simple, putatively childish[77] questions like "Why should people starve when there is food aplenty?" cut through the haze.

But squatting often suffers the same limitations as co-ops, CLTs, and so many other kinds of social or solidarity economy initiatives. Each might be inspiring, effective, useful, cost-efficient, and compelling, but if they are not linked to larger analyses of power they act as lifeboats for a privileged/lucky/resourceful/desperate few. Which is why it is so prescient for Lisa Bates to wonder why housing co-ops tend to be exclusively populated by old white hippies. She's right of course, and not just in Portland, because the alternative and solidarity economy has so often been unwilling to base their work in a real social confrontation with privilege, let alone historicity.

Squatting is kind of a different beast though. It tends by nature to be confrontational, sometimes in a physical sense, but more often in a dual power sense, which makes the very act evocative of a different kind of relationship with ownership and property. When I asked an old friend, Skeeter Wright, about his experience squatting, he talked about how people in the North have always moved from place to place to follow wild game, reflecting the seasons and the migrations of fish and animals. "There were annual gatherings that decided which family group would hunt or trap in what area. While there may not have been a sense of *ownership*, there was a sense of *area use*. In my case and that of my neighbors, the concept of area use was quite strong and to a degree replaced legal 'property rights.'"

77. I mean that in the best sense.

Skeeter has lived as a squatter in the Yukon for over thirty years, which sounds like he's a bushed-out survivalist or something. He's tough and resilient and competent as hell, but really he's a sweet, gentle guy who has worked for the Yukon government for a couple of decades, primarily as a land-claim negotiator. His office is in an unobtrusively bureaucratic building downtown and his house, where he has raised a family, has most of the trappings of (Northern-style) middle-class comfort. He moved up to the Yukon in the 1970s and soon noticed the large tracts of unoccupied, unused, well-treed land within an hour's walk of downtown that provided an opportunity to build a small, unobtrusive cabin. Soon he and a few neighbors had established plots on what is now known as Squatter's Row, and each understood where the others' property extended to: "My neighbours and I, all squatters, established a sense of how far each of our interests reached toward the next resident. The main issue for us was that we occupied a space that was not used by anyone else, and of little or no apparent value to anyone else. There were conflicts when someone started to build too close to one another, but a short conversation usually resolved the difficulty. We had a simple need for low-cost shelter that was matched by an availability of land and building materials (trees)."

Eventually the territorial government realized that their squatter problem wasn't going away, and drafted a policy after considerable consultation with Skeeter and the other squatters. Over time they developed a plan that was "75–80% our ideas," including granting title to reasonably sized lots incorporated into the city of White-horse as the town sprawled. That was supposed to be the end of it though: the government gave ground on existing squatters but formalized their firm opposition to any more squats and drew the line at granting the same privileges to Indigenous nations, despite their millennia of occupation.

Skeeter's experience echoes that of squatters all over the globe: people need cheap shelter and can see the necessary elements around them, so they act. But like any other kind of alternative tenure, they are often just an innovative hustle: an end-run on conventional routes to private landownership.[78] Squats, just like community land trusts or co-ops, are pretty much always inspiring and fun and laudatory, but they only change the game for the rest of us if they overtly challenge the ideological constructions of land and ownership that have made squatting so necessary in the first place: if the fruits of squatters' courage and energy are shared and extended.

It is argued, and mostly correctly, that it's only when alternative land strategies get to certain scales that larger social transformation becomes possible. And that's mostly right, but hardly assured. If we're talking about getting a few folks secure tenure and shelter from market depredations, that's great. But if we want to talk about larger forces of displacement and dispossession, then these kinds of projects are only relevant in the context of social relationships and when situated as dual power: as power against.

It's probably germane to revisit Blackstone here: "Pleased as we may be with the possession, we seem afraid to look back to the means by which it was acquired ... without examining the reason or authority upon which those laws have been built."[79] If co-ops and land trusts can easily get reduced to individualized lifeboats for a privileged few, perhaps the larger danger is that any of these potentially powerful movements fails to note that they are occupying territory that has recently been forcibly cleared of previous residents. It's with the same willful amnesia that white kids theatrically fuss about rents in Albina and settlers blithely occupy Indigenous lands. Squatting, housing co-ops and CLTs are still critically transformative tools— they still really matter to better renditions of the city—but let's

---

78. Typically, the most celebrated squats are the ones who have hung on and resisted long enough that their residents are granted legal title to their property.
79. William Blackstone, *Commentaries on the Laws of England, Book 2, The Rights of Things* (Oxford: Clarendon Press, 1766), 2.

make sure they don't contribute to the narratives of dispossession they are intended to ameliorate. Unsettling property narratives can and should be a lever to larger liberatory politics.

I'm not convinced that the actual *form* of alternative tenure matters all that much. I mean, of course it matters in the specific sense to the people directly involved (we all want our occupancy arrangements to work smoothly), but I suspect that whether initiatives adhere tightly to land trust or co-operative or other principles is sort of inconsequential. Like squatting, they are good reference points or organizational platforms, but they are not fixed categories. All kinds of plausible combinations and variations do and might exist, and places across the globe are employing portfolio approaches.

Consider, for example, the Mutual Home Ownership Society in the United Kingdom, in which a CLT owns the land and leases it to a tenant ownership cooperative. The co-op negotiates a mortgage, and after a place is built, the co-op issues renewable leases to the member-tenants fixed at 35 percent of income, which earns them equity shares in the co-op. These shares appreciate as the co-op's debt is paid down and membership shares can be resold, with capping covenants.[80] It's an elegant construction that evokes all the ways individuals and families contort their finances to help one another out, but one that socializes and institutionalizes the urge to generosity.

All kinds of other formations, possibilities, and combinations are necessary but not sufficient in and of themselves without an ethically animated political milieu. Consider that in late 2014, for example, the City of Paris announced a new plan to confront central-city residential displacement by identifying 257 addresses containing over eight thousand apartments that the city can exercise a "right of first-refusal" to buy on. This means that if any one of these buildings comes up for sale, the city has first crack at it—at market rates (determined by the city, or

80. Michael Lewis, "The Best of Three Worlds," *Canadian Centre for Community Renewal*, 2011, http://communityrenewal.ca/mhos.

by an arbitrator if the owner deems the offer unfair)—and the place can only go on the market if the city declines to purchase. The measure didn't require any new bylaws, and the city plans to use the buildings for subsidized housing, trying to protect working-class neighborhoods and existing lower-/middle-income residents. As a Parisian official put it, they are "choosing diversity and solidarity, against exclusion, social determinism and the centrifugal logic of the market."[81]

This Parisian initiative is a brave one that just might clear the way for other cities (especially global cities being preyed upon by the very rich) to address urban displacements head-on, but it is hardly the only arrow, or the only kind of arrow, in municipal quivers. Rent control, for example, alongside renters' rights provisions are both vital elements of any just housing regime, but neither by itself can do a whole lot to shift the terrain of the debate, aside from restricting rentiers' ability to run roughshod over their tenants, and thus regulating the market to a certain extent. Policy tools are only effective in the context of an aggressive, creative, and flexible push-pull strategy that simultaneously undermines profiteering from land while building attractive nonmarket alternatives that allow for security of tenure, self-management of dwelling, and socializing the value of land. Land value taxes, speculative taxes, affordable housing, community land trusts, co-ops, and squatting are very far from the full portfolio of options—lots of others exist, many more can be dreamed up—but the ground is going to shift only when the starting point is that land *has* to exist outside the predatory market.

I want this chapter to gesture toward a city of generosity. Putting ideas into action, the work of actually figuring out how to make

81. There's no question that it is a potentially expensive measure: If all the buildings in question were purchased, it is estimated that the cost to the city would be a little more than US$1 billion as part of a giant Parisian affordable housing push that's estimated to cost more than US$12 billion. See Feargus O'Sullivan, "Paris Wants to Keep Central Neighborhoods from Becoming Ghettos for the Rich," *Atlantic CityLab*, December 19, 2014.

changes on the ground, often feels grindingly slow under the weight of history. And in some ways it should: so much of our shared urban and landed history is heavy, fraught with dispossessions and shameful acts. But the heart of this chapter is exhortative. It is not enough just to note the damage done, and acknowledgments don't equal restitutions. I am convinced that materially destabilizing ownerships is the predicate to the unsettling of land, to righting past wrongs, and is the route to producing a city air that makes us free. As Ta-Nahesi Coates puts it in "The Case for Reparations": "Perhaps after a serious discussion and debate ... we may find that the country can never fully repay African Americans. But we stand to discover much about ourselves in such a discussion—and that is perhaps what scares us. The idea of reparations is frightening not simply because we might lack the ability to pay."[82] Coates says that the claim to reparations "threatens something much deeper," and this is precisely what I would hope for. Thinking through displacements has to mean calling to account dispossessions of all kinds, taking responsibility for the rationalities that have given permission to the dispersal of Albina's Black community and the clearance of Indigenous nations that predicated it. We have to stand square and face these stories in every city. But taking responsibility to rectify injustice is ultimately to all of our benefit. It is not a burden: it is a move to freedom, differently and incommensurably, from "the republic of property."[83] The tools are at hand, and the city has to be the place to start using them.

---

82. Ta-Nehisi Coates, "The Case for Reparations," *The Atlantic*, June 2014, http://www.theatlantic.com/magazine/archive/2014/06/the-case-for-reparations/361631/.

83. As per Michael Hardt and Antonio Negri, best articulated in *Commonwealth* (Cambridge, MA: Belknap Press of Harvard University Press, 2009).

THE KINDNESS OF NEIGHBORS 4

I have a lot of faith in aggressive and innovative policy. Constructions of alternative tenure remain exciting to me, and the plausibility of suppressing land speculation, and ultimately abolishing profiteering from land, strikes me as critical, even essential, to any rational future. At the same time, it seems absolutely true that no single policy thrust, even a broadly and imaginatively applied land value tax, will be transformative in and of itself. Each of these instruments has to be understood in combination with one another, as part of a larger effort to rethink property and land. And while it is right to argue for "an aggressive push-pull strategy" there is something about that phrase that rubs me the wrong way when I use it—it's too formulaic, or five-year-plan-apparatchikesque or something. It implies that liberal urban democracies just need a couple of civic tweaks here, or a new property bylaw regime there, and everything will be put right. As attractive as that sounds, and as much as I want to focus on boots-on-the-ground everyday routes to organizing and action, it is perilous to rely on policy *over* politics, because what's required is a fundamental shift in social relationships with land, not just a new ordinance here or regulation there.

The current voluminous documentation of common resource and land management opens practical room to talk, a break in the clouds of orthodox property theory. But maybe the real value of the Ostroms (among many others) aggregating, analyzing, and taxonomizing thousands upon thousands of case studies around the globe demonstrating common-pool resource users' ability to manage forests, watersheds, fisheries, and grazing lands is how the landscape begins to shift around property allocation theory: "Case studies left little doubt that, contrary to theoretical expectations, collective action on the commons *is* possible, and *not* merely a vestigial form."[1] That research gives all of us cover for experimentation, participation, or maybe better put, creative production.

The fact that all kinds of people in all kinds of scenarios all over the world have developed multiply held systems to manage complex resources should embolden us. It's not simple: research consistently demonstrates the complexity of collective responsibility, and the need for multiple, overlapping, nested sets of relationships. Any alternative property configurations need constraints on withdrawals from the common pools, and all kinds of agreements on exclusivities, transfers, benefits, and costs. By definition common property can never mean brute open access; it necessarily has to account for difference.

The complexities of common resource management are immediately evident to anyone who has ever lived in a shared house, been part of a formal or informal cooperative, or worked in a collective. Having to make decisions in the face of multiple, overlapping, and shifting usages can be irritating as hell, but that's the burden of the democratic impulse. The easiest, most efficient decision-making approach is always the most authoritarian: dictatorships, fascisms,

1. Amy Poteete, Marco Janssen, and Elinor Ostrom, *Working Together: Collective Action, the Commons, and Multiple Methods in Practice* (Princeton, NJ: Princeton University Press, 2010), 46 (emphasis in the original).

and oligarchies can be tremendously appealing in part because of the clarity of purpose and efficiency of execution they provide. The more user-control or self-management any system attempts, the more complex, sophisticated, and nested power has to become. Anyone arguing in favor of democratizing land and ownership has to be ready to argue against the ease and efficiency of private property. "Where the property-rights school focused on economic incentives for evolutionary changes in property rights and the implications for efficiency, case studies reveal natural resource management as an intensely political matter."[2]

And that's the place to land. Allocation of property is, will always be, and thankfully *has* to be "an intensely political matter." If we get stuck in arguments about efficiency or the minutiae of policy, we're not just outside the ballpark; we're playing the wrong sport.[3] We *do* have to be talking about policy—about the nuts and bolts of how specific approaches to property can and might work, but as an expression of political desire, not an obfuscation or subsumption of it. We can take heart from working examples, and we have to be able to think through tax regimes and infrastructural constructions and organizational platforms, but only if they are levers to and articulations of politicized, justificatory conversations. Any default to rationalities of efficiency is always a reduction of desire to the peripheral, just as private property's core claim is the reduction of social complexity. In reality, all land and property is always subject to multiple, overlapping, contingent, and shifting uses and claims, and governance should reflect that.

Which gets us back to the city. So much of the existing literature around common resource management[4] is focused on small, localized, and inevitably rural examples where the claims and actors of

2. Ibid., 50.
3. As per Jules Winnfield.
4. From Garrett Hardin to the Ostroms and most else between.

ownership and management are relatively transparent and often dehistoricized. In urban environments, however, the densities, the fluidities, the volumes, and the flows, especially of strangers, are presumptively too much for theories of commonality—especially common land—to handle. But I want to argue exactly the opposite.

Cities are our most viable route to an ecological future, not in spite of, but *because* they create the material conditions for incommensurability. Commonality and difference are necessarily bound up with one another, and cities both require and perform a politics of land to embody their social alterity. Or put another way, cities are necessarily always about difference, and incommensurable difference has to be the correct logic of the commons. Far too often the language of commonality gets ground down to a nub of exclusionary logic, a simplistic bordering of who is in and who is out. It is this tendency that makes it reasonable to imagine common management and ownership possible for small, bounded, and exclusive populations, but impossible beyond that. But if we can unmoor the commons from the fixed exclusivities of property, ownership, and dominatory sovereignties, beyond the impermeable us-and-them boundaries, then difference becomes the logic of commonality, not its antipode.

Among the problems of this claim though is finding conversational footholds amid the landslide of signs and signifiers that talking about commonality triggers, and the ahistoricized, apoliticized tendencies of so many of its adherants. We should absolutely embrace destabilized meanings, but that requires a patience I often don't have, especially for the crass repositioning of deeply important ideas in the service of cheaply instrumental ploys. Take "community," for example. I'm not sure there is a more frustrating word around. I can barely move three feet in this city (and I bet yours too) without running into *community* something or other: How many times have you walked past an upscale condo development with a huge sign announcing: "We're building a community"? Is there any nonprofit out there that isn't "working for the community"? Or any business that doesn't "give back to the community"? Or any project that isn't "supporting our community"? Or anyone anywhere who doesn't use the word *community* to describe their own ostensible goodness?

We've got school communities, the downtown business community, gated communities, giving back to the community, community service, communities of interest, online communities, community gardens, community foundations, community colleges, the European Economic Community: as far as I can tell, the word *community* is now deployed to reference *any* affiliation, of any size and in any configuration. It is used as a reflexive invocation of bucolic hominess, social cohesion, and local responsiveness—but really, it's an idea so plasticized, so malleable, so hollowed out that it now means virtually anything, and so of course not much at all. There are some residually warm, pastoral reverberations, but that may be worse than nothing to the cynical late capitalist ear.

Well, so what? We are all inured to marketers, the inevitability of advertising, and the speed of contemporary (social) media. We are so accustomed to the twisting of anything and everything toward capitalization that very few of us have much optimism left to invest heavily in any firmly entrenched linguistic formations because we will inevitably see it hollowed out. For most of us *community* just seems like one more idea that has been essentially abandoned to the semiotic free market. I'm not at all convinced that it is a word worth standing for particularly,[5] but at the very least "community" should be positioned as a political idea that inculcates freedom, not a cultural artifact that constricts it. The key, as Jane Jacobs once wrote, is to eschew sentimentality[6] and I'd add that it's critical to keep reiterating that any evocation of community has to be inseparable from

---

5. To steal a phrase from Wendell Berry, if not the sentiment (suffice to say).
6. Jane Jacobs, *The Death and Life of Great American Cities* (New York: Vintage, [1961] 1992), 112.

social alterity. If we abandon "community" entirely, we lose too much ground on the commons.

But commoning has to contend seriously and simultaneously with liberal renditions of both freedom and justice. Throughout her career and maybe most persuasively in her 1986 book *The Ideal of Community and the Politics of Difference*, Iris Marion Young persuasively argued against community-based politics, which she claimed are based on a negation of difference and "makes it difficult (for people) to respect those with whom they do not identify." I have long found her arguments both challenging and compelling, and very useful.

Young claimed that "community" necessarily draws exclusionary borders and eagerly polices where an "us" ends and a "them" begins. She concluded that not only is the desire for bounded, fixed communities—such as organizing the city around "urban villages"—implausible and unrealistic, but fundamentally repressive of the kinds of mobile, unoppressive freedoms the city is supposed to nurture.[7]

Young's work found confluences with feminist critiques of community for its reliance on nostalgic and distorting "big-home" visions of what a city might be. All too often simplistic evocations of community rest thoughtlessly on romantically extrapolated imaginaries of "home," but for many people, their childhood homes are nothing to be sentimentalized or emulated and in fact were often places of misogynist oppression, violence, and misery. For many people, the city is exactly the escape they dreamed of from small-minded repression and intolerance. I agree with much of this sentiment and that the attempt to reduce cities into a collection of towns is entirely wrong-headed. The correct response here, as much as I admire these critiques, is not to retreat into liberal theory and all its frameworks of tolerant spacing, disinterested distance, and individualism, but to

7. Iris Young, "The Ideal of Community and the Politics of Difference," in *The Blackwell City Reader*, ed. Gary Bridge and Sophie Watson (Malden, MA: Blackwell Publishers, 2002), 431–438.

ask where, how, and why commons theory can be deployed as a vehicle for "denying difference." In some regards Young has set up a two-dimensional rendition of community, but the point she makes is very right, and the challenge is to reconceptualize *commoning* not as small-scale, nostalgically romanticized villagey evocations of a (supposedly) longed-for past, but as a viably *urban* response to ecological and social crises that doesn't just accept alterity but is inseparable from it. That claim doesn't just gesture toward relanding; it has to act on it.

It is the complexities of subjectivities, of governances, of exclusivities, and of incommensurabilities where the commons can be both able and agile. The multiple, nested, fluidly overlapping lines of authority and uses that should be embodied in any commons stand in stark relief against the stiff, fragile simplicities of private property rights. The management, design, and maintenance of any commons has to be emergent: the simultaneously heuristic and discursive embrace of necessarily complicated/complicating and contingent sovereignties. By definition the commons has to be unsettled, and unsettling, to be worthy of its title. Claiming the commons (materially or theoretically) doesn't wipe the slate clean: the primary commitment has to be to resolving standing and landed injustices, a move upon which the integrity of any commons claim rests.

"IF A MAN WILL BEGIN WITH CERTAINTIES, HE SHALL END IN DOUBTS"[8]

I've spent a lot of intellectual and personal energy over the years working with, through, and from the ideas of social ecology and

---

8. "If a man will begin with certainties, he shall end in doubts; but if he will be content to begin with doubts he shall end in certainties." Francis Bacon, *The Advancement of Learning*, book 1, verse 8, 1605.

Murray Bookchin,[9] and I still have a lot of faith in their relevance.[10] The core of Bookchin's work revolves around the assertion that our current environmental crises have to be understood as the products of social relations: that social domination is the root cause of ecological dislocations, and that only a rigorous analysis of hierarchy (in all its forms, not purely class) and an oppositional politics can suffice. This politics is grounded by a *dialectical naturalism*, an idea he coined as a surpassing both Hegelian dialectical idealism and Marx's dialectical materialism: a dialectic that does not conclude in any finality of order, but as a continual, unending, unfolding of differentiation and

9. In many ways, social ecology really *is* Bookchin. Plenty of us have tried to expand and deepen the core insights of Bookchin's work over the years, but frankly I'm not sure how much the theoretical territory has evolved since he died in 2006. There remains significant academic and activist interest in his work, including vibrant pockets in various parts of the world—most celebratedly these days in Rojava, Kurdistan—and via the Institute for Social Ecology in Vermont (where I was part-time faculty for a decade), but the foundations remain firmly (and regrettably rather calcified) as Bookchinite. I mercifully will avoid detailing the machinations of politics and personalities that might explain some of the reasons that this remains so.

10. And I am somewhat unclear (despite considerable investment in the question) as to why his ideas have not yet gained more popular radical purchase (part of this has to be attributed to his uncompromising combativeness that alienated so many allies and foes alike). There seems to be a broad intellectual agreement that there are some critically valuable insights in his work, but not the commensurate energy to engage them seriously. David Harvey exemplifies this sentiment: "Bookchin's proposal [libertarian municipalism] is by far the most sophisticated radical proposal to deal with the creation and collective use of the commons across a variety of scales, and is well worth elaborating as part of the radical anticapitalist agenda." Harvey, *From the Right to the City to the Urban Revolution: Rebel Cities* (Brooklyn, NY; London: Verso, 2013), 85.

I find Harvey's acknowledgment gratifying, as I have put considerable time and energy into this exact project, but also seriously irritating in that Harvey then drops that thread and proceeds to spend the rest of his book asking highly germane questions without returning to the socially ecological theory that might help answer them. I'm going to let that go now, though.

subjectivities, of a social complexity that mirrors the evolution of the natural world.[11]

Bookchin named (and renamed) his political program libertarian socialism, social anarchism, social ecology, and, finally, communalism, in part due to his ongoing battles to separate his thinking from the bulk of contemporary anarchism and socialist thought, but the same essential core remained intact despite repeated rebrandings: a sophisticated post-Marxist ecological socialism. I continually find evidence of his thinking inhered in so much of my own, but what I want to focus on here is his work on the city. Bookchin sought to "redeem the city, to explore it not as a corrosive phenomenon, but as a uniquely human, ethical, and ecological community,"[12] as a socially ecological entity whose complexity and interdependencies mirrored biological mutualism.

The key here is to understand the city as a "creative breach" that allowed humans to transcend biological affinities (like kinship) in favor of social affinities: where former strangers, outsiders, others, even enemies, could set aside historic parochialisms in favor of a shared pluralistic polis necessarily built on mutualism. As an ethical project, the city is thus *the history of the city*, an incremental unfolding of itself, beyond and through the rise and fall of any one particular city.

Though Bookchin was essentially a decentralist, arguing for local self-reliance and local democratic institutions, his vision was confederalist rather than localist. He was convinced that the correct arena for political decision making is the municipality (city, town, village)

---

11. See Bookchin's *The Ecology of Freedom: The Emergence and Dissolution of Hierarchy* (Palo Alto, CA: Cheshire Books, 1982) and/or *The Philosophy of Social Ecology: Essays on Dialectical Naturalism* (Montreal: Black Rose Books, 1990) for a fuller explication.
12. Murray Bookchin, *Urbanization without Cities: The Rise and Decline of Citizenship* (Montreal: Black Rose Books, 1992), xiv.

but that those politics should be articulated via networks of town halls, citizen assemblies, and face-to-face institutions (essentially a rendition of syndicalism, but with social ecology relying on the local assembly instead of the self-managed workplace, and citizen control instead of worker control). He named this libertarian municipalism, and the critical animating element is an insistence that networked power should always flow upward instead of being filtered down.

Drawing on the rich history of confederalism from the Iroquois Confederacy (Haudenosaunee) to the Rhenish League to all kinds of contemporary affiliations, libertarian municipalism is always specifically aimed in antagonism toward the nation state, conceived as a distinctive articulation of popular participatory democratic control that can be scaled and rescaled into mutually beneficial and interdependent affiliations. "It is, above all a network of administrative councils whose members or delegates are elected from popular face-to-face democratic assemblies, in the various villages, towns and even neighbourhoods of large cities. The members of these confederal councils are strictly mandated, recallable and responsible to the assemblies that chose them for the purpose of coordinating and administering the policies formulated by the assemblies themselves."[13] Some renditions of this kind of networked, bottom-up, participatory thinking will surely be familiar to you.

Libertarian municipalism anticipated much of the contemporary participatory planning and budgeting movement; has deep connections to bioregionalism, direct and deliberative democratic movements, alternative economic theories like Parecon; and echoes/is echoed by innumerable social movements from the Landless People's Movement in South Africa, to the Rojava autonomous region, to the Zapatistas, to the recovered factories of Argentina, to Occupy, to

13. Ibid., 297.

many others working in the similar participatory traditions. The famous call from the Paris Commune for a "commune of communes" has been reframed repeatedly in calls for a co-op of coops, a collective of collectives, or Bookchin's community of communities—but the core thematic of confederated bottom-up popular democracy remains entrenched in the radical imaginary.

I'm frankly interested and sympathetic to pretty much all of these articulations and movements. I find social ecology a particularly compelling version, in part due to my weakness for the kinds of abstracted rhetorical flourishes Bookchin tended to trade in—his prose was rife with phrases like "participatory evolution" and the "social metabolism of an ecological society" that speaks to a shift from "independence/dependence to *inter*dependence"—but getting bound up in the procedural infrastructures is both entirely critical in the specific and profoundly distracting in the abstract. When we're organizing on the ground, the details of how power is distributed, exercised, and articulated are of constant interest, but when abstracted, theory often turns solipsistically indulgent and typically highly gendered.

The through line I want to pursue here is not to argue which particular rendition of collective control and management, Bookchinite or otherwise, is the most powerfully useful frame for our purposes. Essentially *every* movement toward the popular democratization of power is at the very least interesting and probably worthy of support. But I want to keep pursuing how social movements and theory can privilege land analytically and practically: to keep acknowledging how constantly stained we are by colonial residues and reflexes, and to keep asking about the ground we're standing on.

Whether it's Bookchin's focus on administrative confederalism or the Ostroms' interest in multiple overlapping governances or any other collective, participatory impulses, there is an (often subtle) implication that radical proposals for democratizing power have sufficient escape velocity to transcend colonial heritages of displacement and dispossession just by virtue of good intentions and sincerities. It is a regrettable tendency that is all too easy to default to, especially for people like me. Here in North America everything we do happens on stolen Indigenous land and in the shadow of slavery and thus we cannot just proceed as if we're all now commonly entitled to so-called common land. Claiming common participation in exercises of power will not heal all wounds.

This is where so much of the literature of participation, including participatory democracy, stalls. Decontextualizing participation from privilege leaves it hollow. We have all seen municipal land-use development "open house" consultations held on Tuesday mornings, or community meetings where only old white guys with easy English skills talk. We have all viscerally experienced the many implicit and explicit ways participation can be limited, or constrained, or manipulated, or excluded. There really has been an impressive amount of sophisticated thinking around ensuring legitimate access to meaningful participation over the past decades that ameliorates some of this, but the issues are not just structural: they are axiomatic.

I'm skeptical, for example, of participatory democratic theory when it leans too heavily on highly structured deliberative mechanisms, whether it's participatory budgeting processes that require endless cage-match meetings, or a libertarian municipalism dominated by "town hall" gatherings. It's not just the Oscar Wilde thing,[14] but because it imputes a certain set of ideas about how "proper" decisions should be made, and about what kinds of behaviors are allocated privileged access to collective decisioning. Social infrastructures organize and regulate space and relationships in very particular ways, and while I am sure that formal face-to-face group meetings will

14. "The trouble with Socialism is that it takes too many evenings" is yet another brilliant Wildeism, but there is no confirmed attribution that I can locate, which works just fine for me.

always have to be a core part of any equitable decision making, they should never be exclusively so.[15]

Participation is a useful trope and sometimes a rupture in entrenched power, but only if it too is broadly understood as fluid, shifting, and politicized: who is participating, what are people being asked to participate in, what are the limits of discussion, and under what terms and what regimes are participants allowed to act. Sherry Arnstein had this exactly right a generation ago in her seminal "Ladder of Citizen Participation"[16] that identified eight rungs of possible participation, moving up the ladder from Manipulation to Informing, through Consultation and Placation, to the top level of Citizen Control, grouped from degrees of nonparticipation to tokenism to citizen power. It remains a tremendously useful model, and one I still use all the time, but it too badly needs context.

As Majid Rahnema has said, the contemporary participatory turn has been predicated on a foreclosure of possibilities outside market development: "In its present context, participation has come to be 'disembedded' from the socio-cultural roots which had always kept it alive. To participate is thus reduced to the act of partaking in the objectives of the economy ... for the modern construct of participation, a person should be part of a predefined project, more specifically an economic project, in order to qualify as a participant."[17]

This is the connection I want to make between participation and the commons: if we are willing to challenge who, and under what conditions, people "qualify" as participants—that is, who is eligible to engage in the production of social space—and are willing to

15. Which, come to think of it, is exactly what Wilde was saying.
16. Sherry R. Arnstein, "A Ladder of Citizen Participation," *Journal of the American Planning Association* 35, no. 4 (1969): 216–224.
17. Majid Rahnema, "Participation," in *The Development Dictionary: A Guide to Knowledge as Power*, ed. Wolfgang Sachs (London: Zed Books, 1992), 120.

consider a radical plurality of participations, then we begin to fill in and substantivize the common. The city is built on and by multiple antagonisms, multiple positionalities, and multiple subjectivities that account for incommensurability. But for the city, *a city*, to emerge as an ethical endeavor, it has to suture itself to multiple, shifting, and complexly nested kinds of participations and productions, to reimagine self-determination in a way that doesn't lose heart in the messy, decenterd, unpredictability of human social life.

All too often, new renditions of governance revert to slippery technocratic languages of efficiency, smart cities, and big data that imagine residents as autonomous smartphone-wielding monads choosing from pull-down menus of policy options. I can be convinced of the productive potentialities of digitally democratic initiatives, but I remain consistently suspicious of those narratives that propose participation as increased/increasing access to consumptive political "choice." The imaginaria of participation has to bind people's commitments together, not techno-innovatively untether them, and it has to be the unfixing of private ownership that breaks the having/being dead end, and releases 'participation' from its imprisonment in property. Then rather than just "participation," we can speak confidently about the creative production of the city.

Thinking a fluidity of productions is bound to the project of imagining multiply overlapping simultaneous sovereignties. As soon as we can unmoor ourselves from fictions of maximally comprehensive authority—whether it's totalitarian, theocratic, plutocratic, or replaced by some democratic rendition—we can acknowledge the tremendous capacities of people to govern and self-govern and produce the city in endlessly reconfiguring formal and informal arrangements. I have no interest in deriding the transformative potentiality of investing town halls or citizen assemblies with real power and real authority as the basis for a grass roots democratic revival: every version of participatory democratic configuration that disperses power is valuable and worthy of investigation and trial. I am interested, however, in displacing the idea that any town hall or citizen's assembly should be sovereign.

I tend to be in favor of sloganeering like "power to the people"—it's warm and fuzzy, the impulse is pretty much always commendable, and we tend to know what it points to—but the obvious corollary is "Which people are you talking about exactly?" and "On what grounds are you suggesting which people should exercise what power?"[18] As soon as the "people" becomes an amorphous objectified thing, we get into trouble. And that's where so much of the language and scholarship around gentrification, displacement, and the city is lacking: organizing ideas around the commons runs into the immediate danger of subsuming a whole city of subjectivities under just another rendition of ahistoricized power that so easily forgets/ignores that essentially every city sits on stolen/colonized land

We cannot, for example, be talking about the transformation of Northeast Portland without mapping the contours of the city within the explicitly racist history of that state, and connecting that history to reparations. Nor can we be talking about displacement in East Vancouver without contextualizing it within a nuanced comprehension of Coast Salish Territories, or any city anywhere without acknowledging ongoing colonialisms. But recognition is far from enough: the multiple, overlapping, and fluid subjectivities in any city have to be matched by similarly imagined participation and thus by multiple, overlapping, and fluid sovereignties.

Glen Coulthard is among the most clear-headed scholars I know on this point; he notes the silence of so much scholarship and organizing when it comes to Indigenous presences: "Translated into practice, my concern is that such an oversight risks anchoring anti-gentrification

---

18. I seriously sound like a grouchy scold here. I love fist-in-the-air, chant-worthy phrasing, but you get my point: the totalizing implications of ideas like "the people" are obscuring at best, and often a lot worse.

efforts against the neoliberal city's further enclosures to a decontextualized and ahistorical notion of 'the commons' that threatens to inadvertently treat settler-colonial cities as urbs nullius: urban space void of Indigenous sovereign presence."[19]

He is being generous with his characterization of commons thinking as "inadvertently" myopic because I suspect many of our blind spots are not so easily ameliorated. The challenge Coulthard throws up here points us in a deeper, more ontologically unsettling direction than it might seem at first glance: "To avoid replicating the originary violence of colonial dispossession in anti-gentrification scholarship and activism, Indigenous sovereignty and land struggles must be situated at the fore of social justice theorizing about and organizing within the city." This admonition is critical because so many of our narratives around the commons are *necessarily* decontextualized: they require a fantasized urban blank slate to hold together theoretically. It is not just Indigenous presences that have to be faced; it is subjectivity as an ideal, not an impediment, that has to anchor any hopes for a commons.

Accounting for the theft of Indigenous land, regimes of slavery, dispossessions, and violence have to be the foundation for any reasonable conversation about property. There's just no way to think about an ethical relationship with land, allocation, and ownership otherwise. It is necessarily the correct starting point to build an intersectionally overlapping set of ideas about participation and the production of a city, not only because it is an ethical imperative, but because it opens up a whole series of new possibilities. I am convinced that taking Indigenous presences, African American reparations, and decolonizing land struggles seriously rips an unfixable tear in the fabric of the ownership model.[20] When Indigenous and

---

19. Personal communication, September 17, 2015.
20. Which I'd guess is at the heart of the furious denials, ideological contortions, hatreds, genocides, and endemic refusals by settlers to deal honestly with in-

Black presences are forced into the conversation, all the Lockean/ Euro-American legitimations for private property via appropriation and occupation are thrown into doubt, and then every other dispossession has be taken equally seriously. But not all displacements are made equal and need to be understood contingently, and in relationship to one another. Colonial dispossessions take very different forms,[21] and gentrifications take on specific characters and contours.

As soon as conversations about dispossession and land are pushed to the forefront, then we are forced to talk about *sovereignty*, which has increasingly become a matter of acute intellectual interest across a whole cross-section of philosophical and social explorations. Opening up imaginatively to different possible renditions of property and ownership necessarily has to mean throwing sovereignty, and possible alternative renditions of sovereignty, on the table too. But what does that mean, what could it mean in praxis, and how might we conceive of a "sovereignty" that informs philosophies of land far beyond simple[22] ownership?

Disputing fixed notions of sovereignty has of course been a constant scholarly and political commitment throughout human history,

digeneity and coloniality and subsequent failures treat Indigenous people as respectful and respected equals. It is not only simple contestations over land and resources that contribute; the (rightful) fear is that Indigenous claims to land cannot be incorporated into existing juridico-political structures without doing significant damage to the quasi-legal claims of colonialism.

21. See, for example, the insightful work Eve Tuck and K. Wayne Yang do in distinguishing settler colonialism from what they call *external* and *internal* forms of colonialism. Tuck and Yang take pains to clarify that their taxonomy is not "exhaustive, or even inarguable; instead, [they] wish to emphasize that (a) decolonization will take a different shape in each of these contexts—though they can overlap—and that (b) neither external nor internal colonialism adequately describe the form of colonialism which operates in the United States or other nation-states in which the colonizer comes to stay." Eve Tuck and K. Wayne Yang, "Decolonization Is Not a Metaphor," *Decolonization: Indigeneity, Education & Society* 1, no. 1 (2012): 5.

22. And fee-simple.

but the idea has been thrust into new kinds of intellectual spotlights with new kinds intensities for a generation or more now. Much of this energy has come from and through Foucault who claimed that the modern age is defined by the eclipse of traditional formations of sovereign power—the right to end life or permit it to continue—by bio-power, or the regulation, control, maintenance and subjugation of bodies via state apparatuses and administrative technique.[23]

The core rendition of sovereignty has always meant "supreme authority within a territory," but each of those three pillars has always been fluidly interpreted: "authority" has taken on countless configurations, the notion of "supreme" has never believably meant absolute or comprehensive, and what constitutes a "territory" is always contested/unstable. In the Anglospheric intellectual tradition, Hobbes's Leviathan[24] is the iconic expression of the sovereign, a claim that the people transfer absolute authority to their ruler via social contract in exchange for security and enforced order, a necessary bulwark against eruptions of the "war of all against all" that living in a "state of nature" entails. In the Hobbesian worldview, life without a sovereign is famously "solitary, poor, nasty, brutish, and short" and the surrender of (certain kinds of) liberty and authority to the sovereign is well worth the resulting peace, security, and commonweal.

Hobbes's rendition of the social contract has been central to the emergence of Westphalian logics of state sovereignty and territoriality that have held dominance ever since. Concluding a slow turn toward a formalized European system of interstate governance, the 1648 Peace of Westphalia (actually a series of treaties all signed consecutively that year) ended both the Thirty Years' War and the Eighty

23. See, for example, *The Birth of the Clinic* (New York: Vintage Books, 1994), *Discipline and Punish* (New York: Vintage Books, 1995), *The History of Sexuality*, vol. 1–3 (New York: Vintage Books, 1990), etc.
24. Originally published in 1651 as *Leviathan, or the Matter, Forme, and Power of a Commonwealth, Ecclesiasticall and Civil.*

Years' War with the Holy Roman Empire, Spain, France, the Dutch Republic, and others agreeing to back off and respect each other's territorially marked borders, including a commitment to noninterventionism and self-determination. The second key Westphalian agreement was the notion of legal equality between states, regardless of their size. Combined with the principles of territorial integrity, this logic has slowly spread to become the foundation for contemporary international orders, through twentieth-century political decolonization and the formal end of colonial rule. Any talk now of sovereignty, philosophical and/or political, is essentially inseparable from the Westphalian water we are all bathed in, but its theoretical and practical conundrums continue to attract tremendous scrutiny.

The celebrated turn in philosophical examinations of sovereignty over the past several decades runs heavily these days through Giorgio Agamben, an Italian philosopher who takes several, occasionally seemingly contradictory routes to and through sovereignty,[25] in part by disputing the clear threshold Foucault draws between traditional life/death sovereignty and newer, modernly articulated forms of power. Agamben suggests that biopolitical control has always been a primary and inseparably integrated aspect of sovereign authority, and the relationship between the two is far from clearly defined. But Agamben's main beef is with sovereignty itself.

Among the most influential pieces of his scholarship is his dragging German jurist and political theorist Carl Schmitt into mainstream philosophical and radical political conversations. Schmitt was an

25. Primarily for English readers: *The Coming Community* (Minneapolis: University of Minnesota Press, 1993), *Homo Sacer: Sovereign Power and Bare Life* (Stanford, CA: Stanford University Press, 1998), *State of Exception* (Chicago: University of Chicago Press, 2005), and Agamben, Lorenzo Chiesa, and Matteo Mandarini, *The Kingdom and the Glory: For a Theological Genealogy of Economy and Government (Homo Sacer II)* (Stanford, CA: Stanford University Press, 2011). There are many more; he is producing books at a ferocious pace.

unrepentant Nazi, lifelong (1888–1985) aggressive anti-Semite, apologist for brutality, and intellectual architect of the dictatorship who argued continually in favor of "decisive action." Schmitt claimed that sovereignty is defined by the capacity to declare a "state of emergency" or better, to decide upon a "state of exception" that frees the sovereign from the normal constrictions of law, up to and including violence. Territoriality and order are delineated by inclusion/exclusion, and the sovereign has to be able to act outside the timorous workings of bureaucrats and the law, to act against enemies (whom Schmitt referenced repeatedly) and to decide upon exceptions to the law. In his defense of the dictatorship, Schmitt claimed that any actions taken outside the explicit agreement of the majority is in fact dictatorial and exceptional, and that while supposedly repugnant to liberal political life, authoritarian rule is in fact always fundamental to sovereign governance and should be embraced.[26]

Agamben's engagement with Schmitt is typically read as picking up Walter Benjamin's unfinished dispute(s) with Schmitt.[27] While agreeing in part with this framing of "the exception," Agamben argues that in contemporary political life the exception has now become the everyday, that crises and states of emergency/exception are the normative political operating standard of sovereignty. But this constantly

---

26. It is possible to find English translations of Schmitt's primary works, the most available usually being *Political Theology: Four Chapters on the Concept of Sovereignty*, trans. George D. Schwab (Cambridge, MA: MIT Press, 1985). However, I have found it fruitful to work through secondary sources, my favorite being Chantal Mouffe, *The Challenge of Carl Schmitt* (Brooklyn, NY; London: Verso, 1999) and Ellen Kennedy, *Constitutional Failure: Carl Schmitt in Weimar* (Durham, NC: Duke University Press, 2004).

27. Walter Benjamin, "On the Concept of History," trans. Harry Zohn, in *Walter Benjamin: Selected Writings*, vol. 4 (1938–1940), ed. Howard Eiland and Michael Jennings (Cambridge, MA: Harvard University Press, 2003); and Marc de Wilde, "Meeting Opposites: The Political Theologies of Walter Benjamin and Carl Schmitt," *Philosophy and Rhetoric* 44, no. 4 (2011): 363–381.

encompassing state of exception is not a circumstantial *misuse* of state power; it is the inevitable unfolding of the logic of the state. Agamben argues that sovereignty is inherent in the state, and that because states have defined themselves as the supreme authority over a demarcated territory, they hold the power to exclude, and thus the power of totalitarianism, whether or not they chose to wield it at any particular moment. So that while nation-states have always been founded on sovereign authority, accelerating and widening state techno and bio-political capacities have necessarily accelerated and widened the statist exercise of sovereignty.

Agamben invokes *homo sacer*, a piece of law from the Roman Empire that allowed people who committed a particular category of crime to be excluded from legal protection. This person could be killed by anyone without consequence, but also could not be sacrificed to the gods, since they were no longer worthy. Thus the homo sacer resides both within and without the law, included and excluded, in a constant state of exception.[28] This is the core of state sovereignty: the ability to decide who and under what terms people deserve what status.[29] Agamben differentiates between bare life (*bios*) and the qualified or politically recognized life (*zoe*) of those who are deemed fully human. He claims that state sovereignty

28. Consider, for example, post-9/11 American logics of confinement and violence. When confronted regarding the US torture of innocent American citizens and foreign nationals, specifically the 2002 death of (the innocent) Gul Rahman, who froze to death after being soaked with cold water and chained to a wall in freezing temperatures, Dick Cheney responded: "I'm more concerned with bad guys who got out and released than I am with a few that in fact were innocent. ... I have no problem as long as we achieve our objective" (http://www.bbc.com/news/blogs-echochambers-30485999). As a side note, the commanding CIA official responsible for Rahman's death not only was not punished or sanctioned, but also received a cash bonus for his "consistently superior work" (http://www.theguardian.com/commentisfree/2014/dec/09/redactions-cia-torture-report-experts).
29. Or, as George Bush helpfully put it in 2006, "I'm the decider, and I decide what is best" (http://www.cnn.com/2006/POLITICS/04/18/rumsfeld/).

entitles itself to decide who falls into which category and what conditions must be met to qualify.

A particularly cold example of this distinction might be the ongoing police violence visited on particular populations. Take, for example, the high-profile killings of Black people in the United States at the hands of police: Michael Brown, John Crawford III, Eric Garner, Kimani Gray, Reynaldo Cuevas, Kendrec McDade, Ramarley Graham, Alonzo Ashley, Raheim Brown, Derrick Jones, Aaron Campbell, Kiwane Carrington, Victor Steen, Shem Walker, Tamir Rice, and Andy Lopez, just to name a few who have been killed within the past three years.[30] Each of these killings is notable for the patent lack of justifiable rationale for the actions of the police and a corresponding lack of prosecution of the perpetrators. I have selected a small number of incidents that unequivocally fall into this category, but there are literally scores more that I could have included in this list, as well as innumerable other police killings of Black people that are slightly less equivocal for any number of reasons. I have also not mentioned the endemic harassment, violence, and incarceration of African Americans at the hands of law-enforcement officials in all kinds of circumstances. In the context of Agamben's thinking, it is particularly poignant that the most prominent contemporary movement resisting police violence is called Black Lives Matter. The fact that this desperately needs to be asserted underlines his point rather starkly.

In Canada the close sister to these particular expressions of state violence is the ongoing lack of police and official action in the cases of hundreds of missing and murdered Indigenous women across the country. In 2014 the Royal Canadian Mounted Police (RCMP) confirmed that their records over the past thirty years indicate 1,186 cases of murdered Indigenous women and 160 who remain missing, including rates of violence three times higher and murder four times

---

30. And by the time you read this, so many more will be added to the list.

higher than that experienced by nonaboriginal women.[31] As of 2015 there have been twenty-five consecutive years of marches across the country calling for concerted action, including demands for a national inquiry into ongoing violence against Indigenous women and girls. The marches are often punctuated by recent high-profile and highly publicized cases, and yet it remains clear that native women retain some exceptional official status, at least in part outside realms of political life that matter to the state.

One of Agamben's key touchstones that he returns to repeatedly in his writing is the concentration camp, a startlingly geographical state of exception where those deemed homo sacer are denied qualified life. But it is not the camp per se that he wants us to resist; it is the capacity of states to declare states of exception, to creates camps anywhere, at any time—the back of police cruisers, Guantanamo, dark sites, borders, NSA surveillance, etc. We have to resist states of exception, but far more than that, we have to understand that because states are built on their sovereign ability to declare exceptions, we have to resist sovereignty and the state itself. His call is for a different kind of post-statist political construction—"the coming community"—that works beyond sovereignty.

But what might a post- or a nonsovereignty look like materially? It's complicated to imagine let alone sketch on the back of a napkin what defying the logic of "supreme authority" might amount to in social organization. The "commonsense" presumption that a supreme final-decider (in some form) is always required is so profoundly enmeshed in our political logics that it takes some work to think outside it. Can we unthink sovereignty? Should we want to? Are multiple renditions of sovereignty possible simultaneously?

Agamben is developing a set of political ideas that rest on communities that are not identity-based but instead rely on conditions

31. Kenneth Jackson, "1,186 Murdered and Missing Indigenous Women over Past 30 Years: RCMP," *APTN National News*, May 1, 2014.

of bare life as singularities. He speaks of a kind of becoming, a passing through current social conditions to new kinds of relationships, beyond commodity fetishisms and normative communicative expectations where "representable conditions of belonging" are impossible, thus defying states of exception. He calls for an "inessential commonality, a solidarity that in no way concerns an essence," a highly radical vision, but not a revolutionary one, as he has no interest in capturing state power or sovereignty, but instead transforming the existing world via subtle shifts.

Agamben's ideas are worthy of much more conversation,[32] but what I want to think about a little more here is his call to dismantle sovereignty. As a philosophical idea, sovereignty is problematic for sure, but in practice it is so embedded in how we think about land as territorialized authority that in the here-and-now it is very far from an ephemeral question. When we think of gentrification, displacement, and/or dispossessions, we inevitably think of power, of the act of deciding, of authority as finality.

I essentially agree with Agamben. But like many others it feels to me that he places an original-sin kind of focus on sovereignty that I am not sure is warranted, in part because it obscures or ignores so many other kinds of power relationships. As Andrew Robinson writes:

> I feel there is a fundamental problem with Agamben's work, and that of several other continental theorists, which stems from an unduly reductive, single- (or at most double-) agent account of social forces, in which sovereignty is treated as a determining instance from which the rest of modern social life

---

32. And have no fear, Agamben is of intense interest in certain circles. Should you be interested, you will be able to find exhaustive conversations from far more agile philosophical scholars than me.

follows (akin to the role of capitalism in Marxist theory, but with capitalism replaced by sovereignty). Agamben explains the current situation mainly through the unfolding of a single dynamic, that of sovereignty. This underestimates the extent to which the state's unfolding is restricted and inflected by other powerful social forces.[33]

This singularly focused insistence on negating sovereignty can also have a corrosive effect on social resistance. What are we supposed to do, how are we supposed to act, if wholesale abandonment of sovereignty and the state is the only thing capable of preventing camps? What if the collapse of the state is not imminent and yet we are called to resist?

Agamben may be correct, but he is not *exclusively* correct, most fundamentally because I resist the characterizations of sovereignty. I accept "supreme authority over a territory" as the historicized rendition and agree with the Schmittian "state of exception" as its expression, but that is far from the whole story. Sutured to my previous concern is that just as fixating on sovereignty as the singularly dominatory dynamic obscures other social forces, it lionizes its workings beyond recognition. Sovereignty is never supreme in any territory, no matter how delineated, no matter how authoritarian. In any place, in any jurisdiction, there are always multiply overlapping, battling, collaborating, relentlessly negotiating, interdependent powers, forces, and actors, far more complexly layered than simple narratives of dominance. Dominatory power constantly attempts to assert itself—to dominate—but there is always

33. Andrew Robinson, "Giorgio Agamben: Destroying Sovereignty," *Ceasefire*, January 21, 2011, https://ceasefiremagazine.co.uk/in-theory-giorgio-agamben-destroying-sovereignty/.

more and there are always resistances, flows of permanence and impermanence, permeability and impermeability. The story of state domination and sovereignty is a real story, but it is not the only story.

Consider our house here on Salsbury Drive. For the most part, our family gets to decide what happens here on a day-to-day basis: who can come in, who stays, the color of the walls, what gets planted in the garden, etc., and we have occupied this house for more than eighteen years now so we have some longer-term relationships and claims. But we do not own the house; we rent it from a landlord whom we have physically laid eyes on only twice. When something major breaks he gets it fixed or replaced. He has owned the house for decades longer than we have been here, and since it is his name on the title he has certain claims, including the right to sell it whenever he feels like it.[34]

But our landlord is not the lord of the land; he is constrained by a dizzying array of municipal permits, bylaws, and regulations about what he can and cannot do. There are any number of city departments who can assert themselves: fire, police, building inspection, water, sewage, and electric offices. Further he is boxed in by provincial and federal laws (maybe especially tax codes), and should one of those levels of government choose to expropriate the land for "public use" he would have to accede. Over and above all that, for time uncounted before colonial intrusions, this was Coast Salish Territoritories, the Musqueam (xʷməθkʷəy̓əm), Squamish (Skwxwú7mesh), Tsleil-Waututh (səlil̓wətaʔɬ), and Sto:lo (Stó:lō) nations, on whose lands Vancouver lies, and since this territory has never been ceded by law or war, and by every legal and ethical logic, it remains so.

34. Hold off a little longer, John!

Making any definitive claim of "supreme authority" on this property gets very messy very quickly, and there's more. My neighbors have some control as well. They can complain about our chickens or bees or our noise, they can enforce social pressure, they can physically intrude on our choices. Furthermore, an entangled lurking web of banks and financial institutions hold claims to the land, and perhaps more than any single entity, the market might claim sovereignty. Any claim to ownership of this little piece of land is problematic, and certainly not fixed or stable, spatially or temporally.

It is not true that all these actors are equal, in any sense, ever. Power and control are constantly being enacted on this property and varying configurations of precarity, dominance, compulsion, regulation, fear, discipline, and capriciousness are shot through the veins of all the relationships. Nor is it true that these actors reside in some kind of Rawlsian mediated bargain, but it is true that even delicate pulls on any one thread can unravel everything. If say, there was an archeological discovery of on-site Indigenous artifacts, or a new municipal rent control bylaw, or a fire, or interest-rate movement, then the whole web of interrelationships will rearrange.

All too often notions of sovereignty are constructed upon retrograde accounts of violent, individualistic, and competitive "states of nature" where sovereign authority becomes the shining beacon of calm and clarity for the huddled masses. Allowing Hobbesian evocations of "all-against-all" inform an articulation and philosophy of land takes us down a dead end alley where only states of exception await us. I want to renounce every rendition of sovereignty that impels "supreme authority" or dominance, in part because that idea is always a fiction that gives permission to all the other fever dreams of exclusive ownership.

I accept an Agambenesque apostasization of "sovereignty," with the caveat that it never really exists in the way he seems to imply. There are always innumerable layerings and complexities of authority, always resistances, overlapping governances, ambiguities, and malleabilities.

Our experiences of sovereignty and control don't always feel complex; they often feel like bluntly unambiguous instruments being brought to bear on us, but any "supreme" authority is always fronting. To use a Deleuze and Guattari metaphor, the enactment of sovereignty is always a lot more like Go than like chess.[35]

Agamben writes of a "coming community," a singular kind of radical social departure where people are made new. I might suggest that we need nothing new, that perhaps the pieces for thinking outside sovereign dominance are all around us, all the time. Perhaps we do not need a coming community, but to see always-coming communities right here, ebbing and flowing, overlapping and refusing, latent and potential, lost and remembered, inscribed in the kindnesses and antagonisms of neighbors. Perhaps we can speak of countersovereignties, or alternative sovereignties, or popular sovereignties, or alternatives to sovereignty—I'm good with all that—but we always have to be willing and able think the social without reducing it to simple narratives of dominance, of who is, or could be, or should be the supreme authority. Capitalism's fetishization of scarcity is mimicked by sovereign arguments in favor of supreme authority. Sovereignty presumes a scarcity of authority: that there

---

35. Let us take chess and Go, from the standpoint of the game pieces, the relations between the pieces and the space involved. Chess is a game of State, or of the court: the emperor of China played it. Chess pieces are coded; they have an internal nature and intrinsic properties from which their movements, situations, and confrontations derive. ... Go pieces are elements of a nonsubjectified machine assemblage with no intrinsic properties, only situational ones. Thus the relations are very different in the two cases. Within their milieu of interiority, chess pieces entertain biunivocal relations with one another, and with the adversary's pieces: their functioning is structural. On the other hand, a Go piece has only a milieu of exteriority, or extrinsic relations with nebulas or constellations as bordering, encircling, shattering. All by itself, a Go piece can destroy an entire constellation synchronically; a chess piece cannot (or can do so diachronically only).
(Gilles Deleuze and Félix Guattari, *A Thousand Plateaus: Capitalism and Schizophrenia* [Minneapolis: University of Minnesota Press, 1987], 352.)

can only ever be one operating in any place. Just as we can surpass capitalist economic fantasies of scarcity, we can think past and beyond scarcities of authority.

In their 2013 book *Dispossession: The Performative in the Political*, Athena Athanasiou and Judith Butler poke at precisely this:

> How might claims for the recognition of rights to land and resources, necessarily inscribed as they are in colonially embedded epistemologies of sovereignty, territory and property ownership simultaneously work to decolonize the apparatus of property and to unsettle the colonial conceit of proper and propertied human subjectivity? The challenge is to advance new idioms for contemporary critical agency by radically questioning the persistent racialized and sexualized onto-epistemologies of self-contained and property-owning subjectivity.[36]

The question they pose here, like all interrogations of sovereignty, can be understood as a contained intellectual exercise, but only with real effort. It would be a lot more pleasant frankly if chattering about sovereignty and propertied subjectivities were just some kind of highbrow diversionism, but living in an era of incipient ecocide with the stains of colonialism everywhere perhaps the most pressing here-and-now conundrum facing us all is how to think about land, territory, and authority. And we have to have these conversations on the fly, picking our way through wreckage while making plausibly existential decisions about carbon loads, bio-collapses, species extinctions, and decolonization.

It's often claimed—popularly and politically—that we have now entered into an anthropocenic ecological emergency where our

---

36. Athena Athanasiou and Judith Butler, *Dispossession: The Performative in the Political* (Cambridge: Polity Press, 2013), 27. *Dispossession* is written as a series of exchanges between the two authors; this quote comes from Athanasiou.

continued existence rests on getting the responses right and there is no time for idle coffee shop repartee. There is significant weight behind the claims that we are in a state of exception to end all states of exception, that what we need is planetary sovereignty and Schmittian decisive action against eco-enemies: recycling must be mandatory, emissions legislated, polluters punished, externalities aggressively internalized, carbon eliminated or at least buried, limits enforced. But even within the claims for decisive, even authoritarian action to right our ecological wrongs, question of scale and jurisdictionality remain: who decides, and how, and for whom? In a globalized landscape where we are apparently all in it together, is it possible that thinking multiple sovereignties, democratic sovereignties, alternative sovereignties is just academicized edutainment for those whose privilege will keep their head above water longer than most? Is it possible that unless somebody takes the sovereign wheel, we are all doomed?

In their 2012 essay "Climate Leviathan,"[37] Geoff Mann and Joel Wainwright consider this in some imaginative depth, and suggest a range of four possible climate change–driven political futures: Climate Leviathan, Climate Behemoth, Climate Mao, and Climate X. They build a tidy 2×2 quadrant divided (roughly speaking) by capitalist/noncapitalist and centralized/decentralized cleavages. Their Leviathan represents a liberal-democratic capitalist planetary sovereignty; Behemoth, a reactionary capitalist Tea-Partyesque mess of localized resistances to planetary climate discipline; Mao, an anticapitalist, state-centered authoritarian regime; and X, an emergent "community of the excluded" that has "defeated the emerging climate Leviathan and its compulsion for planetary sovereignty, while also transcending capitalism."[38] Their "central thesis is that

37. Joel Wainwright and Geoff Mann, "Climate Leviathan," *Antipode* 45 (2013): 1–22.
38. Ibid., 15.

the future of the world will be defined by Leviathan, Behemoth, Mao, and X, and the conflicts between them."[39]

I'm pretty moved by this essay, and where it comes up short it does so for all the right reasons. It generated a series of discussions (within radical geography discourses primarily) some of which fetishized the science or lack thereof, some of which argued for one team or the other, some of which made statist vs. nonstatist claims, some of which fixated on scale—but all were forced to consider sovereignty directly. And while I am unclear on Mann and Wainwright's drive to taxonomize and the contortions necessary to make their categorical partitioning work, theirs is the kind of experimental risk far too few academics are willing to make. They are asking us which kinds of decision-making regimes we are willing to submit to. And what if we choose *wrong*, or even just badly? As they write: "The problems posed at present are not new, despite their novel appearance via atmospheric chemistry and glacial melt-rates. The basic questions which have tormented the left for centuries—the relations between sovereignty, democracy, and liberty; the political possibilities of a mode of human life that produces not value, but wealth are still the ones that matter. The defining characteristic of their present intensity is that they have an ecological deadline."[40]

Winding through the essay, as much as in any radical speculative endeavor, is the return through Hobbes, Hegel, Marx, Schmitt, and carbon to questions of democracy. Mann and Wainwright ask whether democracy and sovereignty are contradictory, possibly antimonies: can there be such a thing as "popular sovereignty" or is that just gibberish? They conclude, more or less, that democracy is the negation of sovereignty, that in its making it refuses to be ruled. They toy around with the Marxist possibility of "non-state sovereignties"

39. Ibid., 5.
40. Ibid., 17.

and conclude that "if the coming climate transition is to be just there can be nothing left of sovereignty in the Hegelian-Schmittian sense."[41]

But is that enough of a starting point to work from? Can we simply say that democracy is the antagonist of sovereignty? Is it enough to say if we can imagine a radically democratic future then that will be enough to suck us out of the quagmires of "supreme authority"? Perhaps that's gesturing in the right direction, but I cannot imagine it is adequate. Amid the ongoing dissolutions of Westphalian certainties and colonialisms, it is hard to deny the grinding suspicion that our increasingly thin renditions of democracy—or even actively robust versions—are ill-equipped to answer ecological complexities.

"Democracy" (especially in its more radical articulations) is certainly a necessary component, but not sufficient for our purposes here, in part because it's useful to remain consistently suspicious of the ritualistic claims for deliberative democratic regimes or something along the lines of Laclau and Mouffe's agonistic narratives.[42] I remain highly

---

41. Ibid., 18.

42. I admire much of Chantal Mouffe's and Ernesto Laclau's work. I believe their insistence on agonistic politics, on there always being countless pluralities that are constantly jockeying without any possibility of a rational final resolution, is excellent. But I part with them fairly cleanly (as you can guess!) when they argue for a new hegemon, some global progressive convergence of leftist forces: "A front of all the progressive forces needs to be established. It is necessary for all the movements of civil society, organized for instance around Attac or the World Social Forum, to work together with the progressive political parties and with the trade unions. A vast chain of equivalences is needed in order to establish the institutional mediations necessary to challenge the hegemonic order." Chantal Mouffe, "An Interview with Chantal Mouffe," in *Agonistics: Thinking the World Politically*, by Chantal Mouffe (Brooklyn, NY; London: Verso, 2013), 135. Honestly, I have no fucking idea what she is talking about here. I suppose in Wainwright/Mannian terms, she is aiming somewhere between Climate Leviathan and Mao, or something, but consider the prospects of a coalition in any one

unconvinced that mass-scale putatively democratic planetary action is an adequate theoretical frame, let alone a faintly plausible political goal. That said, even the best visions for "molecular," decentralized, autonomous, and rhizomatically dense affiliations of networks as per Deleuze and Guattari,[43] or even the Negri and Hardt variants,[44] remain highly troubled crossing size/scale/participation/configuratory terrains of decisioning. Because really, who is going to say no to the tar sands? Who sets carbon limits? Who makes the decisions? Somebody has to, don't they? Or more germane for this book, who says no to displacement? Who decides the city?

In the context of climate change, or species collapses, or racialized dispossessions, we can hardly be faulted for reveries of Schmittian decisive action, can we? Especially if we know our fates may well be sealed without it. Why not dream of a sovereignty, ideally a planetary sovereignty that can right our climate wrongs and maybe fix a few other things along the way? Just for a few years? But beyond all the Agambenesque and gut-level resistances to the sovereign "aporias that explode into open contradictions,"[45] to the states of exception where law decides where the law cannot go, the best antidote to sovereignty has to be acknowledging its inherent futility.

city that brings together all the progressive forces, all the social movements, all the progressive political parties, and all the unions under one banner. And then extrapolate that globally! I'd sooner wait for some progressive, nuclear-fueled superhero to emerge from an underground bunker and unite us all with her unimaginably futuristic powers of reconciliation and leadership. That's going to happen way sooner.

43. See Gilles Deleuze and Félix Guattari, *Anti-Oedipus: Capitalism and Schizophrenia* (New York: Penguin Press, 2009) and *A Thousand Plateaus*.

44. See Michael Hardt and Antonio Negri, *Empire* (Cambridge, MA: Harvard University Press, 2000), *Multitude: War and Democracy in the Age of Empire* (New York: Penguin Press, 2004), and *Commonwealth* (Cambridge, MA: Belknap Press of Harvard University Press; 2009).

45. Giorgio Agamben, *State of Exception*, trans. Kevin Attell (Chicago: University of Chicago Press, 2005), 8.

Any claims of dominatory sovereignty—dictatorial, democratic, or otherwise—rest on fictions, fantasized self-contained impermeabilities of totalities. They are fictions that birth regulating narratives to concretize ever more inventive explanatory fables. The response to metastasized logics of supreme authority and states of exception cannot be to beg for a little more liberal-democratic state sympathy or to replace it with a slightly more user-friendly state apparatus. A free society has to be composed of endlessly unfolding multiplicities of coming communities, but surely there can be no such thing as pluralistic nonstate sovereignty. Sovereignty cannot abide pluralisms. But conversely, if we surrender our reveries of dominatory sovereignty and control, perhaps we can release our white-knuckled grips on ownership and property, democratic or otherwise. As Judith Butler put it (kind of perfectly) in conversation with Athanasiou: "We agree that we have to think about dispossession as one way that subjects are radically deinstituted, as a mode of subjugation that has to be opposed. At the same time, it seems that we are both wondering whether 'possession' is the name of the counter-movement."[46]

Hell, yes. That's exactly what I am wondering. And my answer seems to consistently return to *no*: possession cannot be the answer to dispossessions, and sovereignty cannot be the answer to displacement, but I'm not at all convinced that response is exactly right. In a lot of ways Butler poses precisely the correct question, one that opens itself up even as it anticipates the answer. Butler seems to be gesturing toward a polyphonic, postpossessive, postsovereignty here, an argument I am particularly amenable to when it rests on disownership: a social metabolism of interdependency that mimics the unfolding evolutionary diversity, adaptability, and creativity of the natural world. That said, there is something problematic here about my insistence on disownership. I stand by it for

46. Athanasiou and Butler, *Dispossession*, 28.

disassembling dominatory social structures, but why should that apply to people who have already been displaced and dispossessed of land, who have already been unjustly and violently "disowned"? There has to be a more nuanced, and possibly better, way to think this. That is: to think through difference and incommensurability.

Butler continues: "Surely reclaiming stolen lands is crucial for many Indigenous people's movements, and yet that is something different from defining the subject as one who possesses itself and its object world, and whose relations with others are defined by possession and its instrumentalities ... So if a certain kind of political mobilization, even one against land dispossession, is based on an idea of social interdependency, or on modes of ownership that sometimes seek recourse to sovereignty (as the political movements in Hawaii do), this suggests that land reclamations work with and against traditional notions of sovereignty."[47]

Here Butler seems to push against the exact limits of language so many of us encounter. It seems evident to me that Eurologics of sovereignty resting on "absolute control" are barren of liberatory potential, but it also appears wholly possible to resist and refuse them while supporting the justice of Indigenous and dispossessed claims to land, territory, and autonomy, and to understand them as moves to sovereignty. It should be wholly possible to push against claims of land possession, while simultaneously working with claims to reparations and the repossession of lands that were plundered. Is that not the exact space that thinking incommensurabilty opens?

This is where Indigenous movements are so exciting for so many of us, not just because the clarity of their claims are so evident and decolonizing demands so compelling, but because engaging with indigeneity opens up so much conceptual territory for the rest of us. Listening carefully to various Indigenous relationships with land can

47. Ibid., 28.

offer alternative renditions of sovereignty that may not be available
to us otherwise. So many Indigenous people that I have worked and
spoken with can see it clearly, and often struggle to articulate it in
ways that can be translated easily within settler-rationalities and
languages.[48] Taiaiake Alfred helps significantly:

> "Sovereignty" is inappropriate as a political objective for indig-
> enous peoples ... One of the main obstacles to achieving peace-
> ful co-existence is, of course, the uncritical acceptance of the
> classical notion of "sovereignty" as the framework for discus-
> sions of political relations between peoples. The discourse of
> sovereignty has effectively stilled any potential resolution of
> the issue that respects indigenous values and perspectives.
> Even "traditional" indigenous nationhood is commonly defined
> relationally, in contrast to the dominant formulation of the
> state: there is no absolute authority, no coercive enforcement
> of decisions, no hierarchy, and no separate ruling entity.[49]

It seems unequivocal that Indigenous people must regain control
over lands stolen from them, just as Black people should be compen-
sated for historical injustice, and that colonized people everywhere

---

48. Dylan Miner phrases this nicely: "The opacity of Indigenous sovereignty is
part of what makes it, as a concept, so powerful. Just as Idle No More was
not entirely fixed, so too is Indigenous sovereignty somewhat indeterminate.
It must be noted that sovereignty, in this context, is shorthand for self-determination or self-governance or autonomy and should not be understood in its
purely Westphalian interpretation. Indigenous sovereignties existed long before—and will long after—the nation-state became the dominant global polity." Dylan Miner, "Gaagegoo Dabakaanan miiniwaa Debenjigejig (No Borders,
Indigenous Sovereignty)," *Decolonization: Indigeneity, Education & Society*, October 1, 2015, https://decolonization.wordpress.com/2015/10/01/gaagegoo
-dabakaanan-miiniwaa-debenjigejig-no-borders-indigenous-sovereignty/.
49. Taiaiake Alfred, "Sovereignty," in *A Companion to American Indian History*,
ed. Philip Deloria and Neal Salisbury (Malden, MA: Blackwell, 2002), 464, 467.

are entitled to their sovereign territory. Just as I cannot believe that possession is the answer to dispossession or that ownership is the proper(tied) answer to displaced precarity, I cannot believe that univocal sovereignty is all there is. Other renditions are available, and they speak to an honest accounting of all our difference and all our shared histories. As Coates puts it: "Reparations—by which I mean the full acceptance of our collective biography and its consequences—is the price we must pay to see ourselves squarely. The recovering alcoholic may well have to live with his illness for the rest of his life. But at least he is not living a drunken lie. Reparations beckons us to reject the intoxication of hubris."[50]

It is the insistence on incommensurability, and a thoroughgoing critique of scarcity, that gets me over the hump here. Colonial rationalities insist on erasing and/or assimilating difference into singular narratives of sovereignty. If the right response to monovocality is joyful polyphony, why should repossessive reparations or an Indigenous sovereignty be necessarily incompatible with simultaneous postsovereign settler space? Surely that's not beyond imagining? Eve Tuck and Ruben Gaztambide describe an Indigenous futurity that thinks beyond erasures:

> Anything that seeks to recuperate and not interrupt settler colonialism, to reform the settlement and incorporate Indigenous peoples into the multicultural settler colonial nation state is fettered to settler futurity. To be clear, our commitments are to what might be called an Indigenous futurity, which does not foreclose the inhabitation of Indigenous land by non-Indigenous peoples, but does foreclose settler colonialism and settler epistemologies. That is to say that Indigenous futurity does not

50. Ta-Nehisi Coates, "The Case for Reparations," *The Atlantic*, June 2014, http://www.theatlantic.com/magazine/archive/2014/06/the-case-for-reparations/361631/.

require the erasure of now-settlers in the ways that settler futurity requires of Indigenous peoples.[51]

That's a futurity that does not erase difference, and still, despite everything, is open to a peaceful coexistence, to an alternative, or an alternative-to sovereignty. Each move strengthens the other; each supports complementary logics. In *Red Skin, White Masks*, Glen Coulthard cites Phillip Blake, a Dene from Fort Simpson:

> I strongly believe we have something to offer your nation, however, something other than our minerals. I believe it is in the self-interest of your own nation to allow the Indian nation to survive and develop in our own way, on our own land. For thousands of years we have lived with the land, we have taken care of the land, and the land has taken care of us. We do not believe that our society has to grow and expand and conquer new areas in order to fulfill our destiny as Indian people. ...
>
> We have been satisfied to see our wealth as ourselves and the land we live with. It is our greatest wish to be able to pass on this land to succeeding generations in the same condition that our fathers have given it to us. We did not try to improve the land and we did not try to destroy it.
>
> That is not our way.
>
> I believe your nation might wish to see us, not as a relic from the past, but as a way of life, a system of values by which you may survive in the future. This we are willing to share.[52]

51. Eve Tuck and Ruben Gaztambide, "Curriculum, Replacement, and Settler Futurity," *Journal of Curriculum Theorizing* 29, no. 1 (2013): 80.
52. Glen Coulthard, *Red Skin, White Masks* (Minneapolis: University of Minnesota Press; 2014), 62–63 (emphasis in the original).

Blake is echoing similar sentiments that all kinds of Indigenous people across the globe have been repeating, over and over, in all kinds
of ways, in the face of colonial incursions: dismay and abhorrence at
settler treatment of the land and its inhabitants, reiteration of Indigenous interdependency with the natural world, and generosity,
despite everything, in a willingness to share territory. Blake's articulate clarity is penetrating, but he struggles to explain, to verbalize to
colonizers what is so self-evident to his eyes. I read the same struggle
in Dwamish Chief Sealth's (Seattle's) famous reply in 1854 to Presi-
dent Franklin Pierce's offer to purchase two million acres of Indigenous land:

> How can you buy or sell the sky, the warmth of the land? The
> idea is strange to us.
> If we do not own the freshness of the air and the sparkle of
> the water, how can you buy them from us?
> We will decide in our time.[53]

This is a declaration of total clarity and baffled uncertainty. The
words are comprehensible to me and the sentiment powerful, but
how can a thoroughly settled mind like mine translate Sealth and
Blake's ideas? How can a rigorous ethos of sharing be transposed to
a contemporary politics, to my neighborhood, to Albina, to the city?

Despite near-impossible conditions and confounding communicative gaps, Indigenous people across the globe have adopted all kinds of
sovereignty-based arguments and strategies to assert themselves,
often through the courts and often employing rights-based approaches.
And frequently, certainly here in Canada, real successes occur where

---

53. Rudolf Kaiser, "Chief Seattle's Speech(es): American Origins and European
Reception," in *Recovering the Word: Essays on Native American Literature*, ed. Bri-
an Swann and Arnold Krupat (Berkeley: University of California Press, 1987),
525–530.

legal tactics and assemblages have been acknowledged, and have carved out room for reclamation of lands and territory under certain conditions. But those approaches are necessarily limited by the requisite totalizing colonial languages, colonial political apparatuses, and colonial imperatives, and they ultimately can never truly speak to difference or freedom, because they rest on renditions of sovereignty that are explicitly inadaptable.

The translation to urban displacement struggles is clear. Walking through Albina, John Washington pointed out lot after lot to me where a Black-owned business had been torn down and some giant white-owned monstrosity was being erected in its place: "Look, displacement is just another word for being broke, and we have to stop being broke." He is obviously right: Black people are being pushed out of Northeast Portland in a losing battle on a grossly unfair playing field. So John wants to build the tools so African Americans can get in the competition and win on their own ground. But the field on which he wants to battle is never level or stable, the capitalist market requires displacement in its very construction, and while that fight is the good fight, I'm not at all convinced it's the right fight. But it's still worth fighting.

And I remain convinced that cities are the places to fight. Moving through the city, we are all used to running into overlapping sovereignties, to walking among so many contested, confusing, and unfixed multiplicities. Cities know how to account for difference; they are built by incommensurabilities. We know how to move though shared, shifting, and alternative sovereignties, and we know what restitution should look like.

Planetary-scale empiric capitalism has sanctified the idea of territorial ownership so thoroughly and demanded social discourses that are so saturated with sacramental notions of property that any movements that release us, even fragilely, even temporarily, from the grip of ownership logics are worthy of our time and attention, but only if we understand them as gestures toward a dismantling of colonial sovereign rationalities. I'm in support of counter- or alter-sovereignties, but only if they are ultimately movements toward alternatives-to sovereignty and toward restitution.

 If you tilt your head just right and squint into the horizon, it's possible to see a time where the fictions of "supreme authority" give way to densely fluid webs of authority, mutualism, and interdependence. If the fantasias of sovereignty are predicated on Hobbesian states-of-nature constructions, then perhaps the kindness of neighbors is the right place to begin to reimagine what a city could be for. The generosity and hospitality that so many Indigenous people offered to new arrivals in their territory suggests to me that alternatives to sovereign ownership can be found in relational politics, in the practice of overlapping, multiple, shared uses of territory.

THIS LAND IS OUR LAND, OR, THE PHILOSOPHICAL PROBLEM OF PLACE[54]

This is in part why I am so interested in the Tsilhqot'in (often Anglicized to Chilcotin) decision (also called the William decision) of 2014, a unanimous Canadian Supreme Court judgment granting the Tsilhqot'in Nation title to 1,900 square kilometers of land in central British Columbia. Significant divisions and differences of opinion exist within Indigenous and legal communities as to the ultimate

---

54. "American Indians hold their lands—places—as having the highest possible meaning, and all their statements are made with this reference point in mind. Immigrants review the movement of their ancestors across the continent as a steady progression of basically good events and experiences, thereby placing history—time—in the best possible light. When one group is concerned with the philosophical problem of space, and the other with the philosophical problem of time, then the statements of either group do not make much sense when transferred from one context to the other without the proper consideration of what is taking place." Vine DeLoria, *God Is Red: A Native View of Religion* (Golden, CO: North American Press, 1994), 61–62.

impact and import of the decision, but there is little doubt that something is going on, something worthy of attention happening here. The decision might be a watershed moment in Canadian-Indigenous relationships and a critical moment for settler reconciliation and reparations; it might be one more legality that the Canadian government ignores, perverts, or manipulates; it might be ultimately toothless or a blind alley; or it might instigate another round of revanchist Canadian suppression and disciplining of Indigenous people. The likelihood is that the decision will be all of that, but despite my own profound lack of faith in the courts and laws, I want to pay some real attention.[55]

The Supreme Court ruling confirmed that aboriginal title claims can include a much broader definition of "occupation" than previously acknowledged; instead of the Canadian government's "dots-on-a-map" stance that limited Indigenous settlements to highly prescribed Lockean limits, Indigenous nations are now entitled to huge swaths of land where they have engaged in traditional hunting, fishing, trapping, camping, and gathering practices. Among the critical phrases in the ruling remains the "duty-to-consult," which might be interpreted generously, or not, by future courts, but it appears that from this point on, all levels of government and industry will be exposed to claims for damages and reparations should their activities on Indigenous-titled land not meet the putatively strengthened requirements for consultation. Exactly how this will change, or not, the settler-state's approaches is unclear, but many view this decision as an unequivocal victory for Indigenous autonomy: "As the Court

55. Arthur Manuel, "The Tsilhqot'in Decision and the Indigenous Self-Determination," New Socialist, January 25, 2015, http://www.newsocialist.org/785-the-tsilhqot-in-decision-and-indigenous-self-determination;Martin Lukacs, "The Indigenous Land Rights Ruling That Could Transform Canada," The Guardian, October 21, 2014, http://www.theguardian.com/environment/true-north/2014/oct/21/the-indigenous-land-rights-ruling-that-could-transform-canada.

specifically stated, there is a simple and effective way for government and industry to avoid the uncertainty and risk they now clearly face—obtain the consent of Indigenous people before you mess with their lands and resources."[56]

But it would be unnecessarily naive to think of the Tsilhqot'in (or similar, possibly-promising Canadian court decisions like the *Keewatin* or *Delgamuukw*) as uncomplicated "victories." For its entire existence, Canada has consistently shown a total willingness to violate every one of its own "rules" and fracture "trust" with Indigenous peoples whenever convenient. The history of Canada is littered with precedents: decisions, treaties, proclamations, agreements, and promises that have been violated extravagantly and unapologetically, and Canada's national economy is predicated so heavily on the industrial extraction of oil, gas, and minerals that this duty-to-consult will be challenged and undermined by the state from every possible angle. And if the state cannot find ways around, through, between, or over these court decisions, experience demonstrates it will just plain ignore them.

Even a cursory examination of the Tsilhqot'in decision reveals that the Canadian government will not have to work all that hard to slide out from under the suggested burden of having to deal with Indigenous nations fairly. The ruling allows the state (primarily in this case provincial governments) to infringe on aboriginal title rights if their needs are "substantial, compelling and in the public interest" and meet a series of fairly ephemerally defined conditions. The ruling clearly falls far short of the norms of international law as detailed in the UN Declaration of the Rights of Indigenous Peoples (to which Canada is a signatory) and confirms that "as long as courts privilege the rights of the many at the expense of the few and as long as Indigenous legal orders are conditional on the convenience of Canadians,

---

56. Bruce McIvor, "The Age of Recognition: The Significance of the Tsilhqot'in Decision; Case Comment on Tsilhqot'in Nation v. British Columbia, 2014 SCC 44," *First Peoples Law*, http://www.firstpeopleslaw.com/index/articles/158.php.

the stubborn refusal to take Indigenous jurisdictional claims seriously will persist."[57] The decision highlights how settler states exclusively set the conditions under which their own rule might be challenged, thereby reinforcing and strengthening their own dominance. As Rob Nichols discusses, the process attempts to capture and domesticate resistance, because when justice means closing racialized gaps in access to state-provided benefits, every act of closing that gap reiterates the universality and ubiquity of state power: the prescription is a stronger dose of the same medicine.[58]

Despite all the reasons for cynicism and disbelief that the Canadian court system can ever be commandeered as a vehicle toward freedom (and I am as cynical as any), I remain convinced that the ruling is a significant moment nonetheless. It is one more testament to the resilience and courage of Indigenous nations, and particularly in this case to the Tsilhqot'in people's insistence on anticolonial rationalities and their abilities to continually find new voices to express their claims. The decision is one more sliver of light in redefining how we think of land, ownership, and sovereignty, one more crack in the Lockean logics that have such a stranglehold on our imaginations. And as Thomas King puts it, the question always has to return to land:

What do Whites want?
The answer is quite simple, and it's been in plain sight all along.
Land.
Whites want land.

---

57. Hayden King and Shiri Pasternak, "Don't Call it A Comeback," *Literary Review of Canada*, January–February 2015, http://www.shiripasternak.com/dont-call-it-a-comeback/.

58. Robert Nichols, "Contract and Usurpation: Enfranchisement and Racial Governance in Settler-Colonial Contexts," in *Theorizing Native Studies*, ed. Andrea Smith and Audra Simpson (Durham, NC: Duke University Press, 2014), 99.

Sure, Whites want Indians to disappear, and they want Indians to assimilate, and they want Indians to understand that everything that Whites have done was for their own good because Native people, left to their own devices, couldn't make good decisions for themselves.

All that's true. From a White point of view at least. But it's a lower order of true. ...

The issue has always been land. It will always be land, until there isn't a square foot of land left in North America that is controlled by Native people. ...

Land. If you understand nothing else about the history of Indians in North America, you need to understand that the question that really matters is the question of land.[59]

The most intriguing aspect of the Tsilhqot'in decision—and perhaps the most germane here—is the definitional expansion of "occupation" that is invoked and recognized. The heart of the decision is the court's willingness to employ languages that work beyond the Lockean rationality: "Whatsoever then he removes out of the State that Nature hath provided, and left it in, he hath mixed his Labour with, and joyned to it something that is his own, and thereby makes it his Property."[60] In asserting the title of the Tsilhqot'in to land they do not inhabit consistently, to their authority over territory that they move though fluidly and may not ever stop in for any length of time, almost every component of Locke's famous claim is thrown open. What if title to land does not require

59. Thomas King, *The Inconvenient Indian* (Toronto: Anchor Canada, 2012), 216–218.
60. John Locke, *Two Treatises of Government*, ed. Peter Laslett (London, 1689; Cambridge: Cambridge University Press, 1988), II, paragraph 27.

"*removing* it"? What if "joyning" it to labor does not make it exclusively your own? What if working on land does not make it property? All of these questions relate foundationally to landed questions of who can stay, who decides, and what kinds of activity are permitted, and, thus of course, to sovereignty.

Continual occupation, labor, and ownership are not sufficient frames for permitting the enclosure of land as private property. "Use" is a more appropriate rationality for land allocation: even though the Tsilhqot'in may only pass through selected pieces of the territory at any given time, that use is intrinsic to their self-determination. This broader frame of reference for the concepts of occupation and use is similar to that heard in the Albina Trader Joe's debates, in which current residents claim that displaced African Americans "don't even live here anymore, so why do they get a say in what happens?" The problem is the same in my own neighborhood—and surely in yours—where layers upon layers of displacement are suffused in the soil.

Once use is considered to be a more appropriate relationship to land than ownership, sovereignty as we know it starts to collapse in on itself. Sovereignty insists on the exclusivities and accumulation of private property via an ever-expanding constellation of enforcement and policing, and on the right to declare the exception as a bulwark against threats to those exclusivities. Invoking "use" necessarily means talking about multiple, overlapping, historicized, and contingent claims, about an entangled articulation of relational sharing that takes place on multiple levels simultaneously, about the *right not to be excluded*, about a challenge to the certainties of scarcity.

This is always how all territory is inhabited by human and other-than-humans alike. Frantically attempting to enforce monovocalized sovereignty runs in the face of how any piece of land lives. Supreme authority can never persist because it is always an imaginative fiction. All land is *always* subject to multiplicities of uses. So rather than fantasizing about the imposition of colonial sovereign rationalities, I suggest the languages of difference, multiplicity, and shared, relational use, whether it is Tsilhqot'in, East Vancouver, Coast Salish Territories, Albina, New Orleans, or anywhere. But that "sharing" necessarily has to be generously complex and complexly generous, and speak to land justice. It cannot default to ahistoricity and has to extrovertedly restitute the displacements and thefts on which those places rest. The demands of *shared use*, taken seriously, can and should defy domination and hierarchy, can and should ask after justice, can and should resist claims to scarcity.

DISOWNING DEVELOPMENT

5

I return to Albina once again with a head full of sovereignty. I walk up and down Mississippi and North Williams repeatedly. I see street signs letting me know I've entered a "historic" district.[1] I see artisanal boutiques, Eco-Lofts, Handcrafted Living, Be Nourished, organic pet stores, many blond kids, and local galleries. I see white sorority types in a new Kia convertible blasting Lil Wayne, the deep bass thump ricocheting off buildings for blocks left and right. I see Louisiana-themed condo/loft options: Bayou, Tupelo Alley, the Delta. I see something called Vintage Real Estate. I stop and browse a *Portlandia* book and think about whiteness. I wander up Alberta Street and see a (very attractive) mural telling me "You Are Confined Only by the Walls You Build Yourself." I think: fuck you. I encourage myself to resist too much hostile cynicism; they're probably nice people, and they probably mean well, they just didn't think that one out. There is a Mardi Gras parade on Fat Tuesday, heavily advertised in a

1. These are a recent addition. They seem like an unnecessary bit of triumphalist taunting.

craft store called Gumbo.[2] Looking for some other kinds of insight, I get an Airbnb for a night right in the heart of the neighborhood. The hippie who owns the house mentions in the morning that she has a lot of gardening to do including lifting some heavy rocks and stuff. She looks at me hopefully, waits an extra beat or two, sort of snuffles then says, "Well, I'm going to go get a Mexican for the day." I remind myself again about the hostile cynicism thing and find the affirmation difficult.

The neighborhood is not awful, really not even close. It's actually just beautiful, at least in its built form. The scale is admirable; there is a pleasing diversity of building typologies and ages; there's thoughtful transit, bike and pedestrian-oriented developments, walkably spaced mini-neighborhood centers; the housing stock is attractive and well-maintained; the food trucks pop up serendipitously; and a number of solid community social institutions remain, including the spectacular ReBuilding Centre right in the middle of the Mississippi business strip. There's really plenty to admire here, but why are these kinds of design success stories seemingly inevitably on ethnically cleansed ground?

Tired of gritting my teeth, I wander over to NNEBA world headquarters in an old church just off Fremont to spend another afternoon with John Washington, Joice Taylor, and Fawn Aberson. I ask them about the heavily touted city plan for affordable housing construction and homeownership supports[3] in Albina that the PDC

2. The Disneyfication of Albina is pretty enveloping. The "This Way to Historic Mississippi" signs with big, pointy arrows, combined with the burgeoning numbers of businesses, events, and signifiers playing off the name of the street, lends itself to a well-articulated, theme park vibe. The streets immediately parallel to that one include Montana, Michigan, Missouri, and Massachusetts, but none of these have been subjected to similar indignities.
3. The city claims this will eventually amount to $20 million in new money. That figure, including the sources, routes, and landing spots of that investment, is heavily disputed.

FIGURE 5.1
The author in front of the mural. (Photo by Am Johal)

(Portland Development Commission) really hopes will tone down
some of the rhetoric and activism that has accompanied the Trader
Joe's/Natural Grocers fiasco. John erupts with a stream of startlingly
articulate profanity and describes gentrification as a "three-headed
lion with a long tail": as soon as you cut off one of those heads
another grows, while the tail whips around on you. He says that even
if the city has some kind of success building affordable housing, even
if that lot a few blocks away on MLK gets built up as promised, and
even if they make those units available to low-income Black residents, "What kind of community would these people be getting now
if they stay? Living in a place they can't afford and don't feel comfortable in?"

Paul Knauls is there too, so I ask him what he thinks of all this. Paul is the long-standing, acclaimed "Mayor of the North and Northeast" and a remarkable guy. He moved to Albina in 1963 and has lived in the neighborhood ever since. Eighty-four years old, dressed on point and whip-smart, he describes to me the fifty-plus years of change he has seen in the neighborhood, including his career owning night-clubs: the famous Cotton Club,[4] Paul's, and Geneva's Restaurant and Lounge. Now, and since 1991, he and his wife (who had recently passed away when we were talking) have run Geneva's Shear Perfec-tion and Beauty Parlor, still a center for Black community life in Albina, still a drop-in spot for regulars and celebrities alike.[5]

He told me how the highway construction in the 1950s forced residents and businesses further north and east, then about the sta-dium and hospital constructions that pushed more people out, and then about the real Black exodus beginning in the 1990s when urban renewal destroyed people's homes and all the Section 8 affordable housing they were shuffled to was elsewhere, out in suburban exclaves. I asked him if he thought there was any hope for the neigh-borhood reviving itself as a Black community, and he smiled gently at me. "No. It's not coming back. So what if they build 1,000 new affordable homes here for Black people? There are already more than 10,000 who have left." Paul has documented the ninety-five Black-owned businesses that have failed or abandoned Albina—now only five that remain—and he can remember almost every address, every proprietor, and the circumstances of each enterprise's demise: "We had everything we needed here: TV repair, dry cleaners, clubs, res-taurants, grocery stores, hardware, it was all here." But the sad fact, he says, is that white people just won't support Black businesses.

---

4. Its slogan: "The only nightclub on the West Coast with wall-to-wall soul." As Knauls always puts it, "it was the place to see and be seen."
5. See http://www.genevas.net/sample-page/.

Really, I say, really? Is that *really* true? He holds my gaze for an extra beat and says, "Yeah, it's just true."[6]

After Paul leaves, John, Joice, and I go back to talking about how housing action just isn't enough, how it has to go hand in hand with economic stability. If there aren't enough Black people living in Albina, then Black community institutions and businesses can't make a go of it. But the opposite is true too: if there is not a critical mass of identifiably Black-owned and Black-run cultural and social institutions in the neighborhood, including business enterprises, then African American people don't have much reason to live here. Turning this neighborhood's sharp decline around is going to require so many concerted, articulate, effective responses on so many fronts simultaneously that it's hard to imagine a happy end to this story. But NNEBA is on it, working so hard to figure out adequate responses, and it is hardly alone.

Over and over again on my visits to Portland, I hear people from within and outside Albina talk about the neighborhood in the past tense, celebrating and eulogizing and regretting its history. All the historic markers echo this refrain: come look at what once was. I keep asking and people keep shaking their heads—naw, this place is gone and done. I understand what they are saying for sure, and I've said and thought it myself about gentrified neighborhoods in all kinds of cities, and while there's truth there, I don't think it's quite right. The sentiment is too all-or-nothing, too essentialist, and it doesn't capture the complexity of places fairly. It's tempting to just write off a place, especially one like Albina that is so starkly defined by displacement. But that doesn't do justice to all the good people in every threatened neighborhood who are grinding away, hustling and

6. Look, I know I'm maybe a little naïve and maybe a little doe-eyed, but his comment depresses the hell out of me. Obviously, I know he's right, and obviously I don't believe that we live in a postracial era or anything like it, but that cold reality is just cold.

cornering, trying everything they can think of to stem the tide, to fight the good fight, to save their and their neighbor's homes, to maintain some kind of affordable conviviality for everyday people. The fights may well be ultimately futile, and of course change happens everywhere—nothing stays the same forever—but despite their shock and dismay and pain so many people decide to try and stay and battle. Walidah said the same thing to me the other day, but sharpened it more articulately:

> I think it's important to highlight the pushback, or as Dr. Karen Gibson talks about, the continuous thread of resistance. Black people specifically and communities of color in general have never been just passive victims. The fact that Black communities exist at all here in Oregon is amazing because they were never meant to be here. It's due to constant community building, organizing, and sheer stubbornness that Black communities have created such a vibrant community under such brutal conditions. Black communities specifically in Portland have been displaced again and again historically, and each time they have been displaced, they have been rebuilt.[7]

Many, maybe even most, narratives of displacement tend to cast residents as victims, as swept away by tides bigger than them, relegating people to historical objects and derogating their subjectivities. But that kind of argument defaults to sovereign rationalities, as if decisions made from on high are the only decisions, the only power in operation. But we know that's never the case; formal and informal title cannot simply be extinguished in practice. As Walidah says: "Even if no Black people were to live in Albina (and there are still many, many there), it is *still* the heart of the Black community.

---

7. Personal interview with Walidah Imarisha, March 19, 2015.

FIGURE 5.2
Walidah Imarisha in front of the North Portland Library branch. (Photo by
Am Johal)

Portland will always have a responsibility to the Black community in
North Portland, and even displacing all Black folks won't eradicate
that responsibility. This is the location of the community institutions created to serve the needs of the Black community the larger
society refused to. People come in via transit for more than an hour
to go to Jefferson High School, or to look for jobs at the Urban
League of Portland."[8]

8. Walidah highlighted a really pernicious incongruity here: "The city keeps
playing the numbers game. Portland blatantly and brutally kept the Black
community small—they would have preferred it not existent—and now turns
around and uses the size of the population to justify a lack of attention."

These questions—where to fight, who has voice, for and on what land, what's worth clinging to, when it's time to let it go, what makes a place worth scrapping for—are equally true anywhere that is precarious. This is part of why so many Indigenous land struggles are so compelling for so many: a commitment that is strong enough, through centuries of assault and dispossession, to keep insisting on the land. There is a question here of *place* in an age of fluidity that gestures toward the central question of the book: *What is a city for?* In some ways I am specifically responding to Lewis Mumford's famous 1937 essay, "What Is a City?"

Mumford called the city a lot of things, including "a related collection of primary groups and purposeful associations ... a geographic plexus, an economic organization, an institutional process, a theatre of social action, and aesthetic symbol of collective unity" but at the heart of his vision was the idea of the city as a social staging ground, a performative arena, a dramatic platform: "The city fosters art and is art; the city creates the theatre and is theatre."[9] There is a lot to like about that urban story—a story of diversity, of vibrancy, the ballet of the sidewalk, an overflowing energy. Despite their long-held personal antagonisms[10] Jane Jacobs tended to echo Mumford with lyrical evocations of cities suffused with "everyday diversity of uses and users in its everyday streets" of an urban public dance: "Although it is life, not art, we may fancifully call it the art form of the city and liken it to the dance — not to a simple-minded precision dance ... but to an intricate ballet in which the individual dancers and ensembles all have distinctive parts which miraculously reinforce each other and compose an orderly whole."[11]

9. Lewis Mumford, "What Is a City?," *Architectural Record* 82 (November 1937): 58–62.
10. Mostly fueled by Mumford's highly regrettable sexist condescension.
11. Jane Jacobs, *The Death and Life of Great American Cities* (New York: Vintage, [1961] 1992), 50.

For generations now this vision has acted as the normative progressive narrative that designers and urbanists have consistently reverted to: the city as stage. They have followed (or hoped to follow, or pretended to follow) Jacobs's prescriptions for "exuberant diversity": multiuse districts and multiple-function streets; short blocks; fine-grained typologies of building ages, sizes, and conditions; dense concentrations of people and activities; complete walkable neighborhoods. And in many cases, in many places, planners have found success. But what has it gotten us? A revived interest in nonautocentric design principles. Lots of sweet, pretty urban communities. Sophisticated planning techniques. Some walkable, well-designed urban districts. And it's gotten us three decades of endemic gentrification and urban displacement. It's gotten us Albina, East Vancouver, the Ninth Ward, Brooklyn, the Mission, and every other neighborhood where capital pours in to take advantage of vulnerable but newly attractive stages. It has gotten us cities remade, especially inner cities, as white utopias.

As we sit amid the intellectual wreckage of thirty-plus years of the "new urbanism,"[12] we need to cast a critical gaze not just on the results, but on the apoliticized "diversity" that animates it, an idea so thoroughly pulped that it can now be easily swallowed without chewing.[13] The liberal consensual fantasy of urban diversity has been

12. The influence of new urbanism since its mid-1980s emergence can hardly be understated, driven by architects and designers like Andres Duany, Elizabeth Plater-Zyberk, Peter Calthorpe, Elizabeth Moule, Stefanos Polyzoides, Leon Krier, and many others. In 1993, the Congress for New Urbanism laid out its core tenants clearly: "We advocate the restructuring of public policy and development practices to support the following principles: neighborhoods should be diverse in use and population; communities should be designed for the pedestrian and transit as well as the car; cities and towns should be shaped by physically defined and universally accessible public spaces and community institutions; urban places should be framed by architecture and landscape design that celebrate local history, climate, ecology, and building practice." The Charter of New Urbanism, https://www.cnu.org/who-we-are/charter-new-urbanism.
13. Borrowing a nice bit of shade from Benjamin Bratton here: "What's Wrong with TED Talks," TEDx San Diego, December 30, 2013.

reduced to one more accoutrement of privilege, its perhaps once dangerous potentiality now leveraged in the service of bleached neighborhoods and capital accumulation. The vision of the city as stage is fine, but only if it unfolds on itself, not as a choreographed "dance" but as the built expression of difference that cannot be planned or marionetted but emerges from the everyday lives, antagonisms, and generosities of everyday people.

The urbanist imaginaria that reduces the city to ballet is exactly why Portland and Vancouver[14] are so celebrated as having "gotten it right," while simultaneously clearing the most putatively "livable" parts of their urban landscapes of working- and middle-class, racialized, and poor residents. This is of course what happens—what *has* to happen—when a place insists on doing the design and staging well but effectively ignores the antagonisms of power: a cleansed and securitized playground for privilege. As one of the prime architects of Vancouver's contemporary planned landscape once told me after cataloguing all the city's achievements, "We just missed the affordability part."[15]

14. Among many other cities and parts of cities that adhere to similar development patterns, Vancouver and Portland are perhaps the most lauded new urbanish contemporary cities (certainly in North America). It's no surprise that there are well-circulated and oft-cited books about them, such as Connie Ozawar's *The Portland Edge* (Washington, DC: Island Press, 2004) and John Punter's *The Vancouver Achievement* (Vancouver: UBC Press, 2004).

15. You know this story. You've heard it over and over again. But let me tell you one of my own quickly here: There is a school in New York City that I have visited a number of times, in no small part because they pay generously to have me come say a few words. The school could hardly be more beautiful: small groups of energetically engaged happy kids working with cool, smart, liberal teachers all over the school grounds; two unbelievable buildings with every conceivable piece of high-end equipment; a thoughtful, compassionate, progressive pedagogy; a highly engaged and supportive parent and alumni network; creative, kind administration; all kinds of community and experiential learning; I could go on, but you get the picture. The school is nearly perfect. It's the kind of place you or

Every city evinces and articulates varying patterns of displacement: oftentimes predictable, sometimes not at all; oftentimes systematic, sometimes not at all; oftentimes recognizable, sometimes not at all. In its current form, for example, Vancouver's patterns are less starkly racialized than those in Portland, but more deeply invested in ongoing narratives of colonization with more pronounced housing market contortions, but each city seems committed to a continuous exercise of ahistoricity in the service of privilege. Jane Jacobs seemingly understood the implications of her prescriptions, and on occasion gestured toward a more politicized urbanism: "Cities have the capability of providing something for everybody, only because, and only when, they are created by everybody,"[16] but her "created by everybody" was always an amorphous, aestheticized, cultural production disconnected from social antagonisms, which explains her beatification among liberal planners.

Cities have to be understood as a historically creative breach in social and cultural relations, but that has to extend to a rupture in

your kids would probably love to attend. And it costs a bit more than $47,300 per year per kid, a little more than $45,500 for kindergarten and first grade. They have tuition assistance programs and some scholarships, but essentially it is a playground for intensely privileged kids. It is a lovely, progressive playground that talks openly about equity and white guilt and responsibility and all that, but is an institution that is fundamentally *regressive*, not progressive. It is a place that concretizes and reinforces privilege, one that makes the world a less equitable, more unfair place every day. When I have visited the school, I say this same thing repeatedly, and the lovely, sweet staff all nod and agree with me (seemingly), and nothing ever really changes. (Although come to think of it, it has been quite a while since they've invited me back!) It is a strategy people in Portland are very familiar with. Walidah calls this the "liberal politics of the empty gesture" and "death by listening." Everyone in power in Portland is extremely sympathetic to the plight of Albina and the Black community; they will listen forever, and keep right on doing what they are doing.

16. Jacobs, *Death and Life*, 238.

the certitudes of economic domination. Richard Florida (the instigator of the "creative cities" movement, which is among the very worst renditions of the Jacobian tradition) says that he once asked Jacobs about so-called bad gentrification. In his telling, she said: "The dulling down of one neighborhood, as the diversity of social and economic life was sucked out of it, would lead invariably to the rise of new, energized neighborhoods elsewhere in the city. ... when a place gets boring, even the rich people leave."[17] This is a passively amoral urbanism we should not abide by: one where rich people simply move about fluidly and take what they please, while the best the rest of us can hope for is that they will get bored and go somewhere else after they have trashed a neighborhood.

The "diversity" Jacobs and especially the new urbanists reify is a misapprehension/perversion of difference. What they are calling for is absolutely real and attractive—lively public realms, complete mixed-use neighborhoods, pedestrian/transit/bike-friendly streets, etc.—all those are desirable built forms. But for those goals to be achieved with any stability or resilience or ethics, they have to be the *product* of a city that disowns land: where profiteering and capital accumulation from land is disavowed. Any city that achieves apoliticized but attractive design objectives while allowing its land to be left to the whims of the market will inevitably see its "successes" captured by capital, and quickly destroyed or disemboweled. The neoliberal city is a vampiric city, constantly sucking the vibrancy out of its neighborhoods, and keeping its most alive residents always on the run.

Diversity is the heavily securitized simulacrum of difference. The city has to constantly unfold onto itself, as the creative production of sociability, but a city of difference can only exist where everyday people are not preyed upon and where land is not abandoned to the

17. Richard Florida, "Getting Jane Jacobs Right," *The Atlantic*, April 2, 2010, http://www.theatlantic.com/national/archive/2010/04/getting-jane-jacobs-right/38391/.

market—which is why I am tentative about deferring to *gentrification* as a driving trope of contemporary urban transformations. Antagonism to gentrification all too often strikes me as a defensive action, as working from the presumed inevitability of displacement and dispossession of self-determining subjectivities and then trying to ameliorate the effects. Cities are uniquely constituted to meet that challenge, but can demand so much more, and have every ability to aggressively do so, on land that is not reduced to commodity. And we know how to do just that; we know how to effectively remove land from the market—whether it is speculative or Georgist taxes, nonmarket housing, squatting or co-ops, or any other configurations we can imagine. There is every reasons to believe that cities can be remade as socially creative breaches that by definition seek to repair the injustices their existences are predicated on.

That is what is a city is for.

YOU WANT IT TO BE ONE WAY, BUT IT'S THE OTHER WAY[18]

In some ways a liberatory city, a city that defies displacement, is a precise inversion of contemporary progressive urbanism. Regimes of rational planning purport to choreograph pleasing built-form stages for shows of diversity to parade upon, and then let the market sort out propertied rationalities of access and ownership. And we know what that looks and feels like—the "lively streetscapes" that beckon us from developer-pamphlets, the promises of "vibrancy" and "vitality," the meticulously designed proposals populated with happy, shiny people in pastel golf-wear—we have all encountered these hygienically cleansed environments and blanched.

A city of difference should conclude the opposite: that a city's job is to create space outside of the market, to repair displacements, and

18. As per Marlo Stanfield.

then to allow its own sociability to unfold upon itself. The polyphony that is so attractive as a cultural milieu does not have to be designed or planned; it is inherent to the city. Just as the city, and the history of the city, defies social domination with constantly overlapping, unfixed, and reconstituting social relations, the same rationalities can and should be applied to land. The imagined fixed certainties of sovereign propertied ownerships should be subjected to the same relational unsettling: cities as living, breathing built breaches of domination.

This to me is the promise of the common, but only if we can place those discourses within historico-ontological narratives that privilege reconciliations and restitutions. Reimagining East Vancouver or Albina, or anywhere else, does not allow us to escape our histories of past—and multiple—displacements, and while I do not believe the correct response to dispossession is possession, understanding the kinds of social relations that can articulate alternative sovereignties often means sailing into uncharted and unfamiliar waters.

I continue to find Deleuze and Guattari helpful here. Through many texts, together and separately,[19] they present a bewildering rush of complex ideas and constructions, categories, concepts, and delineations, which seem to pile on top of one another, constantly proliferating and multiplying, frustrating any easy coherence. Once it becomes clear though that this is a deliberate and methodologically productive approach, and that they "encourage readers to pick and choose from their concepts, selecting those which are useful and simply passing by those which are not,"[20] I find reading their work is often intensely useful.

19. Primarily for me their work together, especially *A Thousand Plateaus: Capitalism and Schizophrenia* (Minneapolis: University of Minnesota Press, 1987), *What Is Philosophy?* (New York: Columbia University Press, 1994), and *Anti-Oedipus: Capitalism and Schizophrenia* (New York: Penguin, 2009).
20. Andrew Robinson, "Why Deleuze (Still) Matters: States, War-Machines and Radical Transformation," *Ceasefire*, September 10, 2010, https://ceasefiremagazine.co.uk/in-theory-deleuze-war-machine/.

Perhaps their most popularly extracted trope is the distinction between arborescent[21] (or vertical, hierarchical, monocentric) and rhizomatic (horizontal, planar, interconnected) forms of organization, relations, and approaches to knowledge. Within rhizomatic structures, every point can always be connected to any other point; rhizomes are constantly differentiating into multiplicities, flexible, resilient, and never easily captured. In contrast, arborescent structures all flow from, and constantly refer back to, the dominant trunk with communication between branches always having to return to and through the trunk, and thus all arborescent structures are easily cut down. You can guess all the extrapolations that have been extended from this concept, from brilliant to cringe-worthy, but it remains a good entrée to their thinking.

Deleuze and Guattari constantly seek "the affirmation of difference. This goal is expressed in a theoretical method ... to aid in thinking the world 'otherwise' and bringing a new world into being"[22] Dominatory power constantly seeks to subsume difference under the requirements of order and to reduce multiplicities to essences and fixed, predictable, and classifiable identities. Filtered through the languages of psychoanalytics, they speak of active and reactive forces, blockages, and repressions of flow and desire, constantly counterposing what they call the "royal sciences" drive to reduce, contain, and systematize social and political relations. Theirs is an attempt to think past postmodernism, as a "recomposition of theoretical thought *beyond* the break associated with the critique of metanarratives."[23] In that it is both relentlessly political and intensely hopeful.

---

21. Confusingly (and totally typically), trees do not conform to this description of *arborescent*—and apparently neither Deleuze nor Guattari intended the metaphor to extend to actual trees.
22. Athina Karatzogianni and Andrew Robinson, *Power, Resistance and Conflict in the Contemporary World* (London: Routledge, 2010), 7.
23. Ibid., 11.

This part is often misapprehended, and while I can see it is how it is possible to interpret Deleuze and Guattari as resonating with neoliberal logics, they are clear (or at least as clear as they ever are) that the networked, rhizomatic social relations they speak of are inconceivable within existing statist or "reactive" hierarchical capitalist formations. States exercise what they call "overcoding" or enforcing regimes of meaning-making by fixing certain sets of social relations in place—what they call "axioms"—subsuming those that can be recognized without disrupting statist arborescent power, and marginalizing or destroying those that do not fit so easily. The sovereign state form is constantly enacting antiproduction: tirelessly trying to absorb or marginalize active-networked social relations and seeking to repress creative, or what they call "desiring-production."

Against the state Deleuze and Guattari pose networks and/or war machines. They speak of social production as occurring via the creation of assemblages where various kinds of relations and desires are brought together, not by collapsing themselves, but by associating or grouping in "concerts" or "accords." They call certain kinds of assemblages "war machines"—which is a another pain-in-the-ass appellation because neither are they machines in the mindless mechanical sense, nor are they warring in the militaristic sense. Alternatives have been suggested, the most useful maybe "difference engines" or "differentiation convergences," or even better, "affinities." When autonomous, these "machines" corrode sovereignty, always combining and recombining as active networks of production and reconstituted social relations.

War machines *are* at war though, constantly battling with the state to preserve their own subjectivities. They can be captured or subsumed into the totality of the State via "machinic enslavement," blocked or banished when they cannot be domesticated, but they are always searching for new ways of living and for new spaces, geographical and nongeographical, where autonomous creative production can exist. Autonomous networks organize, disperse, and proliferate, in and out of control, constantly spreading and differentiating, transversaliz-ing, assembling and reassembling, constituting and reconstituting, never attempting to capture state power but actively undermining it, refusing its repressive antiproduction. It is a profoundly different anticapitalism than those that dream of capturing the state, or the renditions of revolt that imagine building new hegemonic alliances and logics.

In important ways Deleuzian politics are not all that new; they are an extension and celebration of existing social relations, a call to deepen and embolden and fertilize the best of these networks, to unthink and dis-enact the state through everyday shared practices, which is part of why it is so attractive to me and why it so easily reso-nates with my thinking about the city as postsovereign space. I'm not particularly invested in whether any of Deleuze and Guattari appeals to you per se, nor am I trying to recruit you for Team D/G, nor am I even convinced I'm on that squad myself. I just know that they open up particular and rousing kinds of imaginative space for me to think outside the hegemony of hegemonies,[24] to think beyond univocal authority of sovereignties.

An endless array of other lines[25] and approaches to the same kinds of territory exist, and in some ways thinking past sovereign domina-tions is incredibly hard. As philosopher Jean-Luc Nancy says: "I am well aware of the fact that all of this does not let itself be conceived of easily. It is not for us, not for our thinking, modeled as it is on the sovereign model; it is not for our warlike thinking. But this is certain: there is nothing on the horizon except for an unheard-of, inconceiv-able task—or war."[26]

24. Nicely put by Richard Day in *Gramsci Is Dead* (London: Pluto Press, 2005).
25. Deleuze and Guattari wrote often of "ligne de fuite," or lines of flight. These are lines not just of escape, but also of creativity, of overcoming, of resistance.
26. Jean-Luc Nancy, *Being Singular Plural*, trans. Robert D. Richardson and Anne E. O'Byrne (Stanford, CA: Stanford University Press, 2000), 141.

But in other ways, maybe better ways, it's not all that hard at all. There are constantly creative, active networks of relation and production all around us, squeezing out, obviating, and rejecting repressive sovereign formations. Think of Walidah's description of how Black communities continue to defy every exclusionary attempt by Oregon and Portland to negate their presences, and how Albina fundamentally remains, despite everything, a Black neighborhood. Think of all the ways Indigenous communities have reconfigured, imaginatively demanding new and old spaces, despite rounds of genocidal assault. Think of so many people's refusal to abide by hetero-normative disciplining of gender and sexuality. Think of all the ways people refuse their designations as states of exception, how social creativities overflow their measures, how endless differentiation, perhaps mimicking bio-evolution, defies sovereignties at every turn.

But this destabilized milieu is hardly all sunshine, rainbows, and unicorns. Think of how easily and explicitly the Israeli army adopted Deleuzian philosophies to invert geometries of military tactics to concretize and deepen their domination of Palestinian lands.[27] Or think of how our cartographics of pseudo-stable sovereign states are being dislocated around us and radically reordered by a "data-shaped planetary epidermis, an ur-infrastructure of extreme biopolitical control," or what design theorist Benjamin Bratton calls the "Google caliphate," the world seen as machine, with all its data "organized and made useful." Our brave new digital worlds are straining every commitment, affiliation, and economic and communicative constraint: "Displacing and replacing the statist functions and repositioning flag-brand loyalties ... Desovereigned lands ruled by Google

---

27. This is well-documented and commented on, not the least by the IDF. Eyal Weizman (author of *The Hollow Land*) has written plenty on it. See, for example, Eyal Weizman, "Walking through Walls," *Transversal*, 2007, http://eipcp.net/transversal/0507/weizman/en.

jurisdictions—the state as para-state reduced to ceremonial monarchical status."[28]

Bratton speaks of new formations, of a cloud polis,[29] the Stack as "a new *nomos* rendered now as vertically thickened political geography,"[30] and of the unimaginably integrated technologies of control and surveillance, compliance and manipulation, blurring and blinding anything we think we may have thought of sovereignties. Listening to Bratton or anyone else who can document/prophesize digital historiographies/futures reminds me of Joice Taylor's description of the clearing of Albina: "And it happened so fast." My point here is not intended as apocalyptic, although surely it could be anthropocenically justified, but as exhortative. The world often changes spectacularly and swiftly, and imagining a postsovereign, postproperty city is hardly the most implausible of futures currently being proposed. Other worlds are absolutely possible, but (put delicately) most of them are not all that appetizing.

In the face of biocatastrophes, we are being forced to act while on the run, with incomplete information, with geoengineering promises ringing in our ears, with new planetary-scale decisioning ready to obviate our sins. It is not a hard sell: maybe we really are in the last gasps of eco-delusions, maybe the earth really is in the midst of rectifying humanity's ingratitude with dramatic climate change, or worse. It strikes me though that it is exactly that unbridled arrogance we

28. Benjamin Bratton, "The Stack: Design and Geopolitics in the Age of Planetary-Scale Computing," October 29, 2014, public lecture, SFU Woodwards, Vancouver, British Columbia.

29. Benjamin H. Bratton, "Some Trace Effects of the Post-Anthropocene: On Accelerationist Geopolitical Aesthetics," *e-flux* 46, June 2013, http://www.e-flux.com/journal/some-trace-effects-of-the-post-anthropocene-on-accelerationist-geopolitical-aesthetics/.

30. Benjamin H. Bratton, "The Black Stack," *e-flux* 53, March 2014, http://www.e-flux.com/journal/the-black-stack/#_ftn3.

have to think beyond, the arrogance that gives permission to every for-your-own-good narrative.

I am convinced, for reasons I hope I have outlined clearly enough, that the city is the right starting place for a necessary rethinking of colonial sovereignty, development, property, and ownership. But I am equally convinced that we require an emotional release from modernist fetishizing of predictability, rational planning, scaled systemizations of efficiency and fixed orders, and all the hubris they require. I think of Patrick Geddes, who in resisting the proposed vast "sanitization" of Indian cities saw how much would be destroyed and called for "conservative surgery" instead of "sweeping clearance."[31] I think of what he would say about Albina, racialized urban "renewals." I think of Emma Goldman who once said: "Finalities are for gods and governments, not for the human intellect."[32] I think of totalitarianisms and states of exception. I think of every scheme that purports to know how land must be improved and developed, regardless of who is there.

If the story I'm trying to tell here—a story of how the city can emerge as a new kind of commons—is going to make any real sense, it has to understand itself polyphonically as the antipode of sovereign domination, as overtly antagonistic to regimes of ownership, to the republics of property that necessarily pit residents one against the other as enemy or coconspirator. And thus any resistance to gentrification has to start much deeper, with the humility to build a city asystematically and asymmetrically, formally and informally, with densely overlapping and simultaneous uses, and it has to start with land.

31. Jacqueline Tyrwhitt, *Patrick Geddes in India* (London: Lund Humphries, 1947).
32. Emma Goldman, "What I Believe," *New York World*, July 19, 1908.

IMPROPRIETIES: LAND AS FREEDOM

But what might this actually mean for the immanent city? Or more pressingly, what might all this mean for my neighborhood, or yours, or any urban area under threat? What might this suggest for that lot at the corner of Martin Luther King Boulevard and Alberta Street? How can we act, not just in producing a social commons full of justice, but in the here-and-now material commons of our lives? I want to conclude with three interlocking ideas.

First, the city has to be able do what the state cannot. The city has to be the right locus for the political. The city is far from the only political entity imaginable in a poststatist future, but jurisdictionally it is uniquely capable of differentiating itself, socially and materially, from state sovereignties. As a creative social breach, cities have the potential to articulate a robust subjectivity that surpasses fixities and by their very nature nurture pluralities. Portland contains within itself every ability to renounce Oregon's racist heritage and choose a different path. There is every capacity for Portland, despite everything, to remake Albina, starting with the corner of MLK and Alberta. Why couldn't the Portland Development Commission turn that property over to a collective of Black community organizations as a foothold for radical neighborhood revitalization on the premise that it remains nonmarket housing and commercial space? They are already giving it away with a two-and-a-half million-dollar subsidy. There is every possibility to privilege that corner as an initial site of reparation and reconciliation. There is every possibility for New Orleans, Vancouver, or any other city confounded by development and displacement to renounce predatory land practices and to make right colonial thefts.

This will take time, patience, and incremental unwinding, starting with an aggressive commitment to protect urban land from the market, and then the city must be allowed, in bits and pieces, through duration and experimentation, to disown itself. Like daylighting a stream or practicing habitat restoration, the city can repopulate itself with a plurality of land stewardships beyond the ownership model, from co-ops to land trusts to shared equity to squats and to anything else that can be imagined.

That unwinding should both rest on and give space for historicized and extroverted exercises of decolonization and reparations, not just as the ethical imperative restitution for Black and Indigenous people, but as the route to shared articulations of new relationships to land. The obligations of reparations and rematriations are not burdens but opportunities for everyone, the clearest route to reallocate and reconfigure our commitments to land. However flawed and potentially disingenuous the Tsilhqot'in decision may be, it might still provide one example, an incremental incursion into Canadian sovereignty, perhaps tenuous and still untested, perhaps incomplete, but it is one more undoing of Westphalian certainties, one more material articulation of something beyond, something else. Extrapolate that experience to the urban, to multiple scales, and imagine other kinds of accords based on nondominatory logics.

Nonstate social organization has been the experience of the vast majority of humankind for most of its history, and it is hardly an extinct form. There are pockets and stretches of people living in nonstate or protostate milieus across the globe, as Clastres,[33] Scott,[34] and so many others have documented, as refugees, fugitives, and conscientious objectors to state repression, taxation, conscription, and/or domination. There are perhaps one hundred million people in Zomia, reaching across maybe 2.5 million sq./km. of the Southeast Asian Massif (southern China, northern India, central Vietnam, Laos, parts of Cambodia, Burma, Pakistan) where social traditions,

33. Pierre Clastres, *Society against the State* (New York: Zone Books, 1987).
34. James Scott, *Seeing Like a State* (New Haven: Yale University Press, 1998).

agriculture, cropping practices, kinship structures, pliable ethnic identification, and essentially everything else have been designed to prevent their societies from being incorporated into state structures or from states springing up among them.[35] With the contemporary stretch of state power, every resisting society is endangered, from Zomia to the Roma to the Ma'dan to the Yanomami to Indigenous societies in every corner of the globe, but the possibility of nonstate society has hardly been extinguished. We live in a profoundly unique era of human existence with unimagined pressures, limited and dwindling resources, and incalculable natural and social challenges to feed, house, and care for so many, and yet the sovereign state cannot be the final word.

Second, our approaches to new forms of social organization should always be tentative, incremental, experimental, and accretive. That may seem a little incongruous given that the future I am imagining invokes a radically different set of relationships to land and to each other, but if the answer to univocality, domination, and monoculture has to be a density of pluralities and multiplicities, then so too should our routes there. If an ethically ecological future is to be a decolonial, postsovereign multiplicity, our organizational philosophies should mimic that. If nondominatory politics is to steer clear of libertarian, protocapitalist Gulchist nightmare fantasias, we have to genuinely believe that every cook can govern, and that the city can unfold patiently onto itself with millions of everyday incremental steps.

Those steps include, but are not encompassed by, *democracy*. I am generally in favor of every kind of legitimately participatory engagement and suspect that we cannot have too much layering of democratic processes and institutions, but contend that it has to be nuanced.

---

35. The best-known text on Zomia is James Scott, *The Art of Not Being Governed: An Anarchist History of Upland Southeast Asia* (New Haven: Yale University Press, 2009). There is a ton of other good research and writing on Zomia. Start with Scott and go from there.

Some forms of democracy—say mass-scale representational voting—often have the effect of squeezing out and marginalizing other forms of politics. By its very nature, representative democratic process tends to hegemonize, and should be subsumed within dense pluralities of participation, which is perhaps a better frame to imagine all the ways, formal and informal, that residents can creatively produce the city.

Participation too is contoured, however, and certain platforms fix certain kinds of participation and define the limits of control and power. Participation as a construct is not unlike democracy—a useful starting point that then has to be immediately subjected to all the tough questions: for whom, under what conditions, what is on the table, who enforces implementation of decisions, etc. And more fundamentally, what are people being asked to participate in, what are frameworks of decisioning, and who controls the processes and for what ends?

A quick glance at participatory budgeting—among perhaps the most encouraging political movements of our era—reveals the malleability and contingency of even the sturdiest of democratic structures. In its contemporary form, participatory budgeting has its origins in Brazil, specifically Porto Alegre beginning in the late 1980s, where sophisticated architectures of citizens' assemblies gather together huge numbers of ordinary residents in year-round sessions to allocate the city's capital expenditures. The Brazilian experience suggests that not only can participatory processes be resiliently scaled to the municipal level, they can be highly effective managing critical and substantial budgets. It also implies that it is the democratic ethics and popular control over local bureaucracies that links the popular assemblies to the heart of political decisioning.

There is lots to be heartened about when looking at Porto Alegre but the participatory budgeting process, which is now emulated across the globe by jurisdictions large and small, rarely travels so well. The idea has been rearticulated and repurposed hundreds of times, and is a darling of the World Bank and the International Monetary Fund (IMF), of retrograde municipal and national governments, and of planners everywhere who seek facades of consultation and placation without ever surrendering any real power. In its transportability participatory budgeting, like all forms of participation, has proven politically compliant and fashionable as a tool for many ends.

This is not to reject the ideals of participation but to suggest that we remain consistently suspicious and constantly problematize to what ends the rhetoric is being leveraged. We can infuse participation into every corner of our lives, formal and informal, piggy-backing on self-governing and self-determining ethics, and the more layers, the more density of plural participations, the more resilient those structures will be.

Consider again the example of Right 2 Dream Too and consider Ibrahim's description of the project as moving homeless people from consumptive to productive lives. He meant that in the conventional sense—getting people into self-reliant economic circumstances—but he also meant it in terms of the everyday production of space as well. R2D2 is a dismayingly complex project with all kinds of uncertainties and constraints, dealing with seriously challenging circumstances with a minimum of support. Yet the project is run beautifully by homeless participants themselves on a volunteer basis and is able to carve out and negotiate shared space on a tiny plot of land. Every day of R2D2 is an exuberant challenge to sovereign state governmentality, a challenge to the normative expectations of homeless people and a challenge to the presumptive limits of social cooperation.

Spending time at R2D2 offers a glance of what a densely participatory postsovereign city might look like. Look one way and it is amazingly structured with firm internal rules and agreements that scaffold its success. Look the other and it is a swirling, free-form of creative production and contingent social relations. But no matter where you cast your gaze, it defies the expectations of planners and rational sovereign orders, it defies the republic of property in its very existence. But you can see those possibilities in cities all over the world, particularly in the Global South, cities that shouldn't "work" by Western standards of efficiency and planning but manage to still produce convivial means of living for the vast majority of their residents.

One of my favorite portraits of a city is *Understanding Cairo: The Logic of a City Out of Control*, which describes a place that for many Western observers presents as a nightmare of a chaotic, overcrowded, cacophonous, confusing, disorganized city beset by inefficiencies, inadequacies, and unsustainabilities.

> And in many ways Cairo is completely out of control, at least by the metric of western urban management. Two-thirds of the city's population now live in neighbourhoods that have sprung up since 1950, devoid of any planning or control, and which are considered by officialdom as both illegal and undesirable. In contrast, there are vast extensions of the urban region that are completely planned and into which the state has poured more and more resources, but perversely these areas remain almost completely devoid of any inhabitants. Housing in Cairo is built, and property exchanged, in contravention of a host of laws; transport functions in strange and apparently contradictory ways; and hanging over all are near-dysfunctional and largely irrelevant bureaucracies. As one academic discussion of Cairo's "master planning" efforts put it, "Greater Cairo has not been mastered or planned."[36]

I don't have any particular interest in valorizing Cairo per se, and you can surely think of all kinds of reasons to be critical of this description of the city, but the point is to acknowledge the surpassing creativity

36. David Sims, *Understanding Cairo: The Logic of a City Out of Control* (Cairo: The American University in Cairo Press, 2010), 3.

of people to manage their own affairs. Some of it may adhere to "democratic" or "participatory" discourses, but mostly it is the everyday capacity of everyday people to creatively produce the city around them. We should rest our ideas of how a good city can emerge on an abiding faith in this capacity: how in fits and starts, unplanned, asystematically, and as an endlessly repeating series of "conservative surgeries," ordinary people can build a city.

Third, and finally, I'd like to end this book with a return, by coming full circle to where I started, with the first line of the preamble to the Code of Ethics and Standards of Practice of the [U.S.] National Association of Realtors: "Under all is the land." The next lines read: "Upon its wise utilization and widely allocated ownership depend the survival and growth of free institutions and of our civilization. Realtors should recognize that the interests of the nation and its citizens require the highest and best use of the land and the widest distribution of land ownership."[37]

I hope you agree that in a time of accelerating biocatastrophes and grotesque colonial inequalities, we probably shouldn't be relying on real estate agents as our moral compasses, nor should we trust their evaluation of what constitutes a just social order. I agree with the National Association of Realtors on one critical point, however—that land is the foundation of society—but entirely reject its prescription of widely distributed homeownership.

In fact, I hope you have read this book as an argument precisely to the contrary. I do not accept Lockean arguments for occupation, nor do I believe that possession is the correct response to dispossession. I believe that when we view land as property, when we reduce it to ownership, we lose the possibility of entering into a legitimate, and

37. Code of Ethics and Standards of Practice of the National Association of Realtors, January 1, 2014, http://www.realtor.org/sites/default/files/publications/2014/Policy/2014-Code-of-Ethics.pdf.

possibly ecological, relationship with it. As Chief Sealth put it, ownership of the land really is a strange idea.

When land or people—urban or otherwise—are viewed as property, as a thing for another's use, the possibility of a relationship is foreclosed. Ownership is the language of possession and dispossession. The desubjectivization of land is intimately bound up with the desubjectivization of people, each ennobling and giving permission to the other: the domination of land is integral to the domination of people, and vice versa.

And that is just as true here in my neighborhood as it is in Albina, or New Orleans, or any/every community threatened by capital. I am frankly unclear on what my next steps here in East Vancouver on Coast Salish Territories will be. I am unsure how I should act in perhaps the least affordable city in the world. I have some ideas maybe, and some sense of how as a settler I might best serve this place, but I do not know what to say exactly about Albina's future. I know Lisa and others are articulating a People's Plan. I know John and Joice and Walidah and Ibrahim and so many others are working hard toward a city that acts as if it is interested in difference, in righting its wrongs.

But I am convinced that if this city, that city, any city is to fulfill its potentiality as a creative breach, it has to be a site of *disownership* and has to recognize that land and freedom are inseparable. Attempting to ameliorate gentrification with the language of property is pouring salt on the wound. The answer to market depredations, displacements, and dispossessions cannot be a desperate expansion of that market; it has to be a refusal, a disavowal. We have to learn as Phillip Blake put it, to be "satisfied to see our wealth as ourselves and the land we live with." With the weight of colonialism on our shoulders and late capitalism right up in our faces that seems a daunting task, but I am not sure I can see another.

INDEX

Page numbers in italics refer to figures.